AFTER THESE THINGS I SAW

A Study of Revelation

AFTER THESE THINGS I SAW

Edward P. Myers, Ph.D.

COLLEGE PRESS
PUBLISHING COMPANY
Joplin, Missouri

Library of Congress Cataloging-in-Publication Data

Myers, Edward P. (Edward Paul), 1946–
    After these things I saw: a study of Revelation /
Edward P. Myers.
        p.   cm.
    Includes bibligraphical references.
    ISBN 0-89900-786-4
    1. Bible. N.T. Revelation—Commentaries. I. Title.
BS2825.3.M94 1997
228'.077—dc21   97-19160
                                                       CIP

Dedication

Richard and Carol Blankenship
Jack and Billie Boustead
Burl and Evelyn Curtis
Morris and Leigh Ellis
Ralph and Verna Mansell
Janice Myers
Richard and Jeanine Peck
Joe and Shirley Segraves
Flavil and Maydell Yeakley

These lovely Christian people are members of the Wednesday Night Home Bible Study with whom I have shared this material in various stages. All of you have been such an encouragement to me in my ministry and Christian walk. I thank you for your love and care for me and my family. You will never know how much each of you mean to me personally. May the Lord richly bless and keep you in His tender care; and may you each remember the encouraging message of this book — WE WIN!

Table of Contents

Preface ✧ ✧ ✧ ✧ ✧ 9

Introduction ✧ ✧ ✧ ✧ ✧ 13

Outline ✧ ✧ ✧ ✧ ✧ 45

Chapter 1 ✧ ✧ ✧ ✧ ✧ 49

Chapter 2 ✧ ✧ ✧ ✧ ✧ 69

Chapter 3 ✧ ✧ ✧ ✧ ✧ 107

Chapter 4 ✧ ✧ ✧ ✧ ✧ 131

Chapter 5 ✧ ✧ ✧ ✧ ✧ 141

Chapter 6 ✧ ✧ ✧ ✧ ✧ 151

Chapter 7 ✧ ✧ ✧ ✧ ✧ 161

Chapter 8 ✧ ✧ ✧ ✧ ✧ 171

Chapter 9 ✧ ✧ ✧ ✧ ✧ 179

Chapter 10 ✧ ✧ ✧ ✧ ✧ 191

Chapter 11 ✧ ✧ ✧ ✧ ✧ 201

Chapter 12 ✧ ✧ ✧ ✧ ✧ 215

Chapter 13 ✧ ✧ ✧ ✧ ✧ 227

Chapter 14 ❖ ❖ ❖ ❖ ❖ 245

Chapter 15 ❖ ❖ ❖ ❖ ❖ 261

Chapter 16 ❖ ❖ ❖ ❖ ❖ 269

Chapter 17 ❖ ❖ ❖ ❖ ❖ 279

Chapter 18 ❖ ❖ ❖ ❖ ❖ 289

Chapter 19 ❖ ❖ ❖ ❖ ❖ 301

Chapter 20 ❖ ❖ ❖ ❖ ❖ 315

Chapter 21 ❖ ❖ ❖ ❖ ❖ 331

Chapter 22 ❖ ❖ ❖ ❖ ❖ 349

Bibliography ❖ ❖ ❖ ❖ ❖ 363

Preface

The book of Revelation is one of John's writings with which I have had a love relationship with for several years. While many years of study have gone into preparation for the writing of this commentary, there are others without whom I could not have completed this project. While I am sure there are more I have failed to mention, I would not want to forget the following:

The Elders and the entire congregation of the McCrory Church of Christ, McCrory, Arkansas. These brethren have provided the necessary funds for a writing ministry for the past two years which has allowed me the access to tools otherwise unavailable for research. Decisions such as this are not always popular because often these kinds of investments take a long time bringing to fulfillment anything that is tangible, such as a book. But they have stood faithfully by me during this ministry and I want to express my grateful appreciation for their help.

Don Shackelford has read every page (some portions more than once) of this commentary and given specific critique. He has worked under a deadline that placed constraints upon his time, but he never once complained but cheerfully read, read, and re-read this material. His keen editorial eye has saved me from many a mistake; but he is not to be faulted for what has slipped through, especially in those areas where I chose not to follow his advice but went my own way.

Lori Lee is my faithful secretary in the School of Biblical Studies at Harding. Putting this project before her and placing it under such a short schedule probably pushed her to the limit on more than one day as we tried to type, correct, print and then turn around and retype, correct, and print all over again to meet the pressing schedule. Thank you, Lori, for being so pleasant to work with in this project.

As Lori left the office to return home to care for small children, Dana Martin stepped in as a temporary secretary. She has shielded me from interference on several occasions and taken responsibilities that allowed me to work uninterrupted. Without her efficiency, I fear this project would have gone on, and on and on. Flowers to you, Dana, you are a marvel.

My wife Janice, as always, has encouraged me in all of my work. She is indeed a "worthy woman" (Prov. 31) and one in whom I find a great deal of delight. She is always saying, "write more." Here, then, is "some more."

John Hunter and Steve Cable have offered a great deal of assistance and are always pleasant to talk with in bringing this project to completion. Their encouragement will always be remembered.

I feel the need to explain what I intend to do in producing this material. The book of Revelation is a highly controversial book. How one interprets the book is dependent on the method of interpretation adopted — and there are many. My purpose in writing this commentary has been to provide a consistent interpretation of the book of Revelation for the average person.

Scholars will be disappointed to find that I have not highly documented every interpretation given to various verses or phrases in the book. My intention has never been to offer all the various alternative explanations of John's Apocalypse. I did not write this for the scholar, but for the man in the pew. For example, I have not given the Amillennial, Premillennial, or Postmillennial interpretations of chapter 20. To do so would have expanded the book considerably and swerved away from my stated intention to provide a consistent interpretation of this mysterious book.

It is my prayer that as you take this commentary and use it in your study of the word of God, you may find fulfillment in the words, "Blessed is he who reads and those who hear the words of the prophecy, and heed the things which are written in it; for the time is near" (Rev. 1:3).

Edward P. Myers, Ph.D.
Professor of Bible & Christian Doctrine
Director, School of Biblical Studies
Harding University
Searcy, Arkansas 72149

Introduction

The book of Revelation is probably the most misunderstood book in all of the Bible. Authors have written volumes trying to make this book understandable to others. However, it should be readily admitted that many times the authors have simply added to the confusion rather than assisting in an understanding.

The book of Revelation is the last book in our Bible. It is couched in highly symbolical language and rests on images from the Old Testament for interpretation. God has given this book to man to understand. The Spirit of God inspired it to be written and understood. The book must have meaning to both the original readers and to man today or else it has no practical value to be studied.

The book portrays the conflict between right and wrong, good and evil, or Christ and Satan. It assures comfort to those who were being persecuted in the first century. It adds strength to our lives in Christ.

The scope of the book is quickly grasped by the serious student of the Word. Though the book may seem difficult at times, the message of an indestructible kingdom of God is obvious. Based on the principles of human conduct and divine moral government, the overruling providence of God in the earth is seen directing the destiny of nations in behalf of ultimate victory for his church.

Historical Background

In dealing with the historical background of a book it is the duty of the writer to deal with such questions as authorship, date, place of writing, recipients and their condition, and the general conditions of the world out of which the book was written.

A. The Author

The author of Revelation is John (Rev. 1:1, 4, 9; 22:8). He refers to himself as the servant of Jesus Christ (1:1), a brother of the Christians of Asia Minor and a fellow sufferer in the tribulation (1:9). He was exiled to the isle of Patmos for the preaching of the word (1:9). He says that he saw and heard the things recorded in this book (22:8).

Facts About John: John was a Jewish Christian who spent a large part of his life in Galilee. He moved to Ephesus and settled there. John was the son of Zebedee (Matt. 4:21) and the brother of James. His mother was possibly Salome and the sister to Mary, the mother of Jesus (cf. Matt. 27:56; Mark 15:40; Luke 23:49; John 19:25). If the preceding is true, then Jesus and John were cousins.

John was a fisherman from Galilee in partnership with his father, Zebedee, and his brother James, along with Peter, Andrew and John their father (Luke 5:7, 10; Mark 1:16-20). As a businessman, he was successful as is evidenced by the facts that: (1) He hired servants, Mark 1:20; (2) His mother seems to have been of the band of women who purchased spices to embalm the Lord, Mark 16:1; (3) He owned his own home, John 19:26-27; and (4) He was known to the high priest, John 18:25.

He was a disciple of John the Baptist (John 1:35-40; Mark 1:16-20) and later became an apostle for Jesus Christ (Matt. 10:2; Luke 5:10). As an apostle, he was one of the inner circle who received special mention on several occasions. He was present (1) when Peter's mother-in-law was healed, Mark 1:29-31; Matthew 8:14-17; Luke 4:38-39; (2) at the healing of Jarius' daughter, Mark 5:37; Luke 9:51; Matthew 9:18-25; (3) at the Transfiguration, Matthew 17:1-5; Mark 9:2; (4) and with Jesus as Christ was questioned about the destruction of Jerusalem, Mark 13:1-3.

Arguments in Favor of John's Authorship: The evidence for the apostle John being the author of the Revelation begins with the Church Fathers who attributed the writing of this book to John. A partial listing is: (1) Justin Martyr, ca. A.D. 140, (2) Irenaeus, ca. A.D. 180, (3) Clement of Alexandria, ca. A.D. 200, (4) Tertullian of Carthage, ca. A.D. 220, (5) Origen of Alexandria, ca. A.D. 223, and (6) Hippolytus, ca. A.D. 240. In fact, until Dionysius of Alexandria, ca. A.D. 190-264, there was no objection found from external sources.

Internal evidence also favors the Apostle John's authorship of this book. The fact that the author simply calls himself "John" would seem to indicate that he was very well known to his readers.

From internal evidence it should also be considered that there are many similarities between the Gospel of John, the Epistles of John, and the Revelation. The most prominent examples within this area of study is the word usages. Such words as: (1) Jesus being called "the Lamb of God," John 1:29; Revelation 5:6, 13. (2) Jesus is called the "logos," John 1:1; 1 John 1:1-3; Revelation 19:13. (3) The "whosoever" doctrine, John 3:16; Revelation 7:9; 22:17.

Arguments Against John's Authorship: There are two other men who are considered to have written the Revelation. One of these is John Mark. Dionysius of Alexandria suggested him and then later rejected the thought because of John Mark's lack of background in Asia.

Some have said that John the Elder was the writer. We do not know what kind of writing John the Elder would have done. Therefore, there is nothing to compare with the Revelation.

Conclusion to Authorship: John, the son of Zebedee, was not questioned until the third century. It is therefore hard to believe those so close to the first century would not have known which John wrote the book. They all agree that John, the son of Zebedee, is the author of the Revelation.

B. The Date

Basically there has been held the view that the book was written during the reign of Nero, Vespasian, or Domitian.

The Neronian Date: A.D. 68. The arguments for the early dating in the time of Nero include the following:[1]

The reference to emperor worship and persecutions was characteristic of Nero's time. The advocates for a later date reply by stating that Domitian is a stronger case for emperor worship than that of Nero.

The number 666 (Rev. 13:18) is a specific identification of Nero. The advocates for a later date reply by stating that if 666 does identify Nero the meaning could very well be that another like Nero, but worse, was about to appear.

The reference (Rev. 17:10) to seven kings of whom "five have fallen, [and] one is" fits Nero Caesar — that is, the count should begin with Julius Caesar, which would make Nero the sixth, the first five having already fallen. The advocates for a later date reply by stating that Julius Caesar was never an emperor and that, therefore, the count should begin with Augustus Caesar.

The temple of Herod was still standing as indicated by the vision (see chapter 11). The advocates for a later date reply by stating that this is not necessarily the case since the Revelation is characterized by symbols which had their roots in Hebrew history and religion.

The author's use of the Greek language is crude, Hebraic, and denotes one who is unskilled in the language; whereas, the Gospel and epistles of John were written in faultless Greek with great literary skill and diction. The advocates for a later date reply by stating that since Revelation is a book of symbols, which grew out of a Hebraic background, the purpose and intent of the book could not have been met otherwise, and that, therefore, the author's use of the Hebraic Greek was deliberate. Those advocates further point out that the argument is a tacit admission that the other four books of John were written at a later date than that of Nero and the destruction of Jerusalem — that is, John learned his Greek after the Neronian persecution and the destruction of Jerusalem.

Problems with the Neronian Date: While the arguments for the Neronian date, at face value, seem to be quite plausible, they are not necessarily conclusive. Certain problems must be taken into account.

There is the problem of accounting for such an early change in the conditions of the churches in Asia from the conditions reflected by Luke in Acts, and by Paul's prison epistles, written in A.D. 60, to Philemon, to the Colossians, and to the Ephesians.

There is the further problem of accounting for the fact that when Paul wrote his first epistle to Timothy in A.D. 64-65, at a time when Timothy was residing at Ephesus, there is absolutely no evidence that John was residing in the province of Asia, or had ever visited there.

There is also the problem of accounting for the fact that when Peter wrote his first epistle to the Jewish Christians who were sojourners throughout Asia Minor, A.D. 64-65, there is absolutely no evidence of anything that would indicate that John was residing, or had resided, at Ephesus, or at any place in Asia Minor.

There is the further problem of accounting for the Nicolaitans, the Antichrists, and the doctrine of Balaam (likely Cerinthus of whom Irenaeus wrote) if John's five books were written at such an early date.

Admittedly, the Revelation could have been written in A.D. 67 or 68, but one thing seems to be rather certain, namely: the subject matter of the Gospel of John and the epistles seem to necessarily infer that they were written much later than A.D. 67-68.

The Vespasian Date: A.D. 78. The basic argument for this date comes from internal evidence, namely a particular exegetical understanding of Revelation 17:9-11. In these verses we read the following, "This calls for a mind with wisdom. The seven heads are seven hills on which the woman sits. They are also seven kings. Five have fallen, one is, the other has not yet come; but when he does come, he must remain for a little while. The beast who once was, and now is not, is an eighth king. He belongs to the seven and is going to his destruction" (NIV).

There are two problems which are evident. First, if this is a discussion of Roman Emperors, which emperor do you begin with in your count? In the popular consensus, Julius Caesar was the first emperor. In the strict constitutional form it was Augustus. Second, there is no evidence that Vespasian persecuted Christians. All external and internal evidence points away from Vespasian.

The Domitian Date: A.D. 96. The traditional view of the dating of the book is that it was written during Domitian's reign. It is the conviction of this writer that a date in Domitian's reign is correct.

External Evidence for Domitian's Reign: The external evidence for the late dating of the book of Revelation is very strong.

Irenaeus, circa A.D. 180, was a student of Polycarp, who was a student of John. Irenaeus wrote that the apocalyptic vision "was seen not very long ago, almost in our own generation, at the close of the reign of Domitian" (*Against Heresies*, V.30).

Clement of Alexandria, circa A.D. 220, says that John returned from the isle of Patmos "after the tyrant was dead," (*Who is The Rich Man*, 42) and Eusebius, known as the Father of Church History, identifies the "tyrant" as Domitian (cf. *Ecclesiastical History*, III, 23.). Clement also speaks of John as being an "old man" which would seem inappropriate if the date of the writing were prior to A.D. 70 At this time, John would have been somewhere in his early sixties, and since Timothy is referred to as a "youth" (1 Tim. 4:12) when in his thirties, it does not seem probable that a man in his early sixties would be addressed in such a manner. Though this is not conclusive within itself, it does add weight to the argument.

Victorinus (circa 3rd or 4th century) was the author of the first known commentary on the book of Revelation. He wrote, "When John said these things, he was in the island of Patmos, condemned to the mines by Caesar Domitian. There he saw the Apocalypse; and when at length grown old, he thought that he should receive his release by suffering; but Domitian being killed, he was liberated."

Jerome, circa A.D. 340-420, said, "In the fourteenth year then after Nero, Domitian having raised up a second persecution, he [i.e., John] was banished to the island of Patmos, and wrote the Apocalypse. . ." (*Lives of Illustrious Men*, 9).

Eusebius (circa A.D. 324), contends that the tradition of his time placed the writing of the Apocalypse at the close of the reign of Domitian (*Ecclesiastical History*, III, 18).

We would agree with the traditional view of the date of the Revelation upon the basis of the external evidence that the date of the writing was sometime during the reign of the Emperor Domitian.

Internal Evidence for Domitian's Reign: There is

also a vast amount of evidence within the book of Revelation to indicate that the date of the writing was circa A.D. 95/96.

The spiritual condition of the churches of chapters two and three seems to be more in harmony with a late date. The church in Ephesus was established by Paul about A.D. 61 and in the book addressed to them, Paul commends them for their love and faith (Eph. 1:5). Yet, when John receives the Revelation they have left their first love (Rev. 2:4). If the early date were ascribed to the Apocalypse this would mean that somewhere within eight years this church had so fallen that such would be said. It does not seem probable that such would take place within the church within that short period of time.

According to the author, the book was written during a time when he was banished on the island of Patmos. It is well known that Domitian had a fondness for this type of persecution (*Ecclesiastical History*, III, 18). Nero, on the other hand, was one who would have rather killed someone than banished him to an island. It was Nero that beheaded Paul and crucified Peter (*Ecclesiastical History*, II, 25). It hardly seems likely that he would have simply banished John to an island when John was one who was so closely attached to the same work as that of Paul and Peter.

The church of Laodicea is reported to have great riches (Rev. 3:17). In A.D. 60 Laodicea was almost completely destroyed by an earthquake. It seems unlikely that they would have been able to rebuild in such a way as to be described as such in the Revelation.

The doctrinal errors described in the Revelation best describe a late date. The Nicolaitans (2:6, 15) were in strong power at the time of John's writing, whereas they were only hinted at in 2 Peter and Jude, circa A.D. 65-66.

It is evident that persecution was on every hand for those who professed Christianity. The churches throughout Asia Minor (Rev. 2 and 3) were having a difficult time through this persecution. Antipas had been killed in Pergamum (Rev. 2:13). Nero's persecution seems to have been confined to the city of Rome and was not a persecution for religious reasons.

Conclusion to the Date: With the evidence that has been presented from both external and internal sources, we believe that the date that best fits the writing of the Apocalypse is that of the later part of Domitian's reign, circa A.D. 95-96.

C. The Place of Writing: The Isle of Patmos

Patmos is a tiny island of the Sporades group twenty-eight miles south of Samos. It is ten miles long and six miles wide at its broadest point. It consisted mostly of volcanic rock and was almost without vegetation. If it were not mentioned in the Bible there would be very few people who would know of its existence. It was such an isolated place that it was a good place for the Romans to use for banishment. Tradition says that John was banished to this island in A.D. 95 under the Emperor Domitian and during an eighteen month period received the visions which are recorded in the book of Revelation.

D. The Recipients of The Revelation

The condition of the Christians who received the Revelation is very crucial. For several years, Christianity had been virtually unnoticed by the Roman government. For the most part it had simply been regarded as a part of the Jewish religion and as such was recognized as a legalized religion of Rome. When it became known that Christianity was not just a part of Judaism but something entirely new and different from Judaism, then Christians found themselves in difficulty with the government as well as with their fellow men. Ray Summers lists the reason for such antagonism directed against Christians as follows:[2]

1. Christianity was an illegal religion. Rome tolerated those whom they conquered so long as they did not proselytize. Christians, of course, existed to save others and this brought Christians in direct conflict with the Roman government.

2. Christianity aspired to universality. With the Romans, the State was the main thing; with Christians, the kingdom of God throughout the world was the principal concern.

3. Christianity was an exclusive religion. Christians refused to mingle freely with heathen social life and customs. It was necessary for them to refuse participation with the pagan world because of the idolatrous practices in which the Romans engaged.

4. Christians were accused of all manner of evil. Because they held meetings at night and were fond of each other, the Romans figured the meetings were for satisfying the lust of the flesh. And when they heard Christians speak of "eating the flesh and drinking the blood" they accused them of being cannibals.

5. Christians refused to go to war. The reasons for this were: (a) A part of the oath and initiation of the soldiers included service to the idols of the state and wearing idolatrous insignias on their uniforms, and (b) Christ had taken their sword from them and had given them ways of peace.

6. Christians were recruited chiefly from the poor and the outcast of society. This caused those who were "respectable" to look down on Christianity.

7. Christians shared with the Jews the contempt which the Romans held for this people. Because Christians refused to compromise they were regarded as worse than the Jews.

8. Christians were viewed as wild fanatics because of their enthusiasm. The dedication of disciples of Christ could not be understood by those of the Roman government.

9. Christianity came in conflict with the temporal

interest of many Romans. When a person became a Christian he changed his relationship with the priest and the idol makers and the vendors of sacrificial animals.

10. Christians refused to worship the emperor. All that was necessary for Christianity to be tolerated was to worship the emperor as the chief deity of the empire. But the Christian could not say, "Caesar is Lord" and at the same time affirm as superior, "Christ is Lord." Because of this attitude, Christians were blamed for all the calamities which befell the empire.

The policy of the government to exterminate Christianity was by itself a sufficient persecution to have brought despair to the heart of the churches. However, this was not all. While this struggle existed from without, there was another danger from within. The problems of Judaism and Gnosticism began to increase within the churches causing bewilderment, controversy, and dissension. It destroyed fellowship, threatened to destroy the permanence of Christianity and broke down the spirit of optimism of the disciples of Christ. When people were being killed, exiled, and robbed of their property for refusal to renounce their religion, when evils were threatening to strike a death blow within the church, the question comes: "Is there any hope for the future?" The Apocalypse is God's answer to this question.

E. The Conditions of the Roman Empire[3]

Since the book of Revelation pictures the church in conflict with the Roman Empire, we need to get a picture of what that Empire was like.

Roman Social Conditions: Rome's boundaries spanned from the British Isles to the African desert on one side, and from the Atlantic Ocean to the Euphrates on the other. She is pictured in the Revelation as a harlot that is sitting "upon many waters" (17:1). These waters are later described as peoples, multitudes, nations, and tongues (17:15). Rome was the worldwide empire of John's day.

Well-trained armies held this empire together. The soldiers were experienced and schooled in the discipline of the Roman army life. These armies brought to Rome the wealth and luxury of the world. The palaces of Rome were rich with their dazzling beauty. Slaves were everywhere to assist their masters and help show off their lords' riches. Slaves often were more cultured and educated than their masters. Fashionable women had a separate slave to apply each shade of makeup. Caligula's wife wore a set of emeralds valued at two million dollars.

On the other hand, there was dire poverty. There was no work for hire; the slaves did it all. The idle poor swarmed to the capital to be fed by the enormous dole system.

Roman Moral Conditions: The teachers of the Roman system were inconsistent in what they taught. They would instruct in purity and live immorally.

According to their own testimony, the Romans cast off everything good and honorable. Crimes multiplied and there was no attempt by anyone to hide vice. Rome was one gigantic monster of lust and wickedness.

Marriage was commercialized. Women began to count their age not in years, but by the number of their husbands. Marriage was held in such contempt that laws against celibacy had to be passed. Children became a burden and were left to the slaves for rearing or sometimes were sold as slaves themselves.

Roman Religious Conditions: The religion of Rome was a mixture of fear, superstition, and ceremony. Most people believed in the existence of many gods, but their faith in these gods vanished when the gods failed to help them. There was much form and ceremony in the religion of Rome.

In the religion of Rome, the emperor was considered divine. A great emphasis was placed on the worship of the emperor especially during the reign of Domitian. The Christian looked upon this as idolatry and utter denial of faith in Jesus Christ. To the emperor, failure to acknowledge his lordship was not as much idolatry as it was to be disloyal to the state of Rome. Thus a Christian who failed to make this vow was held guilty of treason.

An official body was set up in each town to enforce emperor worship. The "Praefectus Urbi" was responsible for punishing those who would not obey the command of worship to the emperor. The "Concillia" was responsible for making images of the emperor, altars, and sponsoring the state religion.

Those who refused to worship the emperor were punished by: (a) being beheaded, (b) being exiled, or (c) having all their property confiscated, thus being reduced to poverty.

The Purpose of the Book

One purpose of the writing of the book of Revelation is to comfort the church in its struggle against the forces of evil and to present and maintain the incentive for the individual Christian to be "faithful to death." This is accomplished in two ways.

The Ultimate Triumph of the Church. The ultimate triumph of the church is seen in three pictures in the book. (1) The Great Multitude: Revelation 7:14-15 shows a great multitude that is said to be "coming out of the great tribulation." Though the saints have been persecuted unto death, this multitude is nevertheless "before the throne of God," Revelation 7:15. (2) Martyrs That Live: On three different occasions we are shown that those who are faithful to Jesus, even though death claims them, live. First is the picture of the souls under the altar, Revelation 6:9. It is said of them that they have been "slain," and yet they "cry out." Second, there are the two witnesses (Rev. 11:3, 7, 11). They are "killed" and yet later raised. Third, there are the souls of them that had been beheaded for the testimony of Jesus (Rev. 20:4). They had died and yet it says, "they lived." The idea behind all this is that even though one might be called to die in his service to God, death does not mean defeat. Little wonder, then, that the Scripture testifies by saying, "Blessed are the dead who die in the Lord" (Rev. 14:13). (3) The Eternal City: The next picture that shows the ultimate triumph of the church is the holy city, New Jerusalem, coming down out of heaven as a bride adorned for her husband (Rev. 21:2, 9-10). This is a picture of the glorified state of the church, which is the bride of Christ, (Eph. 5:22-32; Heb. 12:22-23). Standing triumphant on the other side of the conflict is Christ's church, victorious and glorified.

The Ultimate Defeat of Evil Forces. The comfort continues to be given to the Christians who suffered persecution when they see not only the triumph of the church but also the defeat of the evil forces that have been bringing about this persecution. Two figures are represented from the Apocalypse: (1) The Defeat of Anti-Christian Forces. This picture is taken from Revelation 17:14 and 19:11-16. The battle is not described and yet the adversaries are "killed with the sword which came from the mouth of Him that sat on the horse" (19:21). This means that the defeat of the opposition is inevitable. (2) The Defeat of Satan. From Revelation 12:7-12, it is described "the great dragon was thrown down" and from Revelation 20:10, he is "thrown into the lake of fire and brimstone." The defeat of Satan is presented as complete.

The incentive for the Christian to remain faithful unto death comes when believers are given the assurance that: (a) God sees their tears (Rev. 7:17; 21:4); (b) their prayers rule the world (Rev. 8:3-4); (c) their death is precious in the sight of God (Rev. 14:13; 20:4); (d) their immediate ascent to heaven gives glory that far surpasses the intensity of their suffering here (Rev.

14:13; 20:4); (e) their final victory is assured (Rev. 15:2);
(f) their blood will be avenged (Rev. 6:9; 8:3; 18:20);
(g) Christ lives and reigns forever and as He governs
the world in the interest of His church (Rev. 5:7-8); He
is coming again to take them home with Him in the
"marriage supper of the Lamb" (chs. 21-22). Therefore,
". . . Do not be afraid; I am the first and the last, and
the living One; and I was dead, and behold, I am alive
forevermore, and I have the keys of Death and of
Hades" (Rev. 1:17-18).

Under the fire of severe persecution there had to be
conviction rooted deep in a faith that envisioned an
unalterable triumph of the church and her cause. Only
the belief that world opposition could not prevail
either in time or ultimately, and that the church was
foreordained to prevail in time and eternity, could be
sufficient for maintaining unwavering fidelity in the
face of an otherwise impossible situation.

Therefore, the purpose of the book is to assure us
that Satan and the world cannot win, and that Christ
and the faithful cannot lose. If you want to put it succinctly, Christians can say — *We Win.*

This message is particularly relevant today in that it
presents a call to choose the eternal rather than the
temporal; to resist temptation; to refuse to compromise with pagan secularism; to place the claim of con-
science above all demands against it; to cherish the
confidence of ultimate victory for the kingdom of God,
not only in the reign of Domitian but also in every
other chaotic period of world history, including the
twentieth century.

Methods of Interpretation

Throughout the various periods of Christian history
there have been many methods of interpretation followed in seeking an understanding of the book of
Revelation. Some have approached the book with the

idea that it reveals all the future history from the New Testament times to the consummation of the ages. Others have supposed the book to reveal the history of the apostate church found in Roman Catholicism. Still others find nothing of abiding value in the book and view it simply as a collection of early Christian myth with no significance at all. Another group has sought to point out in the book principles of action by which God deals with man in every age. How are we to interpret this book? What shall be the basis of discussing the meaning of this Apocalypse and give proper significance to its original readers and still have a message for today?

Our understanding of the visions given in this book will depend entirely upon the method of interpretation that will be used. Since this is true, we will briefly study the various theories or methods of interpretation that have been proposed and give our agreement or disagreement to each.

A. The Futurist Method

Mostly (Extreme) Futuristic Method: The "mostly futuristic method" is the extreme view of the futuristic method of interpreting the book of Revelation, a view which is deeply rooted in American evangelical churches. This view sees the dispensational program of God from two different perspectives: one from Israel and one from the church. The seals, trumpets, and bowls of wrath belong to the great tribulation and have to do with Israel and not with the church. In Revelation 2 and 3 the church is seen on earth, but never occurs again in the book (ch. 22:16 being the exception). The twenty-four elders around the throne are the church raptured and rewarded (cf. 4:1) and the people of God who are on earth are the Jews (144,000, Rev. 7:1-7) who preach the gospel of the kingdom during the Tribulation and reach many Gentiles (7:9-17). When the beast (head of the Roman Empire) is restored, the last days begin. The last seven years will begin with a covenant between the Beast (Antichrist) and Israel that the Beast will break in the middle (3 ½ years) and then will turn in anger to persecute the Jews. The great conflict of the book, therefore, is between Israel and the antichrist, not the antichrist and the church. Chapters 4-19 have to do with the Tribulation and do not include the church; only chapters 2 and 3 are for the church and the church age.

Moderate Futuristic Method: One needs to answer the problem of the relationship of the seal, trumpet and bowl judgments to one another in such a way as to provide a solution to the view of history affirmed throughout the rest of the book. It is suggested that the seal judgments represent the forces in history, however long it lasts, by which God works out his redemptive and judicial purposes leading up to the end. In this view the seal judgments are to be going on throughout the church age and the trumpet and bowl judgments are concerned with the time of the consummation. Therefore, from chapters 4-6 you have the church age, and from chapter 7 onward, the end of time. The reason for this is because the contents of the book cannot be opened until the last seal (6:16-17). The seal judgments are seen as parallel to Matthew 24 and the white horse is understood to be the victories won by the gospel in an age characterized by evil and death.

The futurist method of interpretation is the method most often used. This method views the book as almost totally eschatological. The futurist looks upon the book as a volume of unfulfilled prophecy. To some, this book becomes largely a problem of celestial mathematics; and they are more concerned with the calculating of time charts than they are of securing social and economic and political righteousness for their immediate neighbors. The futurist holds that the events from chapters 4-19 are to take place within a brief seven year period that is the same as the 70th week of Daniel 9:24-27. Most futurists are both literalists and millenarians. To them, nothing is symbolical but everything is to be taken literally. For example, when in chapter 11 we read of the measuring of the temple, this is said to mean that the temple is to be rebuilt in Jerusalem before the end of the age. In chapter 11 where there are two witnesses, this means two great prophets will make their appearance near the end of the world.

Objections to the Futurist Method: There are many objections that we have to the futurist method of interpretation. These objections are to the method itself and not to just one or two of the views that result from using this method. The following are objections to the futurist method of interpretation for the book of Revelation:

1. This method of interpretation is inconsistent with John's statement that the things he is writing about "must soon take place" (Rev. 1:1). The Greek word for "must" is the word *dei* and implies a moral necessity. It is morally necessary for the things to be fulfilled shortly in order for God's oppressed people to see his arm revealed and his comfort given in a time of persecution. The same word is used in Matthew 16:21 where Jesus says he must go to Jerusalem to die. This word is also used in regards to the qualifications of bishops in 1 Timothy 3:1ff.

The word "soon" comes from *en taxi* and can be translated either "shortly" or "quickly" and implies an immediate fulfillment. Futurists say this phrase means "certainly." But when compared with 2 Timothy 4:9, where the same word is used this cannot be correct. Paul uses the same word in this passage and tells Timothy to come to him "quickly" (*en taxi*). This does not mean in the next thousand years or so. Allowing Scripture to interpret Scripture we find in 2 Timothy 4:21, that the "quickly" referred to earlier in its context means "before winter." The "soon" was "before winter" or immediately. Therefore, the visions in Revelation were to be fulfilled in the immediate future.

2. This method of interpretation to the book of Revelation divorces the book from its original setting. It takes the message of the book altogether out of relation to the needs of the churches to which it was originally addressed and who received it. A basic rule of interpretation for Scripture is to ask, "What did this mean to the ones to whom it was originally addressed?" We must start with the generation to whom the Apocalypse was addressed and see how the interpretation that we assign to it will give comfort and aid to that audience.

To know that the Apocalypse was written to answer the cry of the Christians under the persecution of Domitian is to know that it was never meant to be a chronology for the Lord's return or a forecast of the apostate Roman Catholic Church.

3. This method of interpretation misses the entire teaching of Christ regarding the nature of the kingdom of God. To assign an interpretation to this book that finds its ultimate fulfillment in an earthly materialistic kingdom is to miss the reason behind the giving of the Apocalypse.

B. The Continuous Historical Method

The Continuous Historical method of interpretation looks upon the Revelation as a forecast in symbols of the history of the church beginning at Pentecost and going until the end of time. People who hold this view are anxious to know exactly where our century is in relationship to the scheme of time for they think they see actual battles, movements, individuals, and events specified in the book. Some even think that with the book of Revelation in one hand, and Gibbon's *Decline and Fall of the Roman Empire* in the other, you should be able to show such the fulfillment of such detail of events that any unbeliever should be convinced of its accuracy. This system makes the book of Revelation prophesy in detail the apostasy of the Roman Catholic Church. It is this method of interpretation that was held by most non-Catholic scholars during the Reformation.

The best example of this method of interpretation that is most familiar today is from *Barnes Commentary on the New Testament.* In his book on Revelation the outline gives the following information and description for chapters 6-11.

Chapters 6-9
1st Seal — Fulfilled in the state of the Roman Empire from the death of Domitian, A.D. 96 to the accession of Commodus, A.D. 180.

2nd Seal — From the death of Commodus, A.D. 193 and onward.

3rd Seal — The time of Caracalla, A.D. 211 and onward.

4th Seal — The time of Decius to Gallienus, A.D. 243-268.

5th Seal — Fulfilled in the Roman Empire in the persecutions particularly in the time of Diocletian, A.D. 284-304.

6th Seal — The invasions of the Barbarians, A.D. 365 onwards.

7th Seal — Fulfilled in the Trumpets, as follows:

1st Trumpet — Invasions by Alaric the Goth, A.D. 395-410.

2nd Trumpet — Invasion by Gensaric the Vandal, A.D. 428-468.

3rd Trumpet — Invasion by Attila the Hun, A.D. 433-453.

4th Trumpet — Final conquest of the Western empire by Odoacer, King of the Heruli, A.D. 476-490.

5th Trumpet — The Mohammedans.

6th Trumpet — The Turks.

Chapter 10

The Great Angel — Announces the Reformation.

The Little Book — The Bible.

The 7 Thunders — The anathemas hurled against the Reformation by the Pope.

Chapter 11

The Measuring of the Temple — The determining of what constituted the true church at the time of the Reformation.

The Two Witnesses — Those who testified against the errors of Rome.

7th Trumpet — The final triumph of the church.

This view of Barnes' interpretation gives an idea of what the whole method under discussion at this time is all about.

Objections to the Continuous Historical Method: The objections that should be considered to this method of interpretation are as follows:

1. This method of interpretation divorces Revelation from the history of the early church and takes the book completely out of touch with the situation of the Christians to whom it was originally written. Of what comfort is it to the persecuted Christian to know that there is going to be an invasion by Attila the Hun in A.D. 433-453? John was writing about things which were "soon to come to pass."

2. This method of interpretation also gives an undue importance to the Roman Catholic Church. It sees the Reformation largely as the one great event since Constantine, and limits the history of the Christian movement to the West. This presents a view of Scripture that has too narrow a horizon. Catholicism is not the only enemy of the church and it would have no significance in those countries where Rome does not have any power.

3. This method of interpretation leads to false calculations of time. It is assumed that the time periods of

Revelation are to be taken as the "one-day = one year" theory (cf. Num. 14:34; Ezek. 4:4-6; Dan. 9:25; 2 Pet. 3:8). Yet this theory has absolutely no proof behind it and should not be used to force an interpretation upon a book which is already the subject of a great deal of uncertainty and misunderstanding.

4. This method of interpretation stoops to details as absurd as those of the futurist school. For Revelation 8:1 it is said the one-half hour of silence is to mean 70 years of no war in Roman history. The lack of war on earth is spoken of as silence in heaven. When asked why, they do not know.

C. The Philosophy of History Method[4]

This method of interpretation looks at the book as highly symbolic. This theory does not apply its message to any particular historical age but sees symbols of descriptions of God's triumph over evil. These symbols refer to forces that are fulfilled over and over again throughout history. Everything is general but nothing is ever specific.

Objections to the Philosophy of History Method: The objections to the Philosophy of History method of interpretation are as follows:

1. This method of interpretation removes the book too far from the situation for which it was originally written. It has no significance to the Christians who first received it. If the visions were mere idealizations rather than actual historical events, what would be the meaning to the original readers?

2. This method of interpretation makes the life and death of early Christians insignificant. Once again it could be said that this method of interpretation also confines the book to a very narrow horizon.

D. The Preterist Method

The Preterist method of interpretation is just the opposite of the Futurist method. The word Preterist means "past or beyond." The Preterists look upon the fulfillment of the visions in Revelation as having taken place in the past. The Preterist school is divided into two main groups:

The Right Wing Preterist: Those who hold this view believe and accept the book as inspired of God. They believe Revelation 6:1-16:21 refers to the immediate history of the church during the age of persecution and that most of the book was fulfilled in the days of the Roman Empire under the reign of Domitian. The final judgment and the perfected state of mankind yet awaits fulfillment. The book of Revelation is only for the days of the persecution in Asia Minor and they feel to a great extent it has only a literary interest for people of our day.

One revision of the right wing preterist position is that while the events depicted in the book of Revelation were for the first century Christians, these visions are not meant to be consecutive but rather repeatable happenings throughout history. For example, the 3 ½ years of the rule of the beast and the harlot represent the "little season" of the dominance of the Roman Empire. The binding of Satan represents the downfall of the persecuting power of Rome. At this time, the cause of the saints is resurrected (the first resurrection) and the thousand years is the longer period of triumph of the biblical faith. The visions symbolize actual historical happenings which are not meant to represent consecutive happenings but are repeatable happenings throughout the history of the church. Most right wing preterists are Amillennial in their view of Revelation 20. In this sense, there is a similarity with the symbolic, spiritual, or idealistic method of interpretation.

The Left Wing Preterist: Those who hold this view do not believe the book of Revelation is inspired. To this group, the Apocalypse is parallel with other apocalyptic literature. The only value to the book is in literature.

Objections to the Preterist Method: The objections to the Preterist method of interpretation are as follows: The left wing Preterist is rejected by the person who believes the Bible is the inspired word of God. The right wing Preterist has more good points than objections. The basic objection is that it finds no present day application or significance. If this is true, then why should one spend his time in study of this book today?

In reality, many commentators today do not subscribe to any one particular view of interpreting the book of Revelation. What you often find is a combination approach where the expositor of the message of this book finds the principles from any of the above mentioned methods and uses them in assisting in our understanding of the text. In keeping with that thought, we would suggest that the best way to interpret the book of Revelation is to understand what was going on during the time in which the book was written (Historical-Background), and having understood that, read, interpret and apply the book of Revelation (a book of prophecy) in much the way you would any prophetic book of the Bible.

E. The Historical-Background/Prophetic Principle

The Historical-Background Method: This method of interpretation might be looked upon as a part of the preterist method. It is desirable to discuss it as a separate division for two reasons: (1) Because the left wing group has left a very undesirable association attached to the entire preterist method of interpretation. (2) Because even some of the right wing group, with which this method has much in common, have held the Apocalypse has no message except to those who first received it. For this reason, the Historical-Background/Prophetic Principle method of interpretation is discussed as a separate method of interpretation.

The principles of this method of interpretation

come from combining the right wing preterist and the philosophy of history interpretation. While no method of interpretation is without objections, this writer believes there are less objections that can be raised here than with any other method. With this in mind, it is good to examine some principles that will assist our understanding of using this method of interpretation.[5]

1. The book of Revelation was written primarily for the encouragement and edification of the Christians in the first century. One must make a close study of the church of that day, the writer of the book, the condition from which he wrote, his relation to those to whom he wrote and any other material significant to the understanding of the background of the day.

2. The book of Revelation is written largely in symbolical language. A symbol is something which suggests something else by reason of relationship or association. In Revelation symbols are used to picture or represent abstract ideas. Revelation is a divine picture book that uses symbols of certain forces which underlie the historical development of the church and its unceasing conflict. Understanding this principle, one must ask two questions: What is the picture? What does it mean? In fact, the order in which these questions are asked is important. Far too often we look at the vision and before seeing the picture, we quickly begin to ask, "What does this mean?" John would have us first observe the picture, that is what he saw, and that is what he wants us to see. Once we see the picture, then we can ask its meaning and then try to work out the details.

3. This book uses Old Testament terminology with New Testament meaning. A symbol used in one place does not necessarily mean the same thing in another. John uses expressions from Daniel and Ezekiel, but they do not necessarily have to mean the same thing. In the book of Revelation there are 278 allusions to the Old Testament.[6]

4. To get the true meaning the reader must seek to grasp the visions or series of visions as a whole without pressing the details of the symbolism. The best policy is to find the central truth and let the details fit in the most natural way.

5. Also, remember that the Apocalypse is addressed chiefly to the imagination. This is in keeping with the way we understand other books from the Bible. The book of Romans has an appeal to the intellect, Psalms to the emotion, and the Commandments to the will. It can certainly be understood that, with the book of Revelation being written in highly symbolical language, it should have an appeal to the imagination.

6. In using this method of interpretation when we have found an event or person to which the prophecy is fairly applicable, we can consider it fulfilled in such a person or event, but not thereby exhausted; for it is intended more for the purpose of showing us the forces for good and evil that make history than for the prediction of particular events.

The Prophetic Principle: The method of interpretation that seems to best fit a proper understanding is to use the Historical-Background and then apply the Prophetic Principle. The author claims to be a prophet of God (22:9) and among other powers of his prophetic office is the ability to predict the future and outcome of all things (10:11; 19:10). This book is called a prophecy (1:3; 22:7, 10, 18, 19). It should be recognized at once that Revelation is a book of prophecy and that the symbols stand for something real. The perspective is not to be limited to a brief period of time, but the way is open, a way not for a reading into it a series of precise historical occurrences, but for doing justice to the truth which lies at the basis of the historical interpretation; namely, that there is in this book prefigured the great crisis in the age-long conflict of Christ and His church with the adversaries.

Prophecy is not for Private Interpretation

A fundamental axiom of biblical interpretation is found within the pages of the Bible itself when Peter writes, "know this first of all, that no prophecy of Scripture is a matter of one's own interpretation" (2 Pet. 1:20). The prophets of the Old Testament received heavenly visions. Their prophecies were interpreted, not by them, but by the Spirit of God. Consider the following:

1. Jeremiah 1:11-15. Jeremiah sees a vision of the rod of an almond tree (vv. 11-12). This signifies Jehovah's diligence to perform His word. He also sees a vision of the boiling pot (vv. 13-15). This signifies judgment upon Jerusalem. The interpretation of these visions are found in the verses and are not the opinion of the prophet but rather, "men moved by the Holy Spirit spoke from God" (2 Pet. 1:21); therefore, the interpretation is the Spirit's.

2. Revelation 1:12, 19-20. John sees a vision of the seven candlesticks (1:12, 20). The candlesticks signify the seven churches. He also sees a vision of the stars (1:16, 20). The seven stars are the angels of the seven churches. The interpretation of the sign was not John's interpretation but rather Christ's.

Signs are to be Interpreted by God

As is true of the Old Testament prophets, so also it is true of the New Testament prophets. When a sign is given, we shall try to allow God to give the interpretation. Those signs whose meanings are not revealed in the text are to be ascertained by observing a like vision in Scripture, the meaning of which is known. Consider the following:

1. The Vision of the Seal of God (Rev. 7:1-4).

The Twelve Tribes of Israel are sealed in their forehead. To interpret this vision one needs to study Ezekiel 9:1-9.

2. The Vision of the Little Book (Rev. 10:5-11) John

was told to eat the book and then to prophesy. To gain an understanding of this vision one should study Ezekiel 2:8-3:3, 14.

In each of the above mentioned cases the visions of Revelation are strikingly similar to the visions in Ezekiel. The meaning of the visions in Ezekiel is obvious. It is safe to conclude that the meaning of the visions in Revelation are similar in nature.

A guiding principle of prophetic interpretation will be: When the meaning of a vision in the book is made known, that meaning will be adopted. When the meaning of a vision is not made known, we will make an appeal to a similar vision from Scripture to interpret that vision.

As you continue to study the book of Revelation you will become aware of the fact that some of the symbols are explained, others are not. Consider the following:

The Unexplained Symbols:
1. The white stone, 2:17
2. The pillar, 3:12
3. The elders, 4:4ff
4. The two witnesses, 11:3ff
5. The woman clothed with the sun, 12:1, 2, 14ff
6. The winepress, 14:20; 19:15
7. The supper, 19:6-9, 17
8. The Great White Throne, 20:11
9. The city of God, 21:2ff

Symbols Explained:
1. The 7 stars = 7 angels of the churches, 1:20
2. The 7 lampstands = the 7 churches of Asia, 1:20
3. The 7 lamps of fire = the 7 spirits of God, 4:5
4. The bowls of incense = the prayers of the saints, 5:8
5. The great multitude = those who come out of the great tribulation, 7:13-14
6. The great dragon = the devil, Satan, 12:9
7. The 7 heads of the beast = 7 mountains, 17:9
8. The 10 horns of the beast = 10 kings, 17:12

9. The waters = peoples, multitudes, nations, and tongues, 17:15
10. The woman = the great city, 17:18
11. The lake of fire = the second death, 19:20; 20:14

Old Testament Imagery: There are also some symbols that are paralleled by Old Testament imagery. While the list is not exhaustive, we offer the following:

1. The tree of life, 2:7; 22:2
2. Hidden manna, 2:17
3. The rod of iron, 2:27
4. The morning star, 2:28
5. The key of David, 3:7
6. The living creatures, 4:7ff
7. The four horsemen, 6:1ff
8. The great angel, 10:1ff
9. The first beast, 13:1-10
10. The second beast, 13:11-18

The Old Testament Background[7]

The language of the Book of Revelation is deeply rooted in the Old Testament. Oddly enough though, there is not one direct citation in Revelation from the Old Testament with a statement that it is quoted from a given passage. However, a count of the significant allusions which are traceable both by verbal resemblance and contextual connection to the Hebrew canon number over four hundred. Often, rather than exact quotations, you will find the Old Testament in citations or allusions.

Symbolism of Numbers[8]

Any study on the book Revelation would be incomplete without trying to understand the significance of the use of numbers throughout the book. Using numbers to signify something has always held a fascination for the oriental mind. In the early days of humanity, language was primitive and vocabulary was meager. Sometimes one Hebrew word was used to mean several things. Under these conditions men came naturally to use numbers as we use words. Certain numbers came to have certain concepts and teach certain truths.

To assist in an understanding of the significance of numbers in the book of Revelation, we offer the following:

1. The Number One: The number one stands for Unity. Man saw a single object and came to associate with the number one the idea of unity or independent existence. It stood for that which was unique and alone. This number does not appear in the book of Revelation.

2. The Number Two: The number two stood for Strength. When a man went out to hunt the wild animal or fight against a foe he found strength and courage in companionship. Two were far stronger and much more effective than one. Thus the number two came to stand for strength, for confirmation, for redoubled energy and courage. In the book of Revelation the truth is confirmed by two witnesses who are slain and rise again. Two beasts are presented as a foe of strength against the cause of Christ.

3. The Number Three: The number three stands for Deity. The number three first came from the home. A man considered father love, mother love, and child love. When it began to be associated with the Greek and Hebrew image of God, it began to carry the thought of the divine, or Deity.

4. The Number Four: The number four is the number for the World. Man believed that the world was flat with four boundaries. There were four winds. A town was surrounded by four walls. So, when man thought of the world, he thought of four. Four becomes the cosmic number. In Revelation, there are four creatures and four horsemen. The world in which men lived and worked and died was symbolized by four.

5. **The Number Five:** The number five is the number for human completeness. A man looked at his hand and counted his fingers and came up with five, a perfect or complete hand. He counted his toes and came up with five, a perfect or complete foot. A perfect or complete man was a man who had his members complete and intact. So the number five doubled to ten became known for human completeness. In Revelation there are ten horns; also the numbers seventy and one thousand appear. These all stand for completeness to the greatest degree.

6. **The Number Seven:** The number seven is God's number for perfection. Man took the perfect world number, four, and added to it the perfect divine number, three, and came up with the number seven, the most sacred number of all. Seven expresses completeness through the union of earth with heaven. Revelation uses the number seven many times. In fact, this number is the most prevalent throughout the Apocalypse.

7. **The Number Twelve:** The number twelve in Hebrew thought came to be the symbol of organized religion. There are twelve apostles, twelve tribes of Israel, twelve gates to the Holy City. Note: 12×12×1,000 = 144,000. A symbol of security.

8. **The Number Three and One-half:** The number three and one-half becomes the number for incompleteness. When you take the number seven (completeness) and cut it in half it becomes three and one-half to symbolize incompleteness. The number three and one-half always stands for indefinite, the incomplete, the dissatisfied; but in it all was the hope and patient waiting for a better day when truth would be delivered from the scaffold and placed on the throne usurped by wrong.

9. **The Number Six:** The number six stands for man's number. The number six is a sinister number.

Six was the charge that met defeat with success just in its grasp. It had within it the stroke of doom. It had the ability to be great but failed to measure up. This is important to keep in mind when we come to the number six hundred and sixty-six. This is man without God; man is doomed to failure.

From this observation it can be said that numbers in the book of Revelation do not have real numeric value but rather are symbolical and we must seek to find their symbolical significance.

NOTES

[1]The following material is outlined in Rex A. Turner, Sr., "Historical Perspectives on the Epistles of John," *Sound Doctrine*, Vol. 3, No. 5, Oct-Nov-Dec, 1978, 8-9.

[2]This is an abbreviated listing from Ray Summers, *Worthy Is the Lamb* (Nashville: Broadman, 1951), 87-88. He cites as his sources Cady H. Allen, *The Message of the Book of Revelation* (Nashville: Cokesbury Press, 1939), 59-63 and A. H. Newman, *A Manual of Church History* (Philadelphia: The American Baptist Publication Society, 1899), I, 148-150.

[3]This material is paraphrased from Ray Summers, 90-93.

[4]This is called by various other names: the "highly symbolic" or "idealist" method of interpretation.

[5]Cf. Summers, 46-51 and Albertus Pieters, *The Lamb, The Woman and The Dragon* (Grand Rapids: the Church Press, 1946), 64-72.

[6]William Hendriksen, *More Than Conquerors* (Grand Rapids: Baker, 1939) 61-62, gives a chart with chapter by chapter summary of the use of the Old Testament in the book of Revelation.

[7]Richard Rogers, *Hallelujah Anyway* (An Outline Study of the Book of Revelation). Lubbock: Sunset School of Preaching, n.d. For further information regarding this area I would recommend Hendriksen and H.B. Swete.

[8]Summers, 21-25 and H.B. Swete, *Commentary on Revelation* (Grand Rapids: Kregel, 1977 reprint), cxxxi - cxxxix.

OUTLINE OF REVELATION

I. INTRODUCTION, 1:1-8.
    A. The Title of the Book, 1:1-3.
    B. The Salutation and Doxology, 1:4-8.

II. JOHN'S VISION OF CHRIST, 1:9-20.
    A. What John Heard, 1:9-11
    B. What John Saw, 1:12-16
    C. What John Did, 1:17-20

III. THE LAMB AND THE SEVEN CHURCHES, 2:1-3:22.
    A. To Ephesus: Loyal but Lacking, 2:1-7.
    B. To Smyrna: Faithful unto Death, 2:8-11.
    C. To Pergamum: Where Satan Lived, 2:12-17.
    D. To Thyatira: Wait for the Star, 2:18-29.
    E. To Sardis: Dead or Alive? 3:1-6.
    F. To Philadelphia: The Church with an Open
       Door, 3:7-13.
    G. To Laodicea: The Church with the Closed
       Door, 3:14-22.

IV. THE THRONE SCENE, 4:1-5:14.
    A. The Glory of God and Creation, 4:1-11.
    B. The Glory of the Lamb and Redemption, 5:1-14.

V. THE LAMB OPENS THE SEALED BOOK, 6:1-8:5.
    A. The First Four Seals: The Four Horsemen, 6:1-8.

B. The Fifth Seal: The Cry of Souls of Martyrs, 6:9-11.

C. The Sixth Seal: Terror of Judgment Announced, 6:12-17.

D. Interlude: 7:1-17.
  1. The Sealing of the 144,000, 7:1-8.
  2. The Innumerable Company, 7:9-17.

E. The Seventh Seal: Introduction to Seven Trumpets, 8:1-5.

VI. THE SEVEN TRUMPETS, 8:6-11:19.

A. The First Trumpet: Land Disasters, 8:6-7.

B. The Second Trumpet: Maritime Disasters, 8:8-9.

C. The Third Trumpet: Land (Fresh Water) Disasters, 8:10-11.

D. The Fourth Trumpet: Heavenly Body Disasters, 8:12.

E. Interlude: Eagle flying in Mid-heaven, 8:13.

F. The Fifth Trumpet: First Woe, 9:1-12.

G. The Sixth Trumpet: Second Woe — Four Angels Loosed, 9:13-21.

H. Interlude: Four Pictures, 10:1-11:13.
  1. Seven Unrecorded Thunders, 10:1-7.
  2. Little "Bitter-sweet" Book, 10:8-11.
  3. Measuring the Temple, 11:1-2.
  4. The Two Witnesses, 11:3-13.

I. The Seventh Trumpet: Third Woe, 11:14-19.

VII. THE CONFLICT BETWEEN GOD AND SATAN, 12:1-13:18.

A. Battle One: The Woman and Her Child, 12:1-6.

B. Battle Two: The War in Heaven, 12:7-9.

C. Interlude: Battle Song of Triumph, 12:10-12.

D. Battle Three: The War on Earth against the Woman and Her Seed, 12:13-17.

E. Battle Four: The Sea Beast, 13:1-10.

F. Battle Five: The Earth Beast, 13:11-18.

VIII. THE FORCES OF THE LAMB, 14:1-20.

A. The Lamb and the Saints, 14:1-5.

B. Four Headline Banners, 14:6-13.

C. The Sickles of Judgment, 14:14-20.

IX. THE WAR WITH THE BEAST, 15:1-16:21.
   A. The Song of Moses and the Lamb, 15:1-8.
   B. The Seven Bowls of Wrath, 16:1-21.
      1. The First Bowl of Wrath: Into the Earth, 16:1-2.
      2. The Second Bowl of Wrath: Into the Sea, 16:3.
      3. The Third Bowl of Wrath: Into the Rivers, 16:4-7.
      4. The Fourth Bowl of Wrath: Upon the Sun, 16:8-9.
      5. The Fifth Bowl of Wrath: Upon the Throne of the Beast, 16:10-11.
      6. The Sixth Bowl of Wrath: Upon the Great River, 16:12-16.
      7. The Seventh Bowl of Wrath: Upon the Air, 16:17-21.

X. THE JUDGMENT OF THE GREAT HARLOT, 17:1-21:8.
   A. The Vision of the Great Harlot, 17:1-5.
   B. The Beast Interpreted, 17:6-11.
   C. The Horns and Woman Interpreted, 17:12-18.
   D. Babylon's Fall Announced, 18:1-3.
   E. The Call to God's People Because of Approaching Punishment, 18:4-8.
   F. The Lament over the City, 18:9-24.
   G. The Hallelujah Chorus after the Fall of the Harlot, 19:1-10.
   H. The Rider on the White Horse: the Conqueror, 19:11-21.
   I. The Thousand Year Reign, 20:1-6.
   J. Satan is Loosed for a Little Season, 20:7-10.
   K. End of Conflict: Final Judgment, 20:11-15.
   L. The New Heaven and New Earth, 21:1-8.

XI. THE VISION OF THE NEW JERUSALEM, 21:9-22:5.
   A. John is Invited to View the Holy City, 21:9-11a.
   B. The City's Outward Appearance, 21:11b-23.

      C. The Inhabitants of the City, 21:24-27.
      D. The Provisions of the City, 22:1-5.
  XI. THE EPILOGUE: CLOSING WORDS, 22:6-21.

Revelation 1

I. INTRODUCTION, 1:1-8

[1]The Revelation of Jesus Christ, which God gave Him to show to His bond-servants, the things which must soon take place; and He sent and communicated it by His angel to His bond-servant John, [2]who testified to the word of God and to the testimony of Jesus Christ, even to all that he saw.

[3]Blessed is he who reads and those who hear the words of the prophecy, and heed the things which are written in it; for the time is near.

[4]John to the seven churches that are in Asia: Grace to you and peace, from Him who is and who was and who is to come, and from the seven Spirits who are before His throne, [5]and from Jesus Christ, the faithful witness, the firstborn of the dead, and the ruler of the kings of the earth. To Him who loves us and released us from our sins by His blood– [6]and He has made us to be a kingdom, priests to His God and Father–to Him be the glory and the dominion forever and ever. Amen.

[7]BEHOLD, HE IS COMING WITH THE CLOUDS, and every eye will see Him, even those who pierced

Him; and all the tribes of the earth will mourn over Him. So it is to be. Amen.

[8]"I am the Alpha and the Omega," says the Lord God, "who is and who was and who is to come, the Almighty."

A. The Title of the Book, 1:1-3

In the opening verses (vv. 1-3), we have an introduction or prologue to the entire book. In this section we learn how and for what purpose the book was written, and a blessing is pronounced on those who read, hear, and take to heart (keep) the things written in this book. We know that this is a different book because it begins by claiming to be a book of revelation, signs, and prophecy.

1:1 The Revelation of Jesus Christ, which God gave Him to show to His bond-servants, the things which must soon take place; and He sent and communicated it by His angel to His bond-servant John,

The word "revelation" comes from the word *apokalypsis* which refers to the act of unveiling or an object which is uncovered. In other uses in the New Testament it refers to something previously unknown but which is now revealed. It is a revelation in the sense that it is an unveiling; a disclosure of truth through a series of visions. For some, the use of the word "apocalypse" does not mean it is a literary classification but rather an indication of the nature and purpose of the book, while others would agree that it "not only describes its contents, but classifies it as a recognized type of literature."[1] As used in the New Testament, revelation may refer to some aspect of making known God's will, whether present or the future (cf. Luke 2:32; Rom. 16:25; Eph. 3:5).

It is stated that this is a revelation "of Jesus Christ," i.e., it is a revelation which God gave Jesus. Jesus is the revealer of the visions which John receives: he addresses the letters to the seven churches in chapters 2-3; he opens the scroll which is the destiny of the churches (5:5, 7); and discloses its contents (6:1, 3, 5, 7, 9, 12; 8:1). The opening verse (1:1) says the revelation is given by Jesus Christ to John as God gave it to him.

The phrase, "which God gave Him to show" indicates that the ultimate source of what Christ reveals is from God. God is the source of all revelation (cf. Dan. 2:28-29, 45). The Revelation did not originate with Jesus but came from God. Therefore, Revelation is called "the word of God" (cf. 1:2; 19:9).

The recipients of the revelation are the "*douloi*," i.e., the bond-servants. In the Old Testament "servant" means prophet (Amos 3:7), but the phrase here seems to refer to those who truly love the Lord and follow His will, i.e., they are God's bond-servants. Eleven times in the book of Revelation, God's people are referred to as servants (e.g., 2:20; 7:3; 22:3). John is one servant receiving the revelation and giving it to other servants. While John may be receiving the visions, they are not for him alone, but also, they are for the community of faith. "What must soon take place" indicates that the events about to take place are for the future; but not the distant future. When Daniel gave his prophecy, he placed the fulfillment of these things "in the latter days" (Dan. 2:28-29, 45). When John receives the revelation, it is something which must "soon" take place. The word "soon" (*en tachei*) means that the visions pertain to John's day. The same word (*tachei*) is translated quickly (Luke 18:8; Acts 12:7; 22:18), shortly (Acts 25:4), soon (Rom. 16:20), and before long (1 Tim. 3:14). It seems, therefore, that this word carries with it a sense of urgency, or near immediate fulfillment.

John was to be shown "what must soon take place." Twice in the opening verse John is told that what he is about to see and write will have immediate fulfillment. In verse 3 he writes, "the time is near." In the closing verses of this book (22:6, 10) the same pattern is found. What John writes must soon take place for the time is at hand. Those who look to the Revelation of John to have a future fulfillment several thousand years from the time it is written have taken the book out of its historical context and missed the meaning to its original readers.

In the midst of the persecution which Christians were facing in John's day, they are told that relief will come "soon" and with this promise they receive comfort.

Our first introduction to the word "angel" is found in the opening verse. It occurs seventy-six times in this book. Angels are involved in praising and serving God. The angel introduced here is not identified for us; we are only told that the angel functions as a messenger who does God's will. The proper chain of revelation is the following: God—Jesus—Angel—John—Servants.

The word "communicated" (made it known, NIV) tells us that what is presented is in language different from ordinary language. The word that is used is a form of the Greek word *semion* which is used by John (in the Gospel) in referring to miracles that Jesus performed. It refers to something shown by signs or symbols.

1:2 who testified to the word of God and to the testimony of Jesus Christ, *even* to all that he saw.

John was to write "all that he saw." That is to say, John was a seer. God's use of one as a seer changed to the use of one as a prophet (cf. 1 Sam. 9:9). A seer was one who saw the vision; a prophet was one who spoke the word of the Lord. John functions in this book as both a seer and a prophet.

1:3 Blessed is he who reads and those who hear the words of the prophecy, and heed the things which are written in it; for the time is near.

This is the first of seven beatitudes found in the

book. "Blessed is he who reads and those who hear the words of the prophecy and heeds those things which are written in it; for the time is near." (The others are found in 14:13; 16:15; 19:9; 20:6; 22:7; 22:14.) The phrase for "he who reads" is singular while the phrase for "those who hear" is plural. This tells us that the Revelation was intended to be read before the church (a practice in synagogue services that probably was carried over into the practice of the early church, cf. Neh. 8:2; Luke 4:16; Acts 13:15). The blessing is not just upon the reading and hearing of the book, but also upon the one who keeps the things which are written in it. It is one thing to hear, but another to do (cf. Matt. 7:21ff).

B. The Salutation and Doxology, 1:4-8

The opening of these verses gives us the salutation and doxology of the book. In these verses we learn of the message and destination of the Revelation given to John.

1:4 John to the seven churches that are in Asia: Grace to you and peace, from Him who is and who was and who is to come, and from the seven Spirits who are before His throne,

The destination of the message is "to the seven churches that are in Asia." These are real cities and real congregations located on the west coast of what is now called Turkey. But they are typical of churches throughout the first century world. The fact that seven churches are chosen probably refers to the number for perfection and indicates that these seven churches are representatives of all the churches. That is to say, what we find in these seven churches we will find also in other churches that are established. We are not to assume, however, that there are only seven churches throughout all of Asia Minor (e.g., Colossae).

The message is one of "grace and peace." In this salutation John combines a religious variation of the normal Hellenistic greeting (grace) with the customary Hebrew greeting (peace). Such a greeting is found in all of Paul's writings (with mercy added in First and Second Timothy). Grace is the divine favor showed to man. It is that unmerited, unearned favor from God. It is the undeserved gift of divine love of God to mankind. Peace is the state of spiritual well-being which follows as a result of grace. It is the harmonious relationship between God and man through the death of Christ on the Cross (cf. Eph. 2:1-22).

The source of his message is seen in the three phrases, 1) "from Him who is and who was and who is to come," and 2) "from the seven Spirits who are before His throne," and 3) "from Jesus Christ." It is interesting to notice that the source of John's message to the churches comes from the entire Godhead.

John emphasizes first the changeless nature of God. The reference to "the one who is and who was and who is to come" is identified for us in verse 8 as "the Lord God." This is a description which is reminiscent of Exodus 3:14, "God said to Moses, 'I AM WHO I AM'; and He said, 'Thus you shall say to the sons of Israel: "I AM has sent me to you."'"

The seven spirits before the throne is a little more difficult to identify. There is probably an allusion here to Isaiah 11:2 and Zechariah 4:10. This phrase is found three more times in the book of Revelation. In 3:1 the seven spirits are identified with the angels of the seven churches. In 4:5 the seven lamps blazing are said to be the seven spirits of God. In 5:6 the seven eyes of the lamb are called the seven spirits of God (cf. Zech. 4:2b, 10b). Robert Mounce says that surveying the places in Revelation where this phrase is found

> . . .fails to provide sufficient information to arrive at a certain understanding of this enigmatic phrase. Although only conjecture, it would seem that they are

perhaps part of a heavenly entourage that has a special ministry in connection with the lamb.[2]

But it seems that this fails to take the context into consideration. The connection with the Father and the Son seems to give reason for accepting the interpretation that the seven spirits before the throne "represents the Spirit of God in the fulness of His activity and power."[3]

1:5 and from Jesus Christ, the faithful witness, the firstborn of the dead, and the ruler of the kings of the earth. To Him who loves us and released us from our sins by His blood —

In verse 5 there are three magnificent titles given to Jesus Christ. Jesus Christ is "the faithful witness" (cf. 3:14; John 3:11; 18:14, 37). A witness is one on whom we can rely. A witness is a person who tells what his eyes have seen and what his ears have heard. Jesus was faithful in fulfilling His mission on earth (Heb. 5:8-9). He came from God, was God, and ascended back to God (cf. John 17:1-4).

Second, "the firstborn of the dead." This is true by virtue of His resurrection (cf. Col. 1:18; Rom. 8:29; 1 Cor. 15:20). The word "firstborn" is *prototokos* which means one with power and honor, or one who occupies the first place, a prince among men. There is no part of the universe, in this world or in the world to come, in life or in death, of which Jesus is not the Lord.

Third, Jesus is "the ruler of the kings of the earth." This is an allusion to Psalm 2:1-9; 89:27; and 110:2. H.B. Swete points out the connection between this title and the temptation scene. The devil took Jesus up into a high mountain and showed Him all the kingdoms of the earth. "All these things I will give you," he said, "if you fall down and worship me" (Matt. 4:8-9; Luke 4:6-7). It was the devil's claim that the world was his and he would give Jesus a share in it. The wonderful thing is that what the devil offered Jesus, but never could have delivered, Jesus obtained for himself in the suffering on the Cross and in the power of the resurrection. As the risen Christ, Jesus is "head over all things" (Eph. 1:22), and rules with a "righteous scepter" (Heb. 1:8), and is able to "RULE THEM [NATIONS] WITH A ROD OF IRON" (Rev. 2:27). Jesus is the exalted Lord over all (cf. Phil. 2:8-11) and the righteous judge over every enemy (cf. Rev. 5:9-10; 11:17-18; 17:14; 19:16 and Psalm 89:27).

1:6 and He has made us to be a kingdom, priests to His God and Father — to Him be the glory and the dominion forever and ever. Amen.

The effect of this message is found in verse 5b-6. The question is: How does Jesus bring about this message of grace and peace? The answer is: By loving us and making us free from our sins. This was done at the cost of His own blood. That is to say, what happened on the cross was one availing act in time which was an expression of the continuous love of God. What happened on the cross in a moment of time is a window into the eternal, unchanging, unceasing love of God.

He made us to be a kingdom of priests to serve His God and Father; i.e., He has given us royalty (cf. Col. 1:13-14), and through His death we have direct access (privileges as a priest) to God (cf. Isa. 61:6). John says that because of what Jesus did, access to the presence of God is no longer confined to priests in the narrow sense of the term but is open to everyone. This expresses the truth of the priesthood of all believers. We can enter boldly into the throne of grace (Heb. 4:16) because there is a new and living way for us into the presence of God (Heb. 10:19-22). Jesus gave us the royalty to those who are sons of God (cf. Gal. 3:26; 4:4-6) and priesthood to those for whom the way to the nearer presence of God is always open.

1:7 BEHOLD, HE IS COMING WITH THE CLOUDS, and every eye will see Him, even those who pierced

Him; and all the tribes of the earth will mourn over Him. So it is to be. Amen.

"He is coming with the clouds and every eye shall see Him" uses language from Daniel 7:13-14, Zechariah 12:10 and Matthew 24:30. The phrase "with the clouds" is used in the Old Testament with reference to judgment (cf. Dan. 7:14; Ps. 18:7-13; 104:3; Isa. 19:1). But Philip Hughes says, "The clouds intended here are not dark storm-clouds which presage divine judgment...but the bright clouds of His transcendental glory. They stand for the glory of the *shekinah* glory of God's presence which caused the face of Moses to shine with supernatural brilliance after speaking with God at Sinai or in the sanctuary (Exod. 34:29ff; 2 Cor. 3:7ff)."[4] The certainty of His coming is recorded with the word, *Amen*, an expression of vigorous approval. A word which shows the solemnity of His return.

1:8 "I am the Alpha and the Omega," says the Lord God, "who is and who was and who is to come, the Almighty."

The closing of this section gives us a description of God that is second to none found anywhere in Scripture. This section ends with a divine self-declaration which incorporates three of the four most important self-designations for God in revelation: the Alpha and the Omega, the Lord God Almighty, and the one who is and who was and who is to come. God is the "Alpha and the Omega," the first and last letter in the Greek alphabet. This imagery is expanded in 21:6 to be "the beginning and the end," an indication of absolute completeness. God is the *A* to *Z* and all the alphabet in between. There are two declarations by God in 1:8 and 21:6; there are also two declarations by Christ in 1:17 and 22:13. The God in whom we trust is the God in whom all things have their being and in whom there is nothing lacking.

He is described as "the one who is and who was and

who is to come." This occurs five times (with variations) in the book of Revelation: 1:4; 1:8; 4:8; 11:17; 16:15. In other words, God is the Eternal One. He was before time began; He is now; He will be when time ends.

And He is "the Almighty." This word is used in reference to God's supremacy over all things. He has dominion over all things; He controls all things; He holds all things in His grasp. The word "almighty" is found ten times in the New Testament. Nine of those times are in the book of Revelation (1:8; 4:8; 11:17; 15:3; 16:7, 14; 9:6, 15; 21:22 [2 Cor. 6:18]).

The opening verses of the Revelation are filled with wonder and awe. We are inspired to set our sights to a higher and loftier plane as we view the visions and notice the symbols in this message that God gives to the lonely seer on the island of Patmos.

II. JOHN'S VISION OF CHRIST, 1:9-20

⁹I, John, your brother and fellow partaker in the tribulation and kingdom and perseverance which are in Jesus, was on the island called Patmos because of the word of God and the testimony of Jesus.

¹⁰I was in the Spirit on the Lord's day, and I heard behind me a loud voice like the sound of a trumpet, ¹¹saying, "Write in a book what you see, and send it to the seven churches: to Ephesus and to Smyrna and to Pergamum and to Thyatira and to Sardis and to Philadelphia and to Laodicea."

¹²Then I turned to see the voice that was speaking with me. And having turned I saw seven golden lampstands; ¹³and in the middle of the lampstands I saw one like a son of man, clothed in a robe reaching to the feet, and girded across His chest with a golden sash. ¹⁴His head and His hair were white like white wool, like snow; and His eyes were like a flame of fire. ¹⁵His feet were like burnished bronze, when it has been made to glow in a furnace, and His voice

was like the sound of many waters. [16]In His right hand He held seven stars, and out of His mouth came a sharp two-edged sword; and His face was like the sun shining in its strength.

[17]When I saw Him, I fell at His feet like a dead man. And He placed His right hand on me, saying, "Do not be afraid; I am the first and the last, [18]and the living One; and I was dead, and behold, I am alive forevermore, and I have the keys of death and of Hades.

[19]"Therefore write the things which you have seen, and the things which are, and the things which will take place after these things.

[20]"As for the mystery of the seven stars which you saw in My right hand, and the seven golden lamp-stands: the seven stars are the angels of the seven churches, and the seven lampstands are the seven churches.

A. What John Heard, 1:9-11

John opens these verses by introducing himself. He does not claim to wear any title or seek for himself any official recognition. He simply claims an identity with those to whom he is writing. He refers to himself as a brother and companion in the suffering they are enduring. His right to speak to them comes from experience. Ezekiel makes a similar claim when he writes, "Then I came to the exiles who lived beside the river Chebar at Tel Abib, and I sat there seven days where they were living, causing consternation among them" (3:15).

It is one thing for a person to speak to others about what he knows, but it takes on a different meaning when a person speaks out of the same experience. John is experiencing the same persecution that his readers are going through. It is a suffering for the sake of the kingdom (cf. 2 Tim. 3:12 and 1 Pet. 4:12-16), and a suffering he patiently endures in Jesus Christ.

1:9 I, John, your brother and fellow partaker in the tribulation and kingdom and perseverance *which are* **in Jesus, was on the island called Patmos because of the word of God and the testimony of Jesus.**

The words "tribulation," "kingdom" and perseverance are very important. "Tribulation" originally meant simply "pressure." In the New Testament use, the word refers to pressure that comes as a result of persecution (e.g., grapes squeezed in a vat; wheat ground in a mill; i.e., the pressure is external). "Kingdom" is a reference to the church. Those who obeyed the gospel of Christ became members of the church, which is God's kingdom (cf. Matt. 16:18; Col. 1:13-14). "Perseverance" is not the patience which sits down with folded hands and bowed head and simply passively submits to the tide of events. This word describes the spirit of courage and conquest which transmutes even suffering into glory. It speaks of courage that takes one through the trials of life keeping an eye on the end of the road. The word used for patience is *hypomonē* — a quality that is constantly connected to Christian living (e.g., Rom. 5:3; 8:35-36; Rev. 2:2-3, 19; 3:10). The way of the kingdom is the way of courage and endurance. No lover of ease and comfort, no coward, no one flabby in body or mind can make that greatest of all journeys.

John is writing from the island of Patmos, a barren rocky island which is ten miles long, five miles wide and forty miles off the coast of Asia Minor. It was the last haven on the voyage from Rome to Ephesus and a common place for political prisoners to be banished. Often they were scourged, mistreated and subject to hard labor. Tacitus refers to the use of small islands, such as Patmos, by the Romans for political banishment.[5] Eusebius mentions that John was banished to Patmos by the Emperor Domitian in A.D. 95. Later, he was released by Nerva.[6] Tertullian says, "The apostle John was banished to the island."[7] Origen says, "The

Roman Emperor, as tradition tells us, condemned John to the island of Patmos for witnessing to the word of truth."[8] Clement of Alexandria tells us, "On the death of the tyrant John returned to Ephesus from the island of Patmos."[9] Jerome says that John was banished in the fourteenth year after Nero and liberated on the death of Domitian.[10]

The reason for John's being on Patmos is "because of the word of God and the testimony of Jesus." This phrase has been understood in several ways: (1) the apostle was sent to Patmos to receive the visions, (2) that John went to Patmos to carry out the Great Commission of making disciples of all nations, and (3) the most probable, that John was a faithful witness, and his being a witness caused him to suffer and be exiled. He is imprisoned because of his loyalty to Christ.

1:10 I was in the Spirit on the Lord's day, and I heard behind me a loud voice like *the sound* of a trumpet,

John describes his experience as being "in the Spirit." This simply means that John was under the influence of the Holy Spirit. He is carried away into the realm of the eternal (out of space/time) cf. 2 Cor. 12:13. In Ezekiel 8:3 we read, "The Spirit lifted me up between earth and heaven and brought me in the visions of God. . ." Therefore, what John is experiencing is not something new for a servant of the Lord. Being in the Spirit refers to the special spiritual gift of prophecy (cf. Rom. 12:6; 1 Cor. 12:10, 28; 13:2; 14:1-39). The experience involved auditions (1:10) and visions (1:12).

The day of this vision is said to be "on the Lord's day." This is the first reference in literature that we have to the Lord's day. Accurate identification of what day is to be identified as "the Lord's day" is very difficult. Some say this has reference to the eschatological day of the Lord referred to by the Old Testament prophets. Others say this phrase refers to Sunday, the first day of the week. Earlier in the New Testament we have examples of the early church recognizing Sunday as a day designated for worship (cf. Acts 20:7; 1 Cor. 16:1-2). John is carried away, not into the future but in an ecstatic state by the Spirit of God.

John hears "a loud voice like the sound of a trumpet." The voice he hears could either be Christ's or the angel from whom John is receiving these visions. The voice is described as like a trumpet. Here is an Old Testament picture. Trumpets were often used to gain the attention of the people (cf. Exod. 19:16). The idea here is the commanding and piercing clarity of the trumpet. The voice of God sounds with unmistakable clearness of the trumpet call to get John's attention.

Two phrases in these verses naturally go together. John was "in Patmos" and he was "in the Spirit." The hardships of Patmos were overshadowed by the glory of the Spirit.

1:11 saying, "Write in a book what you see, and send *it* to the seven churches: to Ephesus and to Smyrna and to Pergamum and to Thyatira and to Sardis and to Philadelphia and to Laodicea."

John is told to "write in a book what you see and send it to the seven churches." The command to "write" is found several times in the book (cf. 1:10, 19; 2:1, 8, 12, 18; 3:1, 7, 14; 14:13; 19:9; 21:5).

These churches are identified by name. What John saw he was to share with others.

B. What John Saw, 1:12-16

What John heard (vv. 9-11) was a voice that sounded like a trumpet. His instruction to write in a book what he sees is significant for what the book of Revelation is all about. John will see visions filled with symbolism, the significance of which is difficult at times to discern. After having heard the voice, he then turns to see the voice, i.e., the person whose voice he heard. What he sees was something for which he was unprepared (v. 17).

1:12, Then I turned to see the voice that was speaking with me. And having turned I saw seven golden lampstands; 13 and in the middle of the lampstands I *saw* one like a son of man, clothed in a robe reaching to the feet, and girded across His chest with a golden sash.

John is the only earthly member in the scene he is about to describe. The picture here of the risen Christ is an echo of another scene from the Mount of Transfiguration (Matt. 17:1-5; Mark 9:2-3). What John has already seen from a hilltop in Palestine, he now sees from a hilltop in Patmos. As John turns to see the one speaking to him, he first sees "seven golden lampstands." These lampstands are identified as the seven churches (cf. 1:20). (There is neither difficulty in seeing, nor difficulty in understanding their meaning.) John tells us the lampstands are the seven churches. Therefore, they should not be represented as meaning anything else. In the OT tabernacle there was a seven-branched lampstand (cf. Exod. 25:31ff). Zechariah had a vision of a seven-branched lampstand that was fed by seven pipes (cf. Zech. 4:10). Christ walks among the churches and if a church fails to repent of wrongdoing, it will have its lampstand removed from out of its place (Rev. 2:6), i.e., the church will cease to have the right to exist as the Lord's church.

The major image in the vision, however, is not the lampstand, but someone, "like a son of man." Here is an allusion to Daniel 7:9-13 and perhaps Acts 7:56 where Jesus is referred to as the "son of man." The title "son of man" relates to Jesus' capacity as judge (cf. John 5:22, 27; Acts 17:31), a function he carries out in Revelation 2-3.

The garments worn indicate both royal, priestly, and prophetic functions. The Lord is robed as a king with a garment down to His feet. The same word used here is used in the Greek Old Testament to describe the robe of the High Priest (cf. Exod. 28:4; Lev. 16:4). Here then is a symbol of the High Priestly character of the work of the risen Lord. But this long robe was also worn by Jonathan (1 Sam. 18:14), Saul (1 Sam. 24:5, 12), and princes of the sea (Ezek. 26:16). It is interesting that the divine figure who came to tell Daniel the truth from God was described as clothed in the same kind of long flowing robe (Dan. 10:5). This is the dress of a messenger of God. Here we see, in the dress of the Risen Lord, the threefold office of Prophet, Priest, and King. The one who brings the truth of God, the one who enables others to enter into the presence of God, and the one to whom God has given the power, dominion, and a throne for ever.

1:14 His head and His hair were white like white wool, like snow; and His eyes were like a flame of fire.

"His head and His hair were white like white wool, like snow" is probably taken from the Ancient of Days (Dan. 7:9) and represents great age, perhaps eternity and also possibly divine purity (as white symbolizes purity, cf. Isa. 1:18).

"His eyes were like a flame of fire" brings to mind the divine figure Daniel saw (10:6) whose eyes were lamps of fire. This represents the penetrating power of the Lord's ability to see and know everything. In the Gospels, we have the picture of the eyes of Jesus sweeping around the circle of people (cf. Mark 3:34; 10:23; 11:11; Luke 22:61). If we take time to read the Gospel story, we learn that one who had seen the eyes of Jesus never forgot them. Perhaps this represents the omniscience (all-knowing) power of deity.

1:15 His feet *were* like burnished bronze, when it has been made to glow in a furnace, and His voice *was* like the sound of many waters.

"His feet were like burnished bronze, when it has been made to glow in a furnace." The picture of His feet were as if they were fired to white heat in a kiln. A similar figure is found in Ezekiel 1:13, 27; 8:2; and Daniel 10:6. In these passages the brightness is connected with the appearance of the glory of God.

"And His voice was like the sound of many waters" describes the glory and majesty of God. Ezekiel describes a similar voice as the voice of God (Ezek. 43:2; cf. 1:24). H.B. Swete says, "The roar of the Aegean was in the ears of the seer."

1:16 In His right hand He held seven stars, and out of His mouth came a sharp two-edged sword; and His face was like the sun shining in its strength.

"In His right hand he held seven stars" which are identified for us as "the angels of the seven churches" (1:20). In the Old Testament and Revelation stars are associated with angels (Job 38:7; Rev. 9:1), or faithful witnesses (Dan. 12:3).

The "sharp two-edged sword" which comes out of the mouth of the Lord is a symbol of judicial authority (cf. Heb. 4:12 and 2 Thess. 3:8). This was a large broad-bladed sword used by the Thracians. The metaphor is important for three reasons: (1) it is seen to be characteristic of Christ several times (1:16; 2:12, 16; 19:15, 21). (2) the word sword (*rhomphaia*) is used only once outside Revelation (Luke 12:35); and (3) there is no scriptural parallel to the expression except in Isaiah 11:4, where it is said that the Messiah will "strike the earth with the rod of His mouth" and "with the breath of His lips He will slay the wicked."[11] This sword is wielded out of His mouth, rather than His hand. The Lord makes war with the Nicolaitans with the sword of His mouth (2:12, 16) and strikes down the rebellious at His coming in the same way (19:15, 21).

"His face was like the sun shining in all its strength." This image is borrowed from Judges 5:31

and may also be reminiscent of the time of the Transfiguration (Matt. 17:1-5) where the face of Jesus shined with the glory of God.

C. What John Did, 1:17-20

The response given by John at this point is somewhat understandable. His vision is of the Risen Christ. The glory and radiance of the figure would cause anyone to stand in awe and fall back with wonder. His speaking begins with words of comfort and then information which allows John to understand some of the vision.

1:17 When I saw Him, I fell at His feet like a dead man. And He placed His right hand on me, saying, "Do not be afraid; I am the first and the last,

The reaction of John was "I fell at His feet like a dead man." This was identical to what Ezekiel experienced (Ezek. 1:18; 3:23; 43:3). But again we can see glimpses of the gospel story (cf. Luke 5:1-11). This is a sign of great respect and awe (cf. Rev. 4:10; 5:8; 7:11; 19:10; 22:8). There is an overwhelming reverence found when one stands in the presence of the Risen Christ.

The response of the Risen Lord was "do not be afraid." Often in the Gospels we read Jesus saying the same thing (cf. Matt. 14:27; Mark 6:50; Matt. 17:7). Reverence and respect are not equal to producing fear. John is told that he should not be afraid and then told why.

"I am the First and the Last." This is a description of God (cf. Isa. 44:6, "Thus says the LORD, the King of Israel And his Redeemer, the LORD of hosts: 'I am the first and I am the last, And there is no God besides me." (cf. also Isa. 48:12). This is also comparable to the "Alpha and Omega" of verse 8.

1:18 and the living One; and I was dead, and behold, I am alive forevermore, and I have the keys of death and of Hades.

Here is a claim and promise of the resurrection of Jesus. Death is conquered, the one who lives and reigns also holds the keys [i.e., power] over death and Hades, (cf. Matt. 16:13-18). "Hades" translates the Hebrew word for "death, grave." Hades sometimes denotes the place of all the departed dead (Acts 2:27, 31); in other Scripture, it is the place of the departed wicked (Luke 16:23; Rev. 20:13-14). Christ has conquered death and Hades. He holds the keys and can determine who will enter death and Hades and who will come out.

1:19 "Therefore write the things which you have seen, and the things which are, and the things which will take place after these things.

The command to write (v. 11) is now repeated and expanded. John is told to write "what you have seen" (i.e., what you have seen up to this point), "what now is" (i.e., the present state of the churches, chapters 2-3), and "what will take place later" (i.e., chapters 4-21).

1:20 "As for the mystery of the seven stars which you saw in My right hand, and the seven golden lamp-stands: the seven stars are the angels of the seven churches, and the seven lampstands are the seven churches.

This is the first place in the book where the interpretation of some of the symbols are given (cf. 17:15, 18). We know the seven stars are the seven angels of the seven churches, and we also know that the seven lampstands represent the seven churches (cf. verse 11 and chs. 2-3 for listing of the seven churches). But what we do not know is what the phrase "seven angels" of seven churches means.

What does the word "angel" refer to? This is extremely difficult to determine. The word for angels (*angeloi*) occurs sixty-seven times in the book of Revelation and in every other reference refers to heavenly messengers. Homer Hailey writes,

> Since the lampstands are the churches — the supporters of the light — viewed externally, the stars may well represent the inward life or spirit of the congregations addressed by Jesus. This position seems to be confirmed by the letters themselves; Jesus addresses each letter to 'the angel of the church,' and concludes with the appeal, 'He who has an ear, let him hear what the Spirit says to the churches.' Whoever is addressed is to hear; the angels are to address; the churches are to hear. It follows that the angels are that part of the church addressed which is to hear, this would be the spirit or active life of the churches.[12]

That is to say, the angels are a way of "personifying the prevailing spirit of the church."[13]

NOTES

[1]G.B. Caird, *A Commentary on the Revelation of St. John the Divine* (New York and Evanston: Harper & Row, Publishers, 1966), 9.

[2]Robert H. Mounce, *The Book of Revelation* (Grand Rapids: Eerdmans, 1977), 70.

[3]G.B. Caird, *A Commentary on the Revelation of St. John the Divine*, 15.

[4]Philip Edgcumbe Hughes, *The Book of Revelation: A Commentary* (Grand Rapids: Eerdmans, 1990), 20.

[5]*Annal* 3.68; 4.30; 15.71.

[6]*Ecclesiastical History* 3.20.8-9.

[7]*On the Prescriptions of Heretics*, 36.

[8]*Homilies on Matthew.*

[9]*Rich Man's Salvation*, 42.

[10]*Concerning Illustrious Men*, 9.

[11]Alan Johnson, *Book of Revelation*, The Expositor's Bible Commentary, vol. 12 (Grand Rapids: Zondervan, 1981), 428.

[12]Homer Hailey, *Revelation: An Introduction and Commentary* (Grand Rapids: Baker, 1979), 116.

[13]Robert H. Mounce, *The Book of Revelation*, 82.

Revelation 2

III. THE LAMB AND THE SEVEN CHURCHES, 2:1-3:22

John now addresses letters to seven different churches located in Asia Minor (2:1-3:22). We are not to suppose that there were only these seven churches located throughout Asia Minor. The significance of the number seven might relate to the symbolism of numbers as used in the book of Revelation itself, or at least relate to the use of numbers which was familiar to the people of John's day. The number seven has been understood to represent perfection and thus when John writes to the seven churches it is as if it would be acknowledging that what is found in these letters is perfectly suited for all churches which might find themselves in similar circumstances.

There is a common literary plan found in each of these letters that consisted of seven parts. Each part is identified as follows:

1. The greeting or the addressee: "To the angel of the church in . . ."

2. The speaker identifies himself; usually this is a

title of the risen Christ taken from chapter 1 (e.g., ". . . the One who holds the seven stars . . .").

3. The knowledge of the speaker is given ("I know your deeds . . .").

4. A compliment or assessment of the church is given (". . . you have left your first love . . .").

5. A correction is given (though not true of Smyrna nor Philadelphia).

6. An exhortation is presented (". . . he who has an ear, let him hear . . .").

7. A promise and reward ("To him who overcomes . . .").[1]

A. To Ephesus: Loyal but Lacking, 2:1-7

[1]"To the angel of the church in Ephesus write: The One who holds the seven stars in His right hand, the One who walks among the seven golden lampstands, says this: [2]'I know your deeds and your toil and perseverance, and that you cannot tolerate evil men, and you put to the test those who call themselves apostles, and they are not, and you found them to be false; [3]and you have perseverance and have endured for My name's sake, and have not grown weary.

[4]"But I have this against you, that you have left your first love.

[5]'Therefore remember from where you have fallen, and repent and do the deeds you did at first; or else I am coming to you and will remove your lampstand out of its place—unless you repent.

[6]'Yet this you do have, that you hate the deeds of the Nicolaitans, which I also hate.

[7]"He who has an ear, let him hear what the Spirit says to the churches. To him who overcomes, I will grant to eat of the tree of life which is in the Paradise of God.'"

When John writes the Apocalypse, Ephesus was not the capital city of Asia Minor but it was a city of great importance. Noted for its magical arts (Acts 19:9), the city also took pride in being the location of the Temple of Diana (Acts 19:19, 35). Charms (referred to as "Ephesian Letters") were supposed to cure illness and bring one good luck. Paul ministered in this city over two years (Acts 19:8, 10). Tradition says John returned to Ephesus after his release from Patmos, and died there.

As John writes these words, Ephesus is at the zenith of her greatness. Commercially she is a city of great importance. Located at a very important spot geographically, Ephesus has one of the best harbors of all of Asia Minor. Three main roads, one from the east, one from the north, and another from the south all converge at Ephesus. Those factors combined to make the city a great trading center. Ephesus was probably the foremost city in Asia Minor for business and trade in the first century.

Politically, Ephesus was granted the status of "free city" which meant they did not have to endure the presence of Roman troops in their city. She was an assize city in which all the important judicial cases were tried. Periodically the Roman Governor would travel to Ephesus for the purpose of hearing important cases, and his visit to the city always stirred up an increase in political activity. Ephesus was also the site of the Panionian games, which rank with our Olympic games. These public games were open to everyone and public officials were so involved and interested they would often bear the cost of the games. Because of this the games soon became political in nature and influence. Commercially and politically Ephesus was a city of great importance.

Religiously, the Temple of Diana, one of the seven wonders of the world, was located in Ephesus. The people of Ephesus considered the Temple of Diana their greatest glory. The Temple of Diana which stood in John's day was the third one built and was a magnificent structure. "The sun sees nothing finer in his course than Diana's Temple."

Being a seaport its population was mixed, and each nationality had its own section of the city. There were Jews, Greeks, and foreigners as well as the original Athenians. The population of the city was of diverse backgrounds. There were six groups. One consisted of the original natives who inhabited the area before the arrival of the Greeks. Then, there were the direct descendants of the original group from Athens. A third group was composed of three other tribes of Greek lineage. Finally, there was a large Jewish population.[2]

Biblically speaking, we know more about Ephesus and what happened there than we do of the other cities mentioned in Revelation 2 and 3. Paul visited Ephesus on his second missionary journey, and left Aquila and Priscilla there to work with the church (Acts 18:19ff). An eloquent man named Apollos, well versed in Scripture, came to Ephesus and began teaching. Knowing only the baptism of John, he had to be taught the way of the Lord more perfectly by Aquila and Priscilla.

While Paul was in Ephesus for two years the gospel was spread throughout Asia (Acts 19:10), and the church was established and strengthened. There is, perhaps, no more tender passage to be found than Acts 20:17-38 where Luke records Paul's farewell to the elders from Ephesus. As Paul leaves Ephesus, according to what the biblical text has to say, the congregation is a glowing, growing, going church. Thirty years later things have changed, and the message that is revealed to the Apostle John calls for repentance.

It has been said that all it takes is one untaught generation for the church to fall into apostasy. All it takes is one generation who have not been taught the fundamentals of the distinct nature of the New Testament church; the distinct nature of Christian worship; the importance of being in a proper relationship with God in obedience to the Gospel of Jesus Christ. All it takes is one generation and the church is in trouble.

In a short thirty-year time period the church at Ephesus had changed. Acts 18-20 tells us of an active, growing church, but the message to the church in Revelation 2 paints a different picture.

2:1 "To the angel of the church in Ephesus write: The One who holds the seven stars in His right hand, the One who walks among the seven golden lampstands, says this:

The letter begins with the address "to the angel of the church" by which we believe he is referring to the heavenly representative to the church (see comments on 1:20). A comparable formula introduces each of the seven letters.

The speaker identifies himself with a reference to 1:13, 16. "The One who holds the seven stars in His right hand, the one who walks among the seven golden lampstands." We know from Revelation 1 that the Lord Jesus Christ is the one who holds in His hand the seven stars which are the seven churches. The word translated "hold" has two different meanings: (1) To hold a book in our hand is to hold a corner of the book rather than enclosing the entire book in our hand. (2) To hold a hazel nut or pecan in our hand is to completely enclose or hold the entire object. The second is the construction which is used. The Lord is saying, "I am the one who holds the church totally, all of it, completely in my hand." The destiny of the church belongs to the Lord Jesus Christ. He wants the church to know who is presenting the message, and identifies himself in such a way as to get their attention. The words spoken here offer reassurance to the original readers of Christ's strong protection and control over the church.

"Says this" (*tade legei*) is used eight times in the New Testament. Seven of these are in Revelation 2-3. In each case it introduces a strong, authoritative, emphatic assertion.[3] *Tade* was used by Persian kings to introduce their decrees, and prophets used it to introduce their prophetic utterances. Such a strong assertion would surely get the attention of the readers.

2:2 'I know your deeds and your toil and perseverance, and that you cannot tolerate evil men, and you put to the test those who call themselves apostles, and they are not, and you found them *to be* false; 2:3 and you have perseverance and have endured for My name's sake, and have not grown weary.

"I know" (*oida*) expresses a claim of knowledge found in each of the seven letters (2:2, 9, 13, 19; 3:1, 8, 15). *Oida* reflects a full and complete knowledge. Such knowledge of the church in Ephesus is reflected in the fact that Jesus "walks among the churches" and therefore knows all things. The Lord's knowledge of their deeds is found in four of the other six messages (2:19; 3:1, 9, 15).

The Lord begins by commending them for what is right in their life. In practice, they were a working, toiling, patient church. Jesus is saying, "I know your deeds," that is, your toil and perseverance. "Toil and perseverance" identify what the work is. They are loyal in doctrine as well. Their toil includes their inability to tolerate false teachers (2:2b).

Their perseverance is further identified in verse 3, "you have perseverance and have endured for My name's sake." Perseverance is translated by some as "patient endurance." This is "the courageous gallantry which accepts suffering and hardship and loss and turns them into grace and glory."[4]

Doctrinal discrimination follows toil and perseverance. They "cannot tolerate evil men." This is not a reference to pagans, but rather to brethren who "call themselves apostles but are not." The problem is within the body, not without. Exactly who these pseudo-apostles are, what they taught, and how the church tested them is not described.

An apostle was one sent with a message. The word is used in the New Testament to refer to the Twelve (Mark 3:14; Acts 1:2, 26); and also of Paul (Gal. 1:1). Miracles were signs of an apostle (2 Cor. 12:12; Heb. 2:4) but miracles also accompanied false apostles (Mark 13:22; 2 Thess. 2:9; 2 Tim. 3:8; Rev. 13:13-14). John warns that we must test or try false teachers (1 John 4:1) and it seems that the way that is to be done today is according to the Word.

2:4 'But I have *this* against you, that you have left your first love.

While there is much for which to commend this church, there is also something to condemn. After the Lord has commended what is right with the church, he turns to state what is wrong. The condemnation is very clear, "you have left your first love." What is this "first love?" This phrase could be understood in one of three ways: (1) the love for God and Christ, (2) the love Christians should have for one another, or (3) the love Christians should have for mankind; i.e., a lost world.

The loss of love was at the root of the problems for the church in Corinth (cf. 1 Cor. 1:10ff; 13:1ff). First *(protos)* love would suggest that they still love, but with a quality of intensity unlike that of their initial love. They had lost their first love, but they had not lost their hatred for evil.

2:5 'Therefore remember from where you have fallen, and repent and do the deeds you did at first; or else I am coming to you and will remove your lampstand out of its place — unless you repent.

Four words that start with "R" summarize the message the Lord has for them: Repent, Remember, Repeat, or I am going to Remove. The road back begins by remembering. The Ephesians are told to reflect on their earlier love. In the story of the prodigal son, the boy left home, wasted everything he had, and ended up feeding pigs. But he *remembered* that even the servants in his father's home were in a better situation than he was, so with deep humility he decided to go home and ask to be simply a servant. His restoration began with remembering.

Remembering is not enough. If we are not careful we could stroll down memory lane toward trouble because we have not repented of our lethargy and gone back to our original zeal. That is exactly what happened at Ephesus. They tightened their belts and girded themselves when it came to false teachers, they manifested works and toil and perseverance, but the Lord said they had lost their first love. They were told to remember and repent.

Then they were told to repeat; i.e., "do again." Repeat in your life what you used to do. Return to that original state of service out of a heart of love. Christ warns that if they do not return to that first state, they are forfeiting their right to exist as a church.

The Lord is saying, "You either remember and repent and repeat or I will remove you from having a right to exist as my people and to represent me on earth."

2:6 'Yet this you do have, that you hate the deeds of the Nicolaitans, which I also hate.

Almost added as a footnote or a "P.S." at the end of a letter is the Lord's comments regarding the Nicolaitans. Who are the Nicolaitans? What did they teach? How were they affecting the church at Ephesus?

There are only two views of identification for the Nicolaitans that we want to mention: (1) The followers of Nicolas of Antioch, one of the seven original deacons (Acts 6:5), a Jewish proselyte, who is said to have fallen into apostasy and taken others with him. (2) A sect that lived a life of lust of the flesh, which began through a misinterpretation of a statement by Nicolas — possibly identified as an early Gnostic sect.

The word Nicolaitans is from the Greek compound *nikos* and *laos* and means "conqueror of the people." Eusebius says the Nicolaitans lasted only a short time (*Ecclesiastical History* 3.29.1), thus probably contributing to our inability to properly identify them. Of the three views mentioned, the first is the most persuasive for many people. Sir William Ramsay identifies the Nicolaitans with those Christians who show identification with the emperor by burning incense in his honor.[5]

2:7 'He who has an ear, let him hear what the Spirit says to the churches. To him who overcomes, I will grant to eat of the tree of life which is in the Paradise of God.'

"He who has an ear, let him hear what the Spirit says to the churches." Even though this was addressed specifically to the church at Ephesus, it was part of a message written to all the churches in Asia Minor. This exhortation is repeated to each of the seven churches. The message is the same to us as well. Christians today need to be careful to stay out of the category of those "who have eyes but do not see; who have ears but do not hear" and instead be those who "hear what the Spirit says to the churches."

Another statement we see repeated in each letter, with some variation, is a promise to the overcomer. This promise is the tree of life. We were introduced to the tree of life in Genesis 2:9 as one of the many trees from which Adam and Eve were cut off from in the Garden of Eden. It is interesting to note that this tree, lost in the garden, is restored in the paradise of God (Rev. 22:19).

B. To Smyrna: Faithful unto Death, 2:8-11

[8]"And to the angel of the church in Smyrna write: The first and the last, who was dead, and has come to life, says this: [9]'I know your tribulation and your poverty (but you are rich), and the blasphemy by those who say they are Jews and are not, but are a synagogue of Satan. [10]'Do not fear what you are about to suffer. Behold, the devil is about to cast some of you into prison, so that you will be tested, and you will have tribulation for ten days. Be faithful until death, and I will give you the crown of life.

[11]'He who has an ear, let him hear what the Spirit says to the churches. He who overcomes will not be hurt by the second death.'

Smyrna is located 35-40 miles north of Ephesus on the western side of the Aegean Sea. It was a metropolitan city of approximately 200,000 people. Smyrna is not mentioned in the Bible outside the book of Revelation. One ancient tradition says that when Paul traveled back to Jerusalem from Galatia, he stayed in Smyrna with Strataeus (*Life of Polycarp* 2).

The letter to the church at Smyrna is unique. Not only is it the shortest of the seven letters; it is one of only two letters which has no words of condemnation. These four short verses are power-packed, containing information and words of encouragement badly needed by the brethren who were the faithful in Christ at Smyrna.

We can better appreciate what is said here if we know something about the city of Smyrna. If we lived in Asia Minor at that time and in the city of Smyrna, what would have been our impressions of the city?

If you had lived in Asia Minor in those days you would have been aware of the fact that Smyrna was a great trade city. She stood on a deep gulf north of Ephesus, and had a magnificent harbor which was especially valuable during times of war because it could be closed. The city stood at the end of a road which served the valley of the river Hermus, and all the trade of the valley passed through its harbor.

Smyrna was an outstandingly beautiful city. She was famous for the wide paved streets which ran from one end of the city to the other. The most well-known of her thoroughfares was called "Golden Street," and along this lovely avenue stood many imposing heathen temples; she was a city filled with religious idolatry. On Golden Street near the sea was the great Temple of Cybele. As the road headed through the city toward the foothills, many other temples lined its way, including temples to the god Asclepius and the goddess Aphrodite. In the inland foothills was the Temple of Zeus. These temples were magnificent structures and added to Smyrna's reputation for beauty and glory.

Smyrna possessed a famous stadium, an impressive library, and claimed to have the largest public theater in all of Asia Minor. She claimed to be the birthplace of the ancient Greek poet Homer, and a monument to him stood in the city. No wonder this splendid city was known as "the glory of Asia."

It may sound like Smyrna was an ideal place to live, but there were two factors that made life there very difficult for Christians.

The first was emperor worship. As Rome conquered more and more of the world, she allowed vassal peoples to govern themselves as long as they were loyal to Rome and faithfully paid their taxes. Rome did, however, strive to unify conquered peoples, and the aim was to accomplish this unity through a national religion. It could not be done with any of the existing religions because of the diversity of gods and practices.

This led to the concept of Dea Roma — the goddess of Rome. The worship of Rome itself as a deity was conceived as a unifying force. Issuing from this was the worship of Caesar. Since the Caesar represented the nation of Rome to the people, the Caesars began to look upon themselves as gods. Early in Rome's history the Caesars were not deified until after their death, but Caligula, who became emperor in A.D. 37, changed that precedent by declaring himself divine during his reign. In the years following, emperor worship became firmly established and Domitian (A.D. 81-96), declared himself to be god in the flesh.

Once a year every citizen of the Roman empire was required to place a pinch of incense on the altar to the emperor, say the words "Caesar is Lord," and receive a token as evidence that the worship had been performed. It was a very brief ceremony, taking perhaps thirty seconds.

Christians were put in a difficult position because refusal to participate in emperor worship resulted in persecution. Some began to use "mental reservation." They rationalized that as long as they acknowledged in their minds that Jesus was Lord, it would be all right to comply with the requirements of emperor worship and be protected against the persecution or even death which might result from their refusal. They felt it would not be wrong to stay "Caesar is lord" under those circumstances, even though they did not agree with the statement. Rome would not object to that — as long as a person went through the motions to demonstrate their loyalty to Rome, it did not matter to the authorities what god he worshiped. Caesar worship was not so much a question of religious loyalty as it was political loyalty.

The conscientious Christian who refused to participate in any way risked political and economic persecution and possible arrest for treason.

The large Jewish population was the second factor which created difficulties for the Christians in Smyrna. The Jews informed on Christians to the local governor, and used their influence to persuade him to unleash an attack on Christianity. This issued in severe persecutions, even to the point of martyrdom for some. The most famous person who died a martyr's death in Smyrna was Polycarp, Bishop of Smyrna. There was a multitude of people that cried for Polycarp to be found, arrested and condemned to death. The Jews cried along with the Gentiles this accusation against Polycarp, "This is the teacher of Asia, the father of Christians, the destroyers of our gods, the one who teaches many not to sacrifice nor to worship."[6] As he entered the arena he was instructed to recant his faith in Christ. He acknowledged that he was a Christian and gave this response, "I have served him eighty-six years and in no way has he dealt unjustly with me; so how can I blaspheme my king who saved me?" [7]

The Jews not only demanded his arrest, but even though it was the Sabbath they led the mob in gathering the sticks to burn Polycarp to death. "You threaten fire which burns for an hour," Polycarp said, "and is soon quenched; for you are ignorant of the fire of the coming judgment and eternal punishment reserved for the wicked. But why do you wait? Come, do what you will!"[8] As he was being burned he prayed, "I bless you because you have considered me worthy of this day and hour to receive a portion, among the number of the martyrs, in the cup of your Christ unto the resurrection of eternal life . . ."[9] And so Polycarp died.

This background material will help us better understand the significance of some of the things said in the letter.

2:8 "And to the angel of the church in Smyrna write: The first and the last, who was dead, and has come to life, says this:

Jesus draws upon His appearance in 1:17-18 for His introduction to the church at Smyrna. "The first and the last" is a title used by Isaiah for the God of Israel (Isa. 41:4; 44:6; 48:12). This title is also used with a similar title "the Alpha and the Omega" (Rev. 22:13). The Lord is speaking of His deity. He was already in existence at the beginning of this and he will continue after all comes to an end. He is "the Eternal One."

Christians in Smyrna faced severe persecutions because of emperor worship and because of the hatred of the Jews. What a great ray of hope it must have been to read, ". . .who was dead, and has come to life." The writer was one who had victory over death, and that was especially meaningful to people who knew they faced the possibility of death.

The slanderous accusations against Christians by the Jewish population were known by Christ. *The Martyrdom of Polycarp* documents this open hostility. When Polycarp confessed he was a Christian "the multitudes of heathen and Jews living in Smyrna cried out with uncontrollable wrath" (xii.2).

2:9 'I know your tribulation and your poverty (but you are rich), and the blasphemy by those who say they are Jews and are not, but are a synagogue of Satan. 10 'Do not fear what you are about to suffer. Behold, the devil is about to cast some of you into prison, so that you will be tested, and you will have tribulation for ten days. Be faithful until death, and I will give you the crown of life.

The word "tribulation" (*thlipsis*) refers to pressure that is brought to bear upon someone from without. Tribulation reflects serious trouble, a burden which crushes. It carries the idea of grapes in a winepress that were crushed by pressure or by trampling of feet. It was used of a man being crushed to death by the weight of a great boulder. G.K. Chesterton has said it was the sign of a real man that he could pass the breaking point and not break. The Lord is telling the Christians at Smyrna He knows what they are going through, and He understands. *Thlipsis* is used in the New Testament in speaking of the calamities of war, of want, of the distress of a woman in childbirth, and of persecution from which Christians would not shrink.

There are two words in the original language for one who is poor. *Penia* means a person who could afford nothing beyond the barest necessities of life. He and his family might have the minimum of food, clothing and shelter, but nothing in addition to that. *Ptōcheia* is the word used here and specifically identifies one who could not even afford the necessities of life. R.C. Trench notes, "The *penēs* has nothing superfluous, the *ptōchēs* has nothing at all."

Why were the Christians in Smyrna that poor? Doing business in Smyrna depended on having that little token which proved a person was loyal to Caesar. People without the token were blacklisted. Merchants were afraid they would be in danger if they dealt with customers who were considered disloyal to the state. The poverty of the Christians at Smyrna which caused their affliction was because of the "blasphemy by those who say they are Jews and are not." This is a direct reference to the slander against Christians from the Jews. Such Jewish agitation is not new. The same thing happened to the Apostle Paul at Antioch of Pisidia (Acts 13:50); at Iconium (Acts 14:2, 5); at Lystra (Acts 14:19); and at Thessalonica (Acts 17:5).

During the first century six types of slander were leveled against Christians: cannibalism, lust and immorality, breaking up of homes, atheism, political disloyalty, and incendiarism.[10]

The result was deep poverty for the Christians at Smyrna. According to the world's standards they are in terrible shape, undergoing persecution and suffering poverty, but by the Lord's standards they are rich. The word for "rich" is the word from which we get the English words "plutarchy," "plutocrat," "plutocracy," etc., conveying the idea of being in a position of power and authority because of wealth. The Lord is telling them that in spite of their situation in the world's eyes, in the eyes of heaven's Banker they are rich in a spiritual way, and have power because of that wealth. In Luke 12:15 Jesus said, ". . . for not even when one has an abundance does his life consist of his possessions" (cf. Matt 6:19-21).

Then Jesus refers to those who blaspheme the Christians in Smyrna — those who claim to be Jews but are not, but are a synagogue of Satan. The word "blaspheme" means "to speak against." We might better understand the thought here if we use the word "slander" — the Christians were being slandered.

The Jews may have had a sign over their place of worship which said "Synagogue of the Lord," but Jesus said they were a "synagogue of Satan." The "synagogue of Satan" reveals the ultimate source of persecution against Christians: Satan (cf. 2:13; 3:9; 9:11; 12:9-10, 12; 13:4; 20:2, 7, 10). They may have claimed to be God's people, but in reality they belonged to the devil. A lot of people claim to be Christians today, but if that is not the Lord's evaluation of them, they belong to Satan.

The Lord's words must have comforted the Christians at Smyrna. He knew the true nature of the Jews, and justice would be done. The Jews would be punished for their blasphemy, and the Christians would be rewarded for their faithfulness.

2:10 'Do not fear what you are about to suffer. Behold, the devil is about to cast some of you into prison, so that you will be tested, and you will have tribulation for ten days. Be faithful until death, and I will give you the crown of life.

The Christians at Smyrna have endured tribulation, poverty, and slander — and there is more to come. Here are people going through tribulation, or pressure beyond what some are able to bear; here are people poverty stricken because they are loyal to Jesus Christ; here are people being blasphemed against. Jesus did not tell them things would get better, but that they would get worse. Some of them are going to be cast into prison by the devil and tried, and they would have tribulation ten days.

"Behold" signals a declaration that is to capture one's attention. It is used five times in these letters (2:10, 22; 3:8, 9, 20). Prison was usually the waiting place for those who would proceed to trial and finally execution. One who is cast into prison must be ready for extreme persecution; indeed, to pay the ultimate price of death.

The phrase "ten days" can be taken to refer to (1) ten literal days, or (2) a comparatively short period of time. It is, however, complete in its persecution. Ten is human completeness doubled. They would have to bear as much persecution as a human could withstand, but only for a short time.

With the tribulation, poverty, slander and persecution also came martyrdom. Verse 10 continues, "Be faithful until death, and I will give you the crown of life." Some take this verse to mean, "Be faithful until the day you die, and I will give you the crown of life." That is a true statement, but not what this verse says. In the construction of the original language here, the word "unto" causes the sentence to mean, "Be faithful knowing that your faithfulness will cause your death."

The reward for faithfulness is the "crown of life." In spite of the serious subject of the letter, it is actually one of hope and consolation. They were promised the "crown of life" if they were faithful unto death. There are two words for "crown" in the Greek. *Diadēma* signified a ruling crown, that which was worn by royalty. *Stephanos* had three applications: (1) the victory crown, given to the winner of a competition; (2) the festal crown, worn at weddings and other festive occasions; and (3) the laurel crown given for faithful civic service. It is the *stephanos* which is promised here.

It is hard for Christians today to relate to the possibility of dying for our faith in Christ. Perhaps if we try to picture ourselves being threatened with death unless we deny Christ, or one of our children being threatened with death unless we deny Christ, we can better understand what the Christians in Smyrna were going through and what this message meant to them.

2:11 'He who has an ear, let him hear what the Spirit says to the churches. He who overcomes will not be hurt by the second death.'

"He who has an ear, let him hear what the Spirit says to the churches." This phrase is found at the close of each of the letters (cf. 2:7, 11, 17, 29; 3:6, 13, 22). The primary instruction found in each letter is for the specific need of that particular church. However, the lessons to be learned are not limited to that particular church but should be for all the churches. In other words, what is said to the church at Ephesus is just as applicable to the other churches and vice versa. The lessons God wants learned at one church are just as important for other churches facing similar situations.

More words of hope and comfort are found in the last part of verse 11. Jesus says, "He who overcomes will not be hurt by the second death." We are given more information about the "second death" in Revelation 20:6. What is that second death? We find it explained in verse 14, "Then death and Hades were thrown into the lake of fire. This is the second death, the lake of fire."

The Christians of Smyrna were told not to fear the death of the body, because those who overcame would not face the second death. Everyone is going to die physically, unless Jesus returns first. But we do not need to be afraid of that death (Heb. 2:14-17). The second death is the one we need to fear, but the Lord promises victory over that death to those who overcome.

It is not likely that many Christians today will face the kind of persecution those at Smyrna faced, but no life is completely free of tribulation. The message for today is the same as the one for the first century. Stand firm and face what has to be faced knowing the Lord understands and will bring about justice; be steadfast in the faith; and be confident of the ultimate reward which is more than worth whatever has to be endured.

C. To Pergamum: Where Satan Lived, 2:12-17

[12]"And to the angel of the church in Pergamum write: The One who has the sharp two-edged sword says this: [13]'I know where you dwell, where Satan's throne is; and you hold fast My name, and did not deny My faith even in the days of Antipas, My witness, My faithful one, who was killed among you, where Satan dwells.

[14]"But I have a few things against you, because you have there some who hold the teaching of Balaam, who kept teaching Balak to put a stumbling block before the sons of Israel, to eat things sacrificed to idols and to commit acts of immorality. [15]'So you also have some who in the same way hold the teaching of the Nicolaitans. [16]"Therefore repent; or else I am coming to you quickly, and I will make war against them with the sword of My mouth.

[17]"He who has an ear, let him hear what the Spirit says to the churches. To him who overcomes, to him I will give some of the hidden manna, and I will give him a white stone, and a new name written on the stone which no one knows but he who receives it.'

Travel north from the city of Ephesus forty miles, then go inland fifteen miles to the Caicus valley, and you will find the city of Pergamum. This city of Mysia had been a capital city since the time of the Attalid Empire (circa 231 B.C.) which was broken up during the days of the rule and conquest of Alexander the Great. In 133 B.C., her dying king bequeathed her to the possession of the Roman Empire, and she became the chief city of the new province of Asia.

Pergamum never attained to the commercial eminence or the trade position of either Ephesus or Smyrna, but she was far superior in historical greatness. In fact, historically she was considered to be the greatest city of Asia Minor. Her prestige caused her to be the site of the first temple of the Caesar-cult, erected to Rome and Augustus in 29 B.C., and a second temple later erected to Trajan. Pliny, the Roman writer, called it *longe clarissimum Asiae*, the most famous city of Asia. Pergamum had the atmosphere of an ancient capital city with the pride of centuries of greatness behind it.

One of Pergamum's claims to fame was her magnificent library of two hundred thousand volumes; a library that rivaled that of Alexandria. This made Pergamum a focal point of intellectual and scholastic activities.

Pergamum was also well-known as a center of worship to the gods Asklepios, Zeus, Dionysus and Athena. The symbol of Asklepios was a serpent, and coins of the city with serpents on them demonstrated the interconnection between religion and politics. A healing cult revolved around Asklepios, and invalids from all over Asia traveled to Pergamum to be healed in his temple. There was a school of medicine connected with the temple. A throne-like altar to Zeus stood on a crag above the city, and the friezes are now in the Berlin Museum. As if Christians in Pergamum would not have been offended enough by the worship of an image of a snake, Asklepios was called "the Savior." The alliance between politics and paganism would have put a lot of pressure on Christians to compromise, and created a favorable climate for Nicolaitanism.

Knowing those things about Pergamum gives us some insight into the message the Lord had for the Christians who lived there.

2:13 'I know where you dwell, where Satan's throne is; and you hold fast My name, and did not deny My faith even in the days of Antipas, My witness, My faithful one, who was killed among you, where Satan dwells.

The Lord has a threefold commendation for this church. (1) "I know where you dwell." In other words, I am aware of the circumstances under which you have to live. (2) "You hold fast to My name" — in spite of the pressures they had not forsaken Christ. (3) You did not deny My faith" — they had not succumbed to emperor or pagan worship. The word "deny" is in the aorist tense and has reference to a particular action completed in past time. Evidently there had been a specific period of persecution and crisis during which the Christians of Pergamum had remained true. They did not deny the faith even though the situation was so critical it resulted in the death of one called Antipas, whom the Lord calls His faithful witness. There is no more information about the death of Antipas except a legend which says he was roasted to death inside a brazen bull.

The Lord told the Christians at Smyrna to be faithful even if it cost them their lives, and their reward would be the crown of life (Rev. 2:10). It seems the Christians here in Pergamum faced a similar situation. In speaking here of the death of Antipas the Lord calls him His faithful witness. Antipas may have suffered a martyr's death, but he gained the martyr's reward. In Revelation 1:5 John refers to Jesus as "the faithful witness." It is noteworthy that Antipas was described with a title which had been applied to the Lord Himself.

The Christians at Pergamum dwelled "where Satan's throne is." The Greek word *thronos* is used in different ways in Scripture and never has reference simply to a place to sit. In Matthew 19:28 it refers to the seat of a judge. In Luke 1:32 it is used in the sense of the throne of a king. It implies a position of power and authority.

Satan did not just exist in Pergamum, he had power and authority there.

"Satan's throne" has been understood to refer to: (1) the great altar of Zeus which crowned the city's acropolis; (2) the sanctuary of the Asklepios whose symbol (a serpent entwined around a staff) was familiar to Jew and Christian alike; (3) a special sense in which Pergamum was the home of the satanic spirit of persecution; (4) as a figurative reference to the power or influence that works against the church and its members; (5) as naming Pergamum as the worst of all the seven cities addressed (Satan had his throne here and ruled as a king — this is evidenced by the temples of at least four prominent Greek gods: Zeus, Athena, Dionysis, and Asklepios); (6) the emperor cult, or emperor worship. The last one here seems to fit the best.

Like Smyrna, Pergamum was the headquarters in which the emperor worship had been organized. One of the oddest titles a city could be given was *neokoros*, or "temple sweeper." When a city erected a temple to a god, its greatest claim to honor was that it officially became the *neokoros*, the temple sweeper of that god. Of course, the sweeping of the temple was the most menial and humble of religious duties. Behind the title lies the lovely concept that it was a city's greatest privilege to render the humblest service to the god who had taken up his residence within it. Pergamum was a city which called itself the *neokoros* of the temple where the emperor was worshiped. She was a city where Caesar worship was at its most intense, a city dedicated to glorying in the worship of Caesar. That, to a Christian, would be nothing less than the worship of Satan.

In Pergamum it was supremely perilous to be a Christian. Some lived in cities where they were relatively safe most of the year and were only in real danger during the time appointed for the ceremony of worship to Caesar. In Pergamum a Christian's life was in jeopardy every day. He put his life on the line for sake of loyalty to Jesus Christ. In other words, on a day-to-day basis, they were living where Satan was in control.

The Greek word that is translated "dwell" in verse 13 is *katoikein* and conveys the idea of a permanent, settled residence; to have one's home or permanent residence in a place. The Christians there were not just visiting or temporarily sojourning; that was their fixed place of abode. And it was Satan's fixed place of abode as well. The Christians could not leave and find a place where they could live in peace — they had to endure where they were. They were living in Hell's Headquarters and the Lord commended them for their faithfulness in the face of such adversity.

2:14 'But I have a few things against you, because you have there some who hold the teaching of Balaam, who kept teaching Balak to put a stumbling block before the sons of Israel, to eat things sacrificed to idols and to commit *acts of* immorality. 15 'So you also have some who in the same way hold the teaching of the Nicolaitans.

In spite of their loyalty and faithfulness in the face of extreme pressure and danger, the Christians at Pergamum needed correction. The Lord said, "I have a few things against you."

The story of Balaam is found in Numbers 22-25. Balaam was a prophet of God with the gift of eloquent speech. He wanted to be true to God, but he also wanted to take advantage of an offer of material wealth and position. As the children of Israel traveled from Egypt to the Promised Land, their numbers and victories struck fear into the hearts of the nations they approached, including Moab and Midian. Balak, king of Moab, conspired with the leaders of Midian to hire Balaam the prophet to curse the Israelites so they might be driven out of the land. Jehovah put the words in Balaam's mouth, and instead of curses, Balaam spoke blessings.

Having failed in his attempts to curse the people of God, he gave Balak advice that would result in their corruption. We know from Numbers 31:16 and Revelation 2:14 that Balaam was responsible for counseling Balak to lead the children of Israel into the immorality and idolatry that is recorded in Numbers 25. As a result of that sin, twenty-four thousand Israelites died. Balaam was killed later when Jehovah ordered Moses to take vengeance on the Midianites.

What is the teaching of Balaam? Balaam probably told the Israelites they could do whatever they wanted without fear of reprisal because they were God's chosen people. He became the prototype of false teachers who would lead Christians into compromise with worldly ideologies. Balaamism would say that Christian liberty allowed participation in worldly activities — being saved by grace meant freedom from the moral law. The word for that doctrine today is antinomianism.

Eating meat sacrificed to idols often involved social occasions. It was not uncommon for the participant to take his offering to the temple, offer a few hairs from the forehead of the animal to the idol, then prepare the rest of the animal for a meal for his family, friends, and neighbors. Invitations might even be issued: "Friend, I invite you to dine with me at the temple of our Lord Serapis." Could a Christian share in a social occasion that was held in the temple of the heathen god? Could a Christian partake of the table of demons as well as the table of the Lord? Paul said no (1 Cor. 10:18-22). The false teachers said yes and encouraged the Christians to compromise.

Fornication and sin were accepted practices in the ancient world. Demosthenes said, "We have courtesans for the sake of pleasure; we have concubines for the sake of daily cohabitation; we have wives for the purpose of having children legitimately, and for having a faithful guardian over our household affairs."

Sexual promiscuity was not shocking; being told it was wrong was shocking. Immorality was the norm, and those who abstained were set apart and looked upon with suspicion. (For comments on the Nicolaitans see 2:6.)

2:16 'Therefore repent; or else I am coming to you quickly, and I will make war against them with the sword of My mouth.

The Christians in Pergamum are given a strong warning, "Therefore repent; or else I am coming to you quickly." What are they to repent of? They were tolerating sin; there were those who were advocating compromise with pagan practices and emperor worship, and the church was looking the other way. The church at Corinth had a similar problem when it tolerated a man's taking his father's wife (1 Cor. 5). The Lord says in essence, "If you don't deal with these Balaamites, I will."

Tolerating what God condemns and looking the other way without taking action is just as much of a sin today as it was then. Christians are to abhor that which is evil, abstain from the very appearance of evil, and not sit by and watch it grow. The church needs to be guarded against the infection of worldliness. Paul said, "A little leaven leavens the whole lump" (1 Cor. 5:6). The Bible teaches that discipline is to be exercised when there is sin in the church (Rom. 16:17; 1 Cor. 5:13; 2 Thess. 3:14; Titus 3:10). It is painful and difficult for all involved but necessary for the purity of the church, and for the restoration of the individuals involved in sin.

The spirit of Balaam gets into the church in many ways. Balaam tried to stand with God and at the same time collect a reward from the ungodly. Today some Christians try to stand with God while at the same time enjoy the pleasures of the world. Paul teaches forcefully in 2 Corinthians 6:14-7:1 that the church is

to be separate from the world. There can be no fellowship between righteousness and iniquity or light and
darkness; there is no harmony between Christ and
Belial; believers have nothing in common with unbelievers; there can be no agreement between Christians
and idols.

**2:17 'He who has an ear, let him hear what the Spirit
says to the churches. To him who overcomes, to him I
will give *some* of the hidden manna, and I will give
him a white stone, and a new name written on the
stone which no one knows but he who receives it.'**

As in all the letters, the Lord says, "He who has an
ear, let him hear what the Spirit says to the churches."
The message is for all to take to heart. The letter closes
with three points made within an exhortation and
promise: (1) the hidden manna, (2) the white stone,
and (3) the new name.

Manna was the food provided by God for the children of Israel as they traveled from Egypt to the
Promised Land (cf. Exod. 16:33-34; Heb. 9:4). The
thought here is similar to Moses' pot of manna which
was to remind the Israelites of God's faithfulness (Ps.
78:24). Those in Pergamum needed to know that God is
faithful to His promises. In John 6:31ff Jesus draws a
parallel between the manna with which God fed the
Israelites and Himself as the bread of life come down
from heaven. The Christians of John's day might have
understood "hidden manna" to be spiritual nourish-
ment provided by the Lord Himself at a time of victory,
as contrasted with the food from sacrifices to idols
which the Balaamites were encouraging them to eat.

The one who overcame was not only going to be
given the hidden manna, but he was also to be given
"a white stone, and a new name written on the stone,
which no one knows but he who receives it." The idea
of the white stone was significant in several different
ways in the ancient world. A white stone symbolized

innocence and might be given to one who had been acquitted of a charge. He could carry that as proof of his acquittal. A white stone was also given to a slave who was granted freedom, and was a sign to all that he was a free man. The victor of a race or contest was sometimes given a white stone. A white stone was given to a soldier or warrior who came back from a victorious battle. Among other customs involving a white stone was its use as admission to a banquet. It may be that all of these concepts are inherent in the Lord giving a white stone to the overcomer. It would symbolize their innocence, freedom in Christ, final victory, and admission to the marriage supper of the Lamb.

There are several views on the identity of the "new name." Some think it is the name of Christ; i.e., the name of Christ Himself, now hidden from the world but to be revealed in the future as the most powerful of all names (3:12; 14:1). Some think it is the believer's new name or changed character through redemption (cf. Isa. 62:2; 65:5; Acts 26:28; 1 Pet. 4:16). And, others think it is the victorious Christian himself.

The Lord said no one would know the name except the one who received it. Whatever the new name is, the Christian will know it when he receives the ultimate reward for overcoming.

The message to the Christians at Pergamum applies to Christians today as well. We can feel very complacent and spiritual when we meet together on Sunday for worship, but after Sunday comes Monday. We are back on the job or back at school — out in the world with influences that constantly bombard us and ask us to compromise our principles in living for Jesus Christ. The Lord knows "where we live." He knows we live in a world under the influence of Satan, but He expects us to overcome — to remain faithful and not compromise (1 Cor. 10:13). The Bible teaches that we are to be a people separated from the ways of this world. It calls upon Christians to live a better life, to walk on a higher plain (2 Cor. 6:14-18). The doctrine of Balaamism would have Christians hold hands with God on one side and the devil on the other, and it will result in the wrath of God today just as it did in Pergamum.

D. To Thyatira: Wait for the Star, 2:18-29

[18]"And to the angel of the church in Thyatira write: The Son of God, who has eyes like a flame of fire, and His feet are like burnished bronze, says this: [19]'I know your deeds, and your love and faith and service and perseverance, and that your deeds of late are greater than at first.

[20]'But I have this against you, that you tolerate the woman Jezebel, who calls herself a prophetess, and she teaches and leads My bond-servants astray so that they commit acts of immorality and eat things sacrificed to idols.

[21]'I gave her time to repent, and she does not want to repent of her immorality.

[22]'Behold, I will throw her on a bed of sickness, and those who commit adultery with her into great tribulation, unless they repent of her deeds. [23]'And I will kill her children with pestilence, and all the churches will know that I am He who searches the minds and hearts; and I will give to each one of you according to your deeds.

[24]'But I say to you, the rest who are in Thyatira, who do not hold this teaching, who have not known the deep things of Satan, as they call them – I place no other burden on you. [25]'Nevertheless what you have, hold fast until I come. [26]'He who overcomes, and he who keeps My deeds until the end, TO HIM I WILL GIVE AUTHORITY OVER THE NATIONS; [27]AND HE SHALL RULE THEM WITH A ROD OF IRON, AS THE VESSELS OF THE POTTER ARE BROKEN TO PIECES, as I also

have received authority from My Father; [28]and I will give him the morning star.

[29]'He who has an ear, let him hear what the Spirit says to the churches.'

It is interesting that the longest letter written in this series of seven letters to the churches is written to the smallest and least important of all of the seven cities. Thirty-five to forty miles southeast of Pergamum lies the city of Thyatira. It is located at the mouth of a long valley which connects the valleys of the Hermus and Caicus rivers. Through it ran a trade route that started in Pergamum and went all the way to Syria.

However, she was not well known for trade, but for manufacturing, and especially industries having to do with cloth — weaving, dyeing, making garments, etc. When the Apostle Paul was in Philippi, he met Lydia, a woman from Thyatira who sold purple cloth (Acts 16:14).

Thyatira was an important manufacturing city and the center of the trade guilds. Trade guilds were organizations formed around people who practiced certain occupations. Wool workers, linen workers, makers of winter garments, dyers, leather workers, tanners, potters, etc., would each have their own guild.

The trade guilds were religious in nature. Each guild had its own god, a guardian god that was supposed to bless those who were members of that guild. To be able to make a living at any trade in Thyatira, one had to belong to that trade's guild, and in order to belong to that guild, he had to participate in the feasts of the guild gods.

There were three parts to the feasts of the guild gods. First, a cup of wine was poured out to symbolize honor and worship to the god. Then a meal was eaten, part of which had been offered in sacrifice to that god. After the meal when most in attendance were drunk there was an orgy, a sexual free-for-all in which all

97

were expected to participate. In order to be a member of that trade guild, a person had to participate in these feasts, and none of the activities could be avoided without incurring persecution. Obviously, the Christian was put in a terrible situation — participate in these ungodly celebrations, or lose his livelihood. With this background we can better understand what the Lord writes to the church at Thyatira.

2:18 "And to the angel of the church in Thyatira write: The Son of God, who has eyes like a flame of fire, and His feet are like burnished bronze, says this:

Robert Mounce writes, "The difficulty in interpreting this letter grows out of the numerous references to details of daily life which have become obscured with the passing of time and the lack of archaeological evidence which would reveal its past."[11] The self-designation in the letter to Thyatira is unique. "The Son of God . . . says this." This is the only letter where direct identification is made. In the first three letters the identification has been indirect with descriptions from the original vision recorded in chapter 1. Perhaps this address is to contrast the true Son of God with Thyatira's false gods, the sons of Zeus.

Like the other letters, however, description is added from the vision recorded in chapter 1, "who has eyes like a flame of fire," might be an allusion to the sun god, Apollo, who was worshiped at Thyatira. Or, it could signify burning penetration — the penetrating power of the Lord to see through deception to the inner person. We will see the significance of that later. The feet like burnished bronze may have to do with bronze which has been refined by fire, and which is an allusion to one of the major trade guilds in the city.[12] Another view is that it gives the idea of strength and splendor.

2:19 'I know your deeds, and your love and faith and

service and perseverance, and that your deeds of late are greater than at first.

The commendation of Thyatira is similar to that directed to Ephesus, i.e., there is a construction in the Greek that we do not see in the English. The words connected by the epexegetic "and" describe what the "deeds" were, rather than being additional items. We could read verse 19 this way: "I know your deeds, that is your work of love, your work of faith, your work of ministry, and your work of patience."

Notice the contrast between what was said to the Ephesians and what is said here. The Ephesians had left their first love and were told to go back to doing the first works (2:14); Thyatira is told that their present works are even greater than their first works (2:19). The Lord's words are quite a tribute to that church. If we knew nothing else about the church at Thyatira, we would think nothing could be wrong with a church which was described in that way.

But the Lord who has eyes like a flame of fire looks inside and sees things that do not appear on the outside. Perhaps an important lesson for us to glean from these letters is that a church might have many things good about it, yet still have characteristics which need correction.

2:20 'But I have *this* against you, that you tolerate the woman Jezebel, who calls herself a prophetess, and she teaches and leads My bond-servants astray so that they commit *acts of* immorality and eat things sacrificed to idols. 21 'I gave her time to repent, and she does not want to repent of her immorality.

The story of Jezebel is found in 1 Kings 16:1-21:29 and 2 Kings 9:1-22. Ahab, king of Israel, married Jezebel, daughter of the king of Sidon. Her father, Ethbaal, had been high priest of Baal until he murdered the king and took the throne. Perhaps that background contributed to her bloodthirsty, power-hungry nature and to her zeal for Baal. She introduced Baal worship into Israel and caused the Israelites to fall away from God. Her influence corrupted Judah as well, when her daughter Athaliah married Jehoram, king of Judah.

Jezebel's intention was to eliminate the worship of Jehovah, and she waged a fierce campaign against his prophets. Elijah dealt a severe blow to Baal-worship in the confrontation on Mt. Carmel, which resulted in the deaths of 450 prophets of Baal (1 Kgs. 18:16-40). However, Jezebel was far from beaten and threatened Elijah's life, causing him to flee.

Her power and ruthlessness was also demonstrated in her ability to involve the elders and nobles of Samaria in a conspiracy to take the life and property of Naboth when Ahab pouted about wanting the property for a garden (1 Kgs. 21:1ff). That event resulted in Elijah's prophecy that Jezebel would die in a grisly and dishonorable manner (2 Kgs. 9:30-37).

Who was the Jezebel at Thyatira? Probably no one in particular but the personification of a teaching or doctrine that encouraged people to compromise their Christian beliefs and participate in the activities of the trade guild feasts. Nevertheless, her teaching was similar to that of the Nicolaitans and the Balaamites at Ephesus and Pergamum. While some commentators would interpret this as a "spiritual adultery" (i.e., idolatry); one should not discount that this could be a reference to cultic fornication (cf. 2:14).

What the Lord had against the church at Thyatira was their toleration of those teaching that doctrine. They were allowing a teaching which resulted not only in acts of sin, but also in an alliance with paganism. It may have been an attractive idea to the Christians at Thyatira because participating in the trade guild feasts would protect their occupations, and that made the teaching all the more insidious. There was no repentant attitude in spite of the Lord's patience, and perhaps for that reason the threatened judgment was severe.

Jezebelism is still with us today, and so is the toleration. There will always be an effort by some to mix Christianity with worldly activities hoping for the benefits of both. And there will always be some who are tolerant of such, not wanting their peace disturbed with negative preaching or confrontation with error. The Lord's judgment on Thyatira should give us some idea how He might feel about that kind of influence in the church today.

2:22 'Behold, I will throw her on a bed *of sickness*, and those who commit adultery with her into great tribulation, unless they repent of her deeds. 23 'And I will kill her children with pestilence, and all the churches will know that I am He who searches the minds and hearts; and I will give to each one of you according to your deeds.

The Jezebelites may have been enjoying the bed of fornication, compromise with immoral pagan practices, but the Lord says their punishment will be the bed of affliction. Those who cooperated in that doctrine would suffer great tribulation — intense suffering — if they did not repent. "Her children," perhaps those who were led astray, would be "killed with death" (ASV, a literal translation from the Greek) a Hebraism that probably means "killed by pestilence." It is possible that the reference to "children" alludes to the slaying of the sons of Ahab as Israel was purged of that family's evil influence.

"I am He who searches the minds and hearts" is an Old Testament description of God (Jer. 11:20; 17:10). From the Garden throughout biblical history, God has always searched for man when he (man) has wandered away. The declaration that God will reward "according to your deeds" is both an Old Testament declaration (Ps. 62:12; Prov. 24:12) and a New Testament affirmation (Matt. 16:27; 2 Cor. 5:10; 11:15).

The persuasive logic of the Jezebelites may have confused many in the church, but He who has eyes like a flame of fire saw through to the hearts and minds, identified the guilty and was going to repay each man for what he had done. A church that in some ways was working — loving, faithful, ministering, and patient — had the serious problem of tolerating evil, and that evil was going to be corrected.

2:24 'But I say to you, the rest who are in Thyatira, who do not hold this teaching, who have not known the deep things of Satan, as they call them — I place no other burden on you. 25 'Nevertheless what you have, hold fast until I come.

The Lord addresses the faithful, those who have not been a part of the heresy, with words of encouragement. Some had not accepted this doctrine — had not known the "deep things of Satan." That expression probably refers to the Jezebelism, and "as they call them" likely means the faithful referred to the teaching as the deep things of Satan. "The deep things of Satan" may be a reversal of a claim by the followers of Jezebel to know divine mysteries, or it may be a repetition of a claim by her followers that one must experience all aspects of pagan society; i.e., "the deep things of Satan" in order to appreciate their Christian walk of life. Johnson writes that this phrase is

> the actual phrase Jezebel used. But could she lure Christians by using such a term? The reasoning of some in the early church (the Nicolaitans) might have gone something like this: This only effective way to confront Satan was to enter into his strongholds; the real nature of sin could only be learned by experience, and therefore only those who had really experienced sin could truly appreciate grace. So by experiencing the depths of paganism ('the deep secrets of Satan'), one would be better equipped to serve Christ, or be an

example of freedom to his brothers (cf. 1 Cor. 8:9-11). Thus the sin of Jezebel was deadly serious because of the depths of its deception. Only a few perceived where the teaching was leading.[13]

The Lord knows they have heavy burdens to bear and He is not going to increase that burden. In fact, He exhorts them to continue to be faithful in the face of the difficulties — "tie a knot in the end of the rope and hold on." The promise of His coming reminds them that they will be rewarded.

2:26 'He who overcomes, and he who keeps My deeds until the end, TO HIM I WILL GIVE AUTHORITY OVER THE NATIONS; 27 AND HE SHALL RULE THEM WITH A ROD OF IRON, AS THE VESSELS OF THE POTTER ARE BROKEN TO PIECES, as I also have received *authority* **from My Father; 28 and I will give him the morning star. 29 'He who has an ear, let him hear what the Spirit says to the churches.'**

In the overcoming passage to Thyatira we learn that he who overcomes is he who keeps the Lord's works until the end. That is a good definition of what it means to overcome. It was expressed another way in the letter to the church in Smyrna when they were told to be "faithful until death" (Rev. 2:10).

Verses 26b and 27 are a rendering of Psalm 2:8-9, which has always been understood to be messianic. Revelation 12:5 and 19:15 use the same imagery, applied to the victorious Christ. The verb means "to shepherd" and the sense of the verse is the Lord will shepherd with an iron staff which can destroy sinners like it can break a clay pot into pieces. Christ will give the overcomer a share of that authority which the Father had given Him (Matt. 28:18), and Christ and His followers will have absolute power over the sinful nations.

Christians today can wield power over the nations as they pray for the leaders (1 Tim. 2:1-3) and intercede with the God of Heaven as He rules this world.

The overcomer is made another promise: "and I will give him the morning star." There are many views as to the identification of the "morning star." It is most likely to be the promise of the Christ, who identifies Himself as the bright, morning star in Revelation 22:16. The overcomer is given the greatest promise of all — the Lord Himself. John 14:1ff records Jesus telling His followers that they would live with Him in a special place that had been prepared for them. Those words would have been of immeasurable comfort and strength to the Christians at Thyatira and would have helped them be steadfast in the face of severe pressures. If they continued to rise above those pressures, they would be victorious and live and rule with Christ Himself.

The message is one of strength and comfort to Christians today as well. The world we live in has its own "trade guilds": pressures to conform, pressures to be dishonest, pressures to be immoral, pressures to make wrong judgments, etc. We must hold fast as the Christians in Thyatira were exhorted to do, and the rewards they were promised will be also ours.

NOTES

[1]In the four last letters the promise is given before the exhortation.

[2]William Barclay, *The Revelation of John, Vol. I* (Philadelphia: The Westminster Press, 1960), 72.

[3]David E. Aune, *Prophecy in Early Christian and the Ancient Mediterranean World* (Grand Rapids: Eerdmans, 1983), 328.

[4]William Barclay, *The Revelation of John, Vol. I* , 75-76.

[5]Sir William Ramsay, M., *The Letters to the Seven Churches of Asia* (London: Hodder & Stroughton, 1904), 300-301.

[6]*The Martyrdom of Polycarp* 12.2 (Nashville: Thomas Nelson Publishers, 1978).

[7]Ibid., 9.3, *The Apostolic Fathers.*

[8]Ibid., 11.2.

[9]Ibid., 14.2.

[10]William Barclay, *The Revelation of John, Vol. I* , 98.

[11]Robert H. Mounce, *The Book of Revelation,* 101.

[12]Colin J. Hemer, *The Letters to the Seven Churches of Asia in Their Local Setting,* Journal for the Study of the New Testament, vol. Supplement Series 11 (Sheffield: The University of Sheffield, 1986), 111-17.

[13]Alan Johnson, *Book of Revelation,* The Expositor's Bible Commentary, vol. 12, 445-446.

Revelation 3

E. To Sardis: Dead or Alive?, 3:1-6

[1]"To the angel of the church in Sardis write: He who has the seven Spirits of God and the seven stars, says this: 'I know your deeds, that you have a name that you are alive, but you are dead. [2]'Wake up, and strengthen the things that remain, which were about to die; for I have not found your deeds completed in the sight of My God. [3]'So remember what you have received and heard; and keep it, and repent. Therefore if you do not wake up, I will come like a thief, and you will not know at what hour I will come to you.

[4]'But you have a few people in Sardis who have not soiled their garments; and they will walk with Me in white, for they are worthy. [5]'He who overcomes will thus be clothed in white garments; and I will not erase his name from the book of life, and I will confess his name before My Father and before His angels.

[6]'He who has an ear, let him hear what the Spirit says to the churches.'

Sardis had been the capital of the ancient kingdom of Lydia, but was declining by the time of the Romans. She was located thirty miles southeast of Thyatira and about fifty miles east of Ephesus. She is historically significant as being the city from where Xerxes invaded Greece, and where Cyrus marched against Artaxerxes.

The city overlooked the valley of the Hermus, and the trade of the valley centered there. Five roads converged at Sardis which gave her commercial advantage. She was the center of a thriving woolen industry.

The major religion of the city was worship of the goddess Cybele, and the rituals involved in that worship were frenzied, hysterical affairs. Fortunately, Christians did not face serious pressure to participate in these pagan activities. Emperor worship was not consequential enough to pose a threat to Christians.

If Sardis had a claim to fame, it was decadence. Even in the pagan world, Sardis was thought of with contempt. A lot of the wealth of the city was due to its trade and industry, and that wealth brought about an emphasis on pleasure and luxury. Sardis was described by the people of her day as a loose-living, pleasure-loving, luxury-laden city.

The Christians at Sardis suffered none of the persecutions faced by the other churches. There was no threat from Caesar worship or pressure to engage in pagan ceremonies. There was no danger from the slander of influential Jews. There was no economic peril from trade guilds. There was not even the hint of any internal heresy within the church. The church at Sardis was completely free from trouble both without and within. She was a church at peace, but the peace she enjoyed was the peace of the dead.

3:1 "To the angel of the church in Sardis write: He who has the seven Spirits of God and the seven stars, says this: 'I know your deeds, that you have a name that you are alive, but you are dead.

The letter comes from the one who has "the seven Spirits of God and the seven stars." We are reminded that the letter to Ephesus came from the one who "holds the seven stars in His right hand" (2:1). The seven stars are identified in 1:20 as the angels of the seven churches.

There is little to commend this church. They are a church that has a name, a good reputation, but they did not live up to that name. Outwardly they gave the appearance of being a faithful, active congregation, but it was in name only.

"That you have a name that you are alive" — There are several factors which may have contributed to a good reputation. The church at Sardis may have had a large membership. Perhaps the church at Sardis was one of the big churches in the brotherhood in Asia Minor. There is a certain distinction attached to large numbers, an attitude that equates a large membership with a fine church. If so many people attend there, it must have much to commend it.

She may have had a name because of wealth. Considering the commerce and industry in Sardis and the reputation the city itself had for riches and luxury, the church there could have been affluent. In societies that respect wealth and position a congregation of wealthy high-placed people might well have a high standing in the community.

It is possible that an attractive worship service contributed to the good name of the church at Sardis. Perhaps people enjoyed attending there because the beauty and structure of the service appealed to them.

Sardis may have had a name because she had sound teachers. We do not read of Balaamites there, or Nicolaitans, or a Jezebel. There were none of those that called themselves to be apostles but were found not to be so.

These things might contribute to the outward appearance of a church and give it a good reputation. Sardis had such a name, but the Lord said that name was unfounded. We see again that it is not what we think about ourselves, or even what others may think about us, but what the Lord thinks about us that is important.

"But, you are dead." The church at Sardis was alive in name only — she was dead in works. Sardis was living in the past — basking in a reputation they may have deserved at one time, but no longer. They may have been alive and vibrant in a material sense, but they were dead or dying spiritually. We will see that there remained a few faithful Christians at Sardis, but apparently the majority had so compromised with the environment of the decadent city they were Christians in name only.

Sardis was not a defunct church with a delapidated building about to close its doors. Its membership was not dwindling and the preacher ready to resign. They could not have had a good reputation unless they had given every appearance of being a thriving congregation. They probably met regularly and had committees galore with lots of activities going on which made it appear to be an active church. But it had no such reputation with the Lord.

A church's health is threatened when it is more concerned with the material than it is with the spiritual — more concerned about the cost than the lost. People can be more disturbed over what may be going on in the fellowship hall than they are that there are people dying in a lost condition. Elaborate building projects and expensive programs can get in the way of preaching the Gospel or feeding the hungry. When a church is more concerned about material things than spiritual things, it has lost a God-designed perspective. The church at Sardis may have been infected with the materialistic attitude of the city around it, and that is a real danger in our time as well.

3:2 'Wake up, and strengthen the things that remain, which were about to die; for I have not found your deeds completed in the sight of My God. 3 'So remember what you have received and heard; and keep *it*, and repent. Therefore if you do not wake up, I will come like a thief, and you will not know at what hour I will come to you.

"Wake up" — Being watchful would have important significance to the people of Sardis. The city was situated on the side of a hill and surrounded on three sides by steep cliffs. She was well-defended against her enemies if the people kept watch. Herodotus, an early Greek historian, tells us of a time when lack of watchfulness caused the city's downfall.

In 549 B.C. Cyrus came through the area on a campaign and intended to take Sardis quickly and move on. He promised a reward to the soldier who could devise a way to get into the city. One of Cyrus' soldiers happened to see a guard up on the cliff drop his helmet, scale down the wall to retrieve it, and scale back up. That night Cyrus' men used that same method and entered the city successfully because there was no guard on duty. The people of Sardis had become complacent because they believed their position to be impregnable, so they were not watchful.

In 216 B.C., it happened again. Antiochus the Great took the city when a Cretan named Lagoras found a vulnerable spot and led a band of men on a daring climb into the city. The city had been taken twice because of a lack of vigilance. With that in their history, being told to "be watchful" would catch their attention. The warning to be watchful applies to Christians today as well as to those in Sardis. There are two areas in which it is important to be watchful. The first area is one's weak points. Each Christian knows where he is the weakest, the most vulnerable to temptation, and he needs to stand guard.

A Christian needs also to be watchful in his strong points. Paul said, "Therefore let him who thinks he stands take heed that he does not fall" (1 Cor. 10:12).

Sometimes a Christian will not put up any guard at all in those areas where he feels he is strong. Satan attacks on all fronts, so the Christian must be watchful on all fronts.

The church at Sardis was told to "strengthen the things that remain." Sardis may have been declared dead, but there was hope of restoration to life. There were some good characteristics and some good works which were ready to die, but they still had a spark of life. None of these good works had been completed, or carried out fully. In other words, breathe life into these dry bones. If we visited the church at Sardis they would give us a tour of the building to show us how good things were. Their membership would be large, their finances in good shape, and we would see a lot of activity. But their is quantity without quality. The salt had lost its savour. They had a reputation that they were alive, but in reality they were dead.

The Christians in Ephesus were also told to remember and repent (2:5). The point was made there that the road back begins with remembering. Newly converted Christians are excited and zealous about the things they can do for the Lord. Their lives have a new spiritual emphasis as they revel in the relationship they now have with the Lord. The church at Sardis was told to remember those things and turn back to them.

The phrase "come as a thief" is used in other places in the New Testament to describe the coming of the Lord as unexpected — with no warning (1 Thess. 5:2; 2 Pet. 3:10). The Second Coming is not being discussed here because that is not contingent upon the actions of the church at Sardis. What is being discussed is judgment that will come upon that church if it does not repent. They will suffer the consequences for their failures and spiritual death, and when it does come, it will be swift and unexpected.

3:4 'But you have a few people in Sardis who have not

soiled their garments; and they will walk with Me in white, for they are worthy.

There were still a few in Sardis who had not been contaminated — who had kept themselves pure from pagan and worldly influences. We see that it is possible for a minority to remain faithful and be acceptable to God even when the majority is not. These Christians were "the salt of the earth" and as such kept the spark of life alive in the church at Sardis. To these faithful the Lord gives four precious promises.

There is no more glorious promise than that the faithful Christian will dwell in the presence of his Lord. In John 14:1ff the Lord said He was going to prepare a place for His disciples, and where He was, they would be also. Paul knew that to leave this body meant to be at home with the Lord (2 Cor. 4:8). He encouraged the Thessalonians by telling them they would be with the Lord forever (1 Thess. 4:17). In Revelation 7:17 the Great Multitude is pictured as being before the throne of God, and in the presence of the Lamb who is their Shepherd and shall guide them to fountains of waters of life.

The Lord told the faithful in Sardis they would walk with Him — they would know the joy of being in His presence. Surely they were strengthened by this promise and better equipped to overcome.

3:5 'He who overcomes will thus be clothed in white garments; and I will not erase his name from the book of life, and I will confess his name before My Father and before His angels. 6 'He who has an ear, let him hear what the Spirit says to the churches.'

Those who had not defiled their garments — the overcomers — would be dressed in white. Seven times in the book of Revelation saints are seen in white garments: 3:6, 18; 4:4; 6:11; 7:9, 13 and 19:14. White symbolized purity, and was also significant as the garment worn by a victorious contestant. Purity is likely the primary thought here with perhaps a secondary application to the victory of those who overcome. Those who kept themselves pure from the defilements of paganism and worldliness would be in the presence of the Lord, dressed in the white garments that represented their purity. They were worthy because they had kept themselves pure and had done nothing to forfeit their salvation.

Our first introduction to a divine register is in Exodus 32:32-33 when Moses asks the Lord to forgive the Israelites, or if not, to blot him out of "Your book which You have written." Jehovah replies He will only blot those who have sinned out of His book. In Psalms 69:28 David asks that his enemies be blotted out of the book of life. Daniel was told that in a time of great distress everyone whose name was found written in the book would be delivered (Dan. 12:1). "The book" was a register of God's people, a roll of the faithful.

In ancient history it was customary to record a person's birth in the city records and then blot that name out when he died. If a criminal's name were removed from the civic register, he lost his citizenship.

Those in Sardis who had compromised and who were dead, were in danger of having their names blotted out of the book of life — being removed from the roll of God's people — losing their citizenship in the kingdom. But the faithful were in no such danger. Their names would not be blotted out; they would retain the status of citizen.

The overcomer's name will be confessed before the Father and His angels. In Matthew 10:32 the Lord said if anyone confessed Him before men, He would confess that one before His Father. What an inestimable blessing it will be. Jesus will say, "Father, this one is mine; this one is faithful and should be admitted into our presence." We can hardly comprehend the significance of that. Think of the blessing of being that overcomer who walks with the Lord in white, whose name is written in the book of Life, and whose name the Lord Jesus in Heaven confesses to the Father.

Sardis was a church in a lot of trouble but not without hope. And even in the midst of a majority that was spiritually dead, there was a faithful minority. That faithful minority was encouraged by the wonderful promises to the overcomer. Being faithful under pressure now meant to be rewarded beyond measure in the life to come.

F. To Philadelphia: The Church with an Open Door, 3:7-13

[7]"And to the angel of the church in Philadelphia write: He who is holy, who is true, who has the key of David, who opens and no one will shut, and who shuts and no one opens, says this: [8]"I know your deeds. Behold, I have put before you an open door which no one can shut, because you have a little power, and have kept My word, and have not denied My name. [9]"Behold, I will cause those of the synagogue of Satan, who say that they are Jews and are not, but lie–I will make them come and bow down at your feet, and make them know that I have loved you. [10]"Because you have kept the word of My perseverance, I also will keep you from the hour of testing, that hour which is about to come upon the whole world, to test those who dwell on the earth. [11]"I am coming quickly; hold fast what you have, so that no one will take your crown.

[12]"He who overcomes, I will make him a pillar in the temple of My God, and he will not go out from it anymore; and I will write on him the name of My God, and the name of the city of My God, the new Jerusalem, which comes down out of heaven from My God, and My new name.

[13]"He who has an ear, let him hear what the Spirit says to the churches.'

Philadelphia, the city of brotherly love, was located twenty-eight miles southeast of Sardis; eighty miles due east of Smyrna. Strategically located, Philadelphia was at the border of three different provinces, Mysia, Lydia and Phrygia. She served as a central point through which Greek culture would be funnelled toward the east in the ancient world. Because of her particular position geographically, she became known as the "Gateway to the East."

Herodotus relates a tradition about the place where Philadelphia one day would stand. When the Persian king Xerxes was on his way to invade Europe, he found shelter at this spot under a tree. He admired and appreciated the tree so much he decked it with costly gifts and left a personal bodyguard there to look after it. It was on this spot some years later that Philadelphia was built.

Philadelphia is not as old a city as the other ones we have studied, dating back only to about 150 years before Christ. Her name was taken from Attalus II, whose loyalty to his brother Eumenes resulted in his being called "Philadelphus," or "brother-lover."

She was founded for the purpose of spreading the Greek language, the Greek culture, and the Greek manner into the east. She was intended to be a missionary city — to promote Hellenism in the land.

Philadelphia lay on the edge of a great volcanic plain, one of the most fertile areas in the world. She was world-famous for her wines and enjoyed an extensive market which brought much prosperity.

The volcanic area also created numerous hot springs which were renowned for their healing powers. People came from far and wide to bathe in the medicinal waters, and this steady flow of visitors added to the wealth of the city.

The very feature which brought good fortune to the people of Philadelphia also brought danger. Because of the volcanic nature of the area, it was subject to frequent earthquakes. The people lived an unsettled life, and at least once, the city had been destroyed.

3:7 "And to the angel of the church in Philadelphia write: He who is holy, who is true, who has the key of David, who opens and no one will shut, and who shuts and no one opens, says this:

The self-designation addressed to the church in Philadelphia is unique. In the other six letters to the churches of Asia the Lord identifies Himself with descriptions we see from chapter one, but that language is not drawn on for the identification to the Philadelphians.

He "who is true," is a very significant phrase. There are two words for "true" in the original language. *Alēthēs* refers to something that is true as opposed to something that is false. *Alēthinos* means something which is genuine as opposed to that which is counterfeit. The latter is the word used here. The Lord is saying He is real — genuine — not an illusion or counterfeit.

He "who has the key of David." The Lord draws on a passage from the prophet Isaiah to further identify Himself. From Isaiah 22 we learn that Eliakim, the faithful steward of Hezekiah, was given the key to the royal palace. He completely controlled access to the palace and to the presence of the king. Anyone who would enter had to go through him. In speaking of Eliakim, Isaiah writes in verse 22, "Then I will set the key of the house of David on his shoulder, When he opens no one will shut, When he shuts no one will open." Jesus here describes Himself as one who has the authority to open and close the door. Access to the heavenly palace and its king is through Jesus and none other. In John 14:6 Jesus said, "I am the way, and the truth, and the life; no one comes to the Father, but through Me."

3:8 'I know your deeds. Behold, I have put before you an open door which no one can shut, because you have a little power, and have kept My word, and have not denied My name.

It is possible the church at Philadelphia was referred to as having "a little power" because it was a small congregation and did not have much impact on the city. In spite of their little strength they had been faithful, and that had not gone unnoticed by their Lord. Every one of the letters to the seven churches has an "I know" statement. It is important for us to remember that the Lord knows what is happening, both with the church collectively and with Christians individually.

The parenthetical phrase "behold, I have put before you an open door" has been interpreted various ways. The most common explanation is in a missionary context. Paul uses this particular language, for instance, in 1 Corinthians 16:9 when he says, "for a wide door for effective service has opened to me." In 2 Corinthians 2:12 he says that in Troas, "a door was opened for me in the Lord." He asks the Colossians to pray for him and his companions that "God will open up to us a door for the word" (4:3).

Perhaps the term is even more meaningful in light of Philadelphia's geographical location. As the "Gateway to the East," situated at the eastern end of a valley leading to the great central plain, it had a unique opportunity to carry the Gospel to the cities beyond. It would have been significant and encouraging to this church, perhaps small and not very strong, that the Lord was going to present them with greater opportunities for service.

Christians today need to be watchful for doors of opportunity. It behooves us to ask the Lord to open doors of opportunity for service and be ready to go through those doors when they are opened. Sometimes doors of opportunity are opened unexpectedly, and a walk of faith is necessary to get us through the door.

The church at Philadelphia had faithfully kept the Lord's word and not denied His name in spite of their little power and whatever difficulties they faced. Pergamum received similar praise (2:13). Being obedient to the word of the Lord is how we show our love for Him (John 14:15). We will be judged according to that word (John 12:48-50).

In spite of pressures brought to bear upon them, in spite of their "little power," the Christians in Philadelphia had remained faithful. Their faithfulness would be rewarded.

3:9 'Behold, I will cause *those* **of the synagogue of Satan, who say that they are Jews and are not, but lie — I will make them come and bow down at your feet, and** *make them* **know that I have loved you.**

One of the future rewards of the faithful is going to be victory over their foes. We see that here in verse 9. The church in Philadelphia was apparently having some of the same kind of difficulties that faced the Christians in Smyrna. The Jews of the day thought they were the people of God, and mistreated Christians in the name of religion. The time will come when those Jews will acknowledge the Christ and His love for His church, and the faithful Christians will be vindicated.

3:10 'Because you have kept the word of My persever- ance, I also will keep you from the hour of testing, that *hour* **which is about to come upon the whole world, to test those who dwell on the earth.**

The Christians in Philadelphia had kept the Lord's command to endure patiently, and as a reward for this they would be kept from the hour of trial that was to come.

God never promised His people that when they

become Christians they will be vaccinated against tribulation. They are not exempt from hard times. When the Lord promises Christians He will keep them during trial, He means that He will see them through it — help them stay faithful through it — and bring about their ultimate victory. Exemption from tribulation does not fit with the rest of the picture in Revelation.

Later in the book, in chapters 7 and 14, we find the redeemed of God pictured as 144,000 servants who have the seal of God upon their foreheads. They are sealed because they came through persecution and will be vindicated when God brings judgment on the earth. They had to endure the persecution but because they were faithful through it, they were sealed. In the Judgment they will be signified as belonging to the Lord.

The Lord is telling the Christians in Philadelphia they will be kept because they kept His word. He is the keeper — the holder of the key — and will be the one who keeps them.

In the trial which is about to come upon the Roman Empire, Christians are going to face persecutions. There will be many temptations to turn from the faith. But Christ is promising here that faithful followers will be protected and able to persevere during this "hour of testing." The "hour of testing" is not a period of time but a designation of the trial itself. "Those who dwell on the earth" refers to the non-Christian world (cf. Rev. 11:10).

3:11 'I am coming quickly; hold fast what you have, so that no one will take your crown.

The phrase "I am coming quickly" indicates the promised judgment is not far off. To further sustain this, John later will write that the things written in this book "must soon take place" (22:6) for "the time is near" (22:10). The crown referred to is a reminder of the victor's crown which the athletes received if they won at the games. These brethren were already reigning as kings (Rev. 1:5-6), and as victors, were wearing the victory crown which the Lord promised (cf. 2 Tim. 4:8).

3:12 'He who overcomes, I will make him a pillar in the temple of My God, and he will not go out from it anymore; and I will write on him the name of My God, and the name of the city of My God, the new Jerusalem, which comes down out of heaven from My God, and My new name.

This idea of a pillar is very significant. A pillar has one special function — it is to support the edifice of which it forms a part. The church is the temple of God (1 Cor. 3:16-17), and that ties in with the description of faithful Christians as "pillars." There are at least two ideas involved in pillar. One is incorporation: a pillar is an integral part of the structure to which it belongs. These Christians in Philadelphia are promised they will be an integral part of the heavenly temple if they overcome. Second is the idea of permanence and stability. They were told they would become part of the temple of God and not go out any more.

Then the Philadelphians are promised a beautiful threefold inscription: (1) "I will write on him the name of my God." That inscription would identify the Christian as belonging to God. (2) "And the name of the city of my God, the new Jerusalem." The Christian not only belongs to God, he is a citizen of the kingdom, the New Jerusalem. (3) "And my new name." The third inscription identifies the Christian as one who has a special relationship with Christ, and perhaps implies that after the Second Coming, when the Christian is freed from the mortal body, he will have fuller knowledge and understanding of the Christ.

3:13 'He who has an ear, let him hear what the Spirit says to the churches.'

Churches today must heed what the Spirit says to the churches just as these churches of Asia were told to do. Being small in number, or having "little power," should not prevent a congregation from taking advantage of the doors that are opened for it. Even a handful of people can have a mighty impact on society if they are zealous and diligent.

Christians today have the same promises that were made to the church in Philadelphia. If we remain faithful, we will be vindicated and victorious in the eyes of unbelievers; we will be "kept" through every trial; we will be a permanent, stable part of the heavenly temple and will be identified as children of God, citizens of the kingdom, and brethren of Christ.

G. To Laodicea: The Church with the Closed Door, 3:14-22

[14]"To the angel of the church in Laodicea write: The Amen, the faithful and true Witness, the Beginning of the creation of God, says this: [15]'I know your deeds, that you are neither cold nor hot; I wish that you were cold or hot. [16]'So because you are lukewarm, and neither hot nor cold, I will spit you out of My mouth.

[17]'Because you say, "I am rich, and have become wealthy, and have need of nothing," and you do not know that you are wretched and miserable and poor and blind and naked, [18]I advise you to buy from Me gold refined by fire so that you may become rich, and white garments so that you may clothe yourself, and that the shame of your nakedness will not be revealed; and eye salve to anoint your eyes so that you may see. [19]'Those whom I love, I reprove and discipline; therefore be zealous and repent.

[20]'Behold, I stand at the door and knock; if anyone hears My voice and opens the door, I will come in to him and will dine with him, and he with Me. [21]'He

who overcomes, I will grant to him to sit down with Me on My throne, as I also overcame and sat down with My Father on His throne.

[22]"He who has an ear, let him hear what the Spirit says to the churches.'"

Forty miles southeast of Philadelphia, three famous cities clustered in the valley of the river Lycus. To the north of the river was the city of Hierapolis; to the south of the river were the cities of Laodicea and Colossae, about ten miles apart. Laodicea was founded about the middle of the third century B.C. by Antiochus II and named for his wife, Laodice.

Laodicea was the location of a very famous health resort. Hot mineral springs found in the area were reputed to be soothing and restorative. The famous medical center there was the source of a well-known Phrygian eye salve which was in great demand.

Laodicea, having access to a fine soft wool from the black sheep of the valley, was famous for its wool industry. Because of its commercial prosperity, its health resort, and the medical facilities, Laodicea was a popular place for wealthy people to retire. Those things combined to make the city a famous banking center.

The wealth of the city caused her to be proud and self-sufficient, so much so that in A.D. 60 when she suffered a severe earthquake, she refused any outside help in rebuilding the city. We will see that pride, self-sufficiency and dependence upon material wealth were big factors in the Lord's denunciation of the Laodicean church.

The church at Laodicea is mentioned in Colossians 4:16. Paul apparently had written letters to both the church at Colossae and at Laodicea, and in his closing in the letter to the Colossians, he instructs that the two churches exchange and read each other's letters.

The congregation at Laodicea was not infected with the poison of a specific sin, nor was it troubled with either heretics or persecution. Laodicea had one problem and one problem alone — she was half-hearted in her devotion to God. There is an important lesson in this letter for the church today.

3:14 "To the angel of the church in Laodicea write: The Amen, the faithful and true Witness, the Beginning of the creation of God, says this:

This letter opens, as do the others, with a phrase that identifies the writer. *Amen.* The word "amen" affirms a statement as being absolutely true, absolutely reliable. We are familiar with statements of Jesus that begin, "verily, verily," or "truly, truly." In the original language it is *"amēn, amēn"* — coming from Hebrew to Greek to English untranslated. We use "amen" to close prayers, affirming the truth of what has been expressed. Sometimes a preacher's audience will say "amen" to indicate agreement with what has been said.

Jesus refers to Himself as "the Amen." In John 14:6 He said He was the way, the truth and the life. Jesus is not only the one who speaks the truth, He is the truth itself. The idea is further expanded and defined by the phrase, "the faithful and true witness of God."

"Beginning" is not the best understanding of the Greek word *archē*. There are some people in the religious world who have taken this passage along with a few others to teach that Jesus was created first, and then He created everything else. That is not what this word means. *Archē* means "source or origin" — Jesus is the source or origin of all creation. In Colossians 1:15ff, Paul writes that Jesus is preeminent over all creation, all things being created in Him through Him and unto Him. John expressed the same truth in John 1:3. This is Jesus who is true, who is the very source or origin of all things that God has created, who is speaking and writing these words.

3:15 'I know your deeds, that you are neither cold nor hot; I wish that you were cold or hot. 16 'So because you are lukewarm, and neither hot nor cold, I will spit you out of My mouth.

The Lord has no words of commendation for the church at Laodicea. Even this first phrase, "I know your works," cannot be understood as words of commendation as they were to the church at Ephesus when He told them He knew their works and toil and patience (2:2).

He gets swiftly to the point. "I know your deeds, that you are neither cold [that is, icy cold] nor hot [the word means burning hot]. . . . because you are lukewarm . . . I will spit you out of My mouth."

This vivid portrayal has long been interpreted against the local background. The city of Hierapolis, six miles across the Lycus valley from Laodicea, was famous for its hot springs. The waters flowed over a wide plateau and were lukewarm by the time they reached the edge. The waters were considered medicinal and beneficial while they were hot but were nauseating when they were lukewarm.

The adjectives "hot" and "cold" are not to be taken as describing spiritual fervor or lack of fervor. The contrast is between the medicinal waters of Hierapolis and the cold pure waters of Colossae, another neighboring city. The hot waters were healing, the cold waters refreshing — both having value to those who drank them.

The church in Laodicea "was providing neither refreshment to the spiritually weary, nor healing for the spiritually sick. It was totally ineffective, and thus distasteful to its Lord." This explanation solves the problem of why the Lord would prefer a church to be "cold" rather than "lukewarm."

3:17 'Because you say, "I am rich, and have become wealthy, and have need of nothing," and you do not

know that you are wretched and miserable and poor
and blind and naked,

The Laodiceans claimed to be rich, to have gotten
riches, and to have need of nothing (v. 17). Their were
finding their security in their wealth; they were complacent, self-satisfied, and self-sufficient. Not only were
they smug in their trust in material wealth, but they
also arrogantly claimed to have accomplished it themselves and to need nothing more than what they had
been able to gain.

Jesus' condemnation directly parallels the reasons
for their self-satisfaction. In spite of living in a city
noted for its health resort, they were "miserable." They
lived in a city noted for its wealth, but they were
"poor." Their medical center was world-renowned for
its eye salve, but they were "blind." One of their
sources of wealth was textiles, yet they were "naked."
Their material prosperity did not keep them from
being spiritually destitute, and their reliance upon
their material wealth resulted in spiritual poverty.

**3:18 I advise you to buy from Me gold refined by fire
so that you may become rich, and white garments so
that you may clothe yourself, and that the shame of
your nakedness will not be revealed; and eye salve to
anoint your eyes so that you may see.**

The Laodiceans thought they had everything they
needed, when in reality, they desperately needed what
the Lord had to offer. "Buy from Me gold refined by fire
so that you may become rich." They needed the spiritual
riches available through Christ to be genuinely rich.
"And white garments so that you may clothe yourself."
In contrast with the black wool of Laodicea's textile
industry, the Christians there needed the white robe of
righteousness to cover their spiritual nakedness. "And
eye salve to anoint your eyes so that you may see." The
famous eye salve of Laodicea was not healing their spiritual blindness. They needed the healing of the Lord.

Material wealth is not wrong in and of itself, but it can present a serious danger. Paul addresses this in 1 Timothy 6:9-17. It was not the mere possession of wealth which got the Laodiceans in trouble, but the fact that their hope was set on their material riches instead of on God. The remedy was to turn to the Lord for the true riches.

3:19-22 'Those whom I love, I reprove and discipline; therefore be zealous and repent. 20 'Behold, I stand at the door and knock; if anyone hears My voice and opens the door, I will come in to him and will dine with him, and he with Me. 21 'He who overcomes, I will grant to him to sit down with Me on My throne, as I also overcame and sat down with My Father on His throne. 22 'He who has an ear, let him hear what the Spirit says to the churches.'"

"Tough love" is a popular phrase today. It means showing love for another in ways that are best for that person, even if it means correction, reproof or even punishment. The Lord said hard things to the Laodiceans and called for their repentance, but it was out of love for them and a desire for what was best for them.

The word for "love" in this verse is *phileō* — feelings of affection. Jesus is expressing personal affection for them and that love moves Him to do what is necessary to bring about a correction of their spiritual deficiencies. Their confidence in His love should motivate them to take His admonitions to heart, just as we can much more easily accept correction from one who loves us than from one who does not have our welfare at heart.

Holman Hunt painted a picture of Jesus entitled, "The Light of the World." It pictures Jesus standing and knocking at a door with no knob. The door represents the door of the heart, and the knob is on the inside. The Lord never forces Himself on anybody. He stands and knocks, patiently waiting for the door to be opened and for Him to be invited in.

"If any one hears My voice and opens the door, I will come in to him and will dine with him, and he with Me." In the ancient world the first two meals of the day were functional — a hurried breakfast at the beginning of the day and some lunch caught during a break from the day's activities. The evening meal, the supper meal, was that time a man spent eating leisurely and socially. The day's activities had been taken care of, and in a relaxed atmosphere he could enjoy dining with his family and friends at a meal that often lasted for hours.

In Oriental lands eating together was very significant. It meant a strong bond of affection and companionship. That background caused the common meal to be used as a symbol of the intimacy to be enjoyed in the kingdom of the Lord. The Lord offers that kind of intimacy and fellowship to those who open the door for Him.

In this last letter as in the other six, there is a promise to the overcomer. "He that overcomes, I will grant to him to sit down with Me on My throne, as I also overcame and sat down with My Father on His throne." Christ was victorious over Satan and death, and sat down with the Father to reign with Him. The Christian is promised the same reward — overcoming persecution and overcoming Satan will result in victory and the opportunity to sit with Christ on His throne and reign with Him. Paul writes in 2 Timothy 2:11-12, "It is a trustworthy statement: For if we died with Him, we will also live with Him; If we endure, we will also reign with Him; If we deny Him, He also will deny us."

For the seventh time we read the exhortation, "He who has an ear, let him hear what the Spirit says to the churches." The messages to the churches in Asia were not just for them in their time but for the church through the ages. Laodicea had to overcome complacency, materialism, lukewarmness, and dependence on their material wealth. No one can deny that those ills plague the church today. For the church to overcome and go on to victory, each Christian must overcome the attitudes that diminish enthusiasm and result in stale, lukewarm, or no performance for the Lord. We cannot mistake the call to commitment sent out to each of these seven churches and the same call comes to us. The final reward is worth each Christian's zealous, enthusiastic, faithful service.

There has been a different emphasis in each one of these letters to the seven churches. In the letter to the church at Ephesus, the emphasis was the importance of returning to its first love. The church at Smyrna was warned against compromising and told to be ready to suffer. The emphasis in the letter to Pergamum was the need to champion the truth in the face of error that was all around them. Thyatira was told to follow righteousness even in the face of evil. The emphasis in the letter to the Christians at Sardis was they should be on the inside what they appear to be on the outside. The letter to the church in Philadelphia stressed the open door of opportunity to evangelize that was available to them in spite of their size. To the church at Laodicea, the emphasis will be a combination of strong denunciation of their complacency and loving appeal for wholeheartedness. This letter is one of the sternest, if not the sternest, of the seven letters.

Revelation 4

IV. THE THRONE SCENE, 4:1-5:14

A. The Glory of God and Creation, 4:1-11

¹After these things I looked, and behold, a door standing open in heaven, and the first voice which I had heard, like the sound of a trumpet speaking with me, said, "Come up here, and I will show you what must take place after these things."

²Immediately I was in the Spirit; and behold, a throne was standing in heaven, and One sitting on the throne.

³And He who was sitting was like a jasper stone and a sardius in appearance; and there was a rainbow around the throne, like an emerald in appearance.

⁴Around the throne were twenty-four thrones; and upon the thrones I saw twenty-four elders sitting, clothed in white garments, and golden crowns on their heads.

⁵Out from the throne come flashes of lightning and sounds and peals of thunder. And there were seven lamps of fire burning before the throne, which are the seven Spirits of God;

⁶and before the throne there was something like a sea of glass, like crystal; and in the center and around the throne, four living creatures full of eyes in front and behind.

⁷The first creature was like a lion, and the second creature like a calf, and the third creature had a face like that of a man, and the fourth creature was like a flying eagle.

⁸And the four living creatures, each one of them having six wings, are full of eyes around and within; and day and night they do not cease to say, "HOLY, HOLY, HOLY IS THE LORD GOD, THE ALMIGHTY, WHO WAS AND WHO IS AND WHO IS TO COME."

⁹And when the living creatures give glory and honor and thanks to Him who sits on the throne, to Him who lives forever and ever,

¹⁰the twenty-four elders will fall down before Him who sits on the throne, and will worship Him who lives forever and ever, and will cast their crowns before the throne, saying,

¹¹"Worthy are You, our Lord and our God, to receive glory and honor and power; for You created all things, and because of Your will they existed, and were created."

In the Letters to the Seven Churches we were introduced to three different directions from which temptations come. As we continue to study this book, we will find that these avenues of temptations are constantly used by the Devil in an effort to try to cause man's fall. First, there are the anti-Christian forces (cf. 2:9; 3:9). These forces form persecution against the people of God. This will later find identity with the beast which comes up from out of the sea (13:1-10) representing the civil persecuting power of the Roman Empire. Second, there are the anti-Christian religions (cf. 2:6). This is found in the cult of emperor worship (cf. 2:13). Identity will be found here with the beast which comes up from out of the earth (13:11-18) and also will be referred to as the false prophet (cf. 13:13-14; 16:13; 19:20). Third, there is worldliness (cf. 2:14-15; 3:17-18). There is the appeal to the flesh, to compromise, and to make one's social position acceptable. This will later be seen in the great harlot (chapter 17).

There is a central theme found in chapters four and five. That theme is: God rules, not man. In chapter four the message is centered around the glory of God and the creation. In chapter five the message is the glory of the Lamb and redemption. These will be evident from a reading of the two chapters. Another way of saying this is that chapter 4 is God the Creator, and chapter 5 is God (Christ) the Redeemer.

One item of focus in this picture is the "throne." This word is found seventeen times in chapters four and five; thirteen of which are in chapter four.

4:1 After these things I looked, and behold, a door *standing* open in heaven, and the first voice which I had heard, like *the sound* of a trumpet speaking with me, said, "Come up here, and I will show you what must take place after these things."

The phrase "after these things" introduces a new aspect of the message following that started in Revelation 1:1 and is found frequently (e.g., 7:1; 18:1; 19:1). This is not to be taken that the Revelation was given in parts, but is simply used as a point of emphasis (cf. 7:1, 9; 15:5; 18:11; 20:3).

A door in heaven is opened (cf. Ezek. 1:1-28). We are never told whether John went through the door or simply looked through the door. The fact that a door is opened may be suggestive that the vision was only for John and not for angelic hosts.

This is similar to what Paul writes about in 2 Corinthians 12:1-4. The language and imagery of John's throne room scene are similar to Ezekiel's (1:1-28), an echo of which is also found in the writing of

1 Enoch 14:15; 3 Maccabees 6:18; and Testament of Levi 5:1.

The voice John heard as a trumpet was heard earlier (cf. 1:10) and indicates the sound of authority. We will have more to say about trumpets in Revelation 8. Most commentators identify this voice with that of Christ in 1:10.

"What must take place after these things" is taken to mean that chapters 1-3 indicate what is happening in the present as John writes the book, and from chapter 4 to the end is indicative of future events. We must remember, however, that these are future events from the *time* in which John writes, not future events from our perspective.

4:2 Immediately I was in the Spirit; and behold, a throne was standing in heaven, and One sitting on the throne.

John sees the vision "in the Spirit," (cf. 1:10). This reminds us of Ezekiel when he was lifted up between heaven and earth and was taken to the city of Jerusalem (Ezek. 8:3). Being in the Spirit means he does not see with the physical eye nor hear with the physical ear, but his body and soul are wholly fixed on heavenly things.

John sees a throne set in heaven and someone sitting on the throne. Three out of every four times the word "throne" is mentioned in the New Testament is found in the book of Revelation. The reference to the one "sitting on a throne" occurs twelve times in the book of Revelation and is John's way of speaking about God. He is the one whom the prophet Isaiah saw ". . . sitting on a throne, lofty and exalted" (Isa. 6:1). The description of the heavenly temple (vv. 2-8) is similar to the throne of Ezekiel 1.

4:3 And He who was sitting *was* like a jasper stone and a sardius in appearance; and *there was* a rainbow around the throne, like an emerald in appearance.

The one seated on the throne is later identified for us as "the Lord God, the Almighty" (4:8-9). The description of the throne occupant in Ezekiel's vision is "a figure with the appearance of a man" (1:26), but for John's vision there is no form mentioned, rather a description is given of three stones: jasper, sardius, and a rainbow (resembling an emerald). The jasper and sardius portray the supernatural splendor of God while the rainbow conveys the impression of God's encircling brilliance. Jasper and sardius vary in appearance from dull yellow to red or green. The term "emerald" is an interpretation of a word which varied in color from green to a colorless state. The rainbow imagery is suggestive of the covenant nature of God (cf. Gen. 9:8ff). These help us to see the beauty and glory signified about God who is seated on the throne. Frequently in the Old Testament, heaven is described as God's throne (Isa. 66:1; Ps. 11:4). Here we are shown the throne room of God in heaven's court. The imagery of the rainbow may be a reminder of God's covenant with Noah (Gen. 9:12-17).

4:4 Around the throne *were* twenty-four thrones; and upon the thrones *I saw* twenty-four elders sitting, clothed in white garments, and golden crowns on their heads.

Around the throne are twenty-four other thrones with elders seated on them. Who are these elders? Throughout the book they are pictured as falling down before God in worship and devotion (cf. 5:14; 11:16; 19:4). There are some who interpret the twenty-four elders as the twenty-four priestly orders enumerated in 1 Chronicles 24:4ff and the twenty-four Levitical orders of 1 Chronicles 25:1; suggesting the function of the twenty-four elders is that of adoring and serving the Lord of the universe. We view these as the "overcomers" addressed earlier in the letters to the churches. There are several points of identity which make this true: (1)

they sit on thrones (cf. 3:21), (2) they are arrayed in white (cf. 3:5), (3) they have crowns of gold (cf. 2:10, and (4) they are in the place of overcomers, i.e., in heaven. The representation is that of the redeemed of both covenants. The number twenty-four is usually understood as representing the Twelve Patriarchs (or the Twelve Tribes of Israel) and the Twelve Apostles. These represent all of the redeemed covenant people of God in heaven after death (cf. 7:1-8; 12:1; 21:12-14).

The elders are dressed in white robes, which represents either the holiness of Christ with which they are covered, or purity and victory (cf. 3:4f, 18; 7:9, 14; 19:8, 14). They are wearing golden crowns (which symbolizes they are reigning with Christ, cf. 3:21). These crowns are cast down before the throne (4:10) as they worship the one seated on the throne. This indicates their devotion and worship to the one on the throne.

The elders are associated with the four living creatures. They engage in acts of worship to God and to the Lamb (cf. 4:10-11; 5:11-14). Golden crowns are referred to in 4:4, 10; 9:7; 14:14. They are always distinguished from the saints of God on earth (5:8; 11:17-18; 19:1-4).

4:5 Out from the throne come flashes of lightning and sounds and peals of thunder. And *there were* **seven lamps of fire burning before the throne, which are the seven Spirits of God;**

The flashes of lightning, and the rumblings and peals of thunder symbolize the divine power, majesty and glory which are intensely awesome to the beholder (cf. Exod. 19:16-19). God reveals himself in the activity in nature frequently in the Old Testament (cf. Ps. 18:12ff; 77:18). Slight variations of this picture occurs four times in the book (cf. 4:5; 8:5; 11:19; 16:18). In every passage except this one (4:5), the lightning and thunder appear with an earthquake at the conclusion of a series of judgments when God is about to be disclosed in glory.

The seven lamps blazing are interpreted as the "seven Spirits of God." This has already been mentioned in 1:4 and 3:1 and will be again in 5:6. While there are various interpretations given to this phrase we feel the one most appropriate is that the reference here is to the Holy Spirit. Seven is the divine number and fire is often associated with the Holy Spirit (cf. Acts 2). This also fits the context of this section and makes the picture (through chapter five) complete with each member of the Godhead represented in the scene in heaven.

4:6 and before the throne *there was something* like a sea of glass, like crystal; and in the center and around the throne, four living creatures full of eyes in front and behind.

This heavenly crystal sea occurs in Ezekiel's vision of the Lord's throne (Ezek. 1:22, 26). The next mention of the "sea of glass" is in 15:2, where it is mixed with fire, eloquent of impending judgment. Those who are victorious stand by it (reminding us of the Israelites at the Red Sea, Exodus 14:1-15:21) and sing the Song of Moses and the Lamb (which is a Song in Praise of God's Judgment).

Caird says this sea is identical with the sea in 13:1 and 21:1. He identifies it with a "reservoir of evil." Glass, however, may symbolize the fact that before the sight of God all is revealed (cf. Heb. 4:13).

The sea of glass could represent separation. As there is a separation, by the Aegean Sea, between John and his brethren in Asia Minor, so also there is a separation between the twenty-four elders and the one who is seated on the throne. There is yet no intimate fellowship between the redeemed and God. The sea of glass is pictured as removed in chapter 20, thus indicating the full and final fellowship God will sustain with the redeemed.

The four living creatures stand out in the picture

and can tend to be overwhelming if we forget the over-all scene. While we might be tempted to stand in awe of these creatures, we are reminded that the center of the picture is the main throne and the one seated on it. The description of these living creatures continues in the next verse.

4:7 The first creature *was* like a lion, and the second creature like a calf, and the third creature had a face like that of a man, and the fourth creature *was* like a flying eagle. 8 And the four living creatures, each one of them having six wings, are full of eyes around and within; and day and night they do not cease to say, "HOLY, HOLY, HOLY *IS THE* LORD GOD, THE ALMIGHTY, WHO WAS AND WHO IS AND WHO IS TO COME."

The description of these creatures reminds one of Ezekiel 1 where similar creatures are described. In both they are called "living" ones (Ezek. 1:5; Rev. 4:6); in both the symbolic number, four, is used (Ezek. 1:5; Rev. 4:6); in both the faces are compared to those of a man, lion ox [calf], and eagle (Ezek. 1:10; Rev. 4:6); in both they are associated with a throne (Ezek. 1:26; Rev. 4:6); in both, a rainbow encircles the throne with which these living ones are associated (Ezek. 1:28; Rev. 4:8). But, who are these creatures?

Ezekiel calls them the cherubim ("These are the living beings that I saw beneath the God of Israel by the River Chebar; so I knew that they were cherubim," Ezekiel 10:20). But linking this with the next verse (Rev. 4:8) these creatures are also identified with Isaiah's seraphim (cf. Isa. 6:1-6). It seems likely, then, that these creatures are heavenly messengers (angels?) of God involved in worship to the one who is seated on the throne.

Each creature's face is representative of the creation of God. Rabbi Abahu (c. A.D. 300) taught that the lion represents the wild beast of which the lion is king; the ox (calf, bull) represents the domesticated beasts of which he is king; the face of man represents all animate creatures of which man is king; and the eagle represents the birds of the air of which he is king. These four living creatures represent the whole order of animate creation. To describe these creatures as covered with eyes all around is indicative of their knowledge and their conscious awareness and vigilance to do the Lord's will. With their wings they are able to move swiftly to do God's bidding.

4:9 And when the living creatures give glory and honor and thanks to Him who sits on the throne, to Him who lives forever and ever, 10 the twenty-four elders will fall down before Him who sits on the throne, and will worship Him who lives forever and ever, and will cast their crowns before the throne, saying, 11 " Worthy are You, our Lord and our God, to receive glory and honor and power; for You created all things, and because of Your will they existed, and were created."

These creatures sing a song of praise to the Lord God Almighty and describe Him as the one "who was and who is and who is to come." This is the first of several songs that is sung throughout the book (cf. 4:8, 11; 5:9-10, 12, 13; 7:12, 15-17; 11:15, 17-18; 12:10-12; 15:3-4; 16:5-7; 18:2-8; 19:2-6). Five hymns are sung in chapter four and five. The first two are addressed to God, the next two are to the Lamb, and the last hymn is addressed to both.

As the four living creatures finish their song of praise, the twenty-four elders fall down before the throne of God, casting down their crowns (acknowledging where and how they got their thrones) and sing the song of creation. Crowned as overcomers they ascribe all glory and honor to the one who lives forever and ever (cf. 2:10; 4:4; 2 Tim. 4:8; James 1:12; 1 Pet. 5:4).

"By Your will" (NIV) is better translated "because of Your will" things were created and have their being.

God is praised for His glory, honor, and power for He created all things. This song acknowledges that God is the source and sustainer of all things (cf. Ps. 33:6-9; 102:25; 136:5ff).

Revelation 5

B. The Glory of the Lamb and Redemption, 5:1-14

[1]I saw in the right hand of Him who sat on the throne a book written inside and on the back, sealed up with seven seals. [2]And I saw a strong angel proclaiming with a loud voice, "Who is worthy to open the book and to break its seals?" [3]And no one in heaven or on the earth or under the earth was able to open the book or to look into it. [4]Then I began to weep greatly because no one was found worthy to open the book or to look into it; [5]and one of the elders said to me, "Stop weeping; behold, the Lion that is from the tribe of Judah, the Root of David, has overcome so as to open the book and its seven seals."

[6]And I saw between the throne (with the four living creatures) and the elders a Lamb standing, as if slain, having seven horns and seven eyes, which are the seven Spirits of God, sent out into all the earth. [7]And He came and took the book out of the right hand of Him who sat on the throne. [8]When He had taken the book, the four living creatures and the twenty-

four elders fell down before the Lamb, each one holding a harp and golden bowls full of incense, which are the prayers of the saints.

[9]And they sang a new song, saying, "Worthy are You to take the book and to break its seals; for You were slain, and purchased for God with Your blood men from every tribe and tongue and people and nation. [10]"You have made them to be a kingdom and priests to our God; and they will reign upon the earth." [11]Then I looked, and I heard the voice of many angels around the throne and the living creatures and the elders; and the number of them was myriads of myriads, and thousands of thousands, [12]saying with a loud voice, "Worthy is the Lamb that was slain to receive power and riches and wisdom and might and honor and glory and blessing."

[13]And every created thing which is in heaven and on the earth and under the earth and on the sea, and all things in them, I heard saying, "To Him who sits on the throne, and to the Lamb, be blessing and honor and glory and dominion forever and ever." [14]And the four living creatures kept saying, "Amen." And the elders fell down and worshiped.

Though we have a new chapter beginning, the picture remains the same. John now describes, in closer detail, actions of the ones associated with the throne and the one seated on it (i.e., God). The focus moves in this chapter from God, who is the one seated on the throne, to the Lamb, standing as though it had been slain.

5:1 I saw in the right hand of Him who sat on the throne a book written inside and on the back, sealed up with seven seals.

In the right hand of the one who sits on the throne is held a scroll written on both sides and sealed with seven seals. Often messages were sealed more than once, but seven seals means this scroll is totally secure. The imagery reminds one of Ezekiel 2:9f, where the message was "lamentations, mourning and woe." In this scene John is anticipating seeing what he had been promised would "shortly come to pass" (1:1; 4:1).

What exactly does this scroll represent? Interpretations vary from (1) the Lamb's book of life (3:5; 13:8; 17:8; 20:12, 15; 21:27), (2) the entire Old Testament, (3) a testament which insures inheritance for the saints, (4) a doubly inscribed contract deed, and (5) the revealing of coming events throughout the Revelation. The scroll represents God's plan for man; i.e., God's preordained plan for His world, to be revealed and carried out by the Lamb. To be sealed means that no one was to tamper with it and that this plan was unexecuted. To remove the scrolls and open the book means that this plan is executed. This reminds us of Isaiah's vision which became "like the words of a sealed book." When someone was handed the book to read, he answered, "I cannot, for it is sealed" (Isa. 29:11). Sealed with seven seals could also indicate the scroll was sealed by God himself.

5:2 And I saw a strong angel proclaiming with a loud voice, "Who is worthy to open the book and to break its seals?"

A strong angel (Gabriel?) asks who is "worthy" to break the seals and open the scroll. We will meet this angel again in 10:1, where he straddles the sea and cries with the voice of a roaring lion, and in 18:21, where he casts a great millstone into the sea. The question is not, "Who has the strength to break the seals? or, "Who is ready to break the seals? or, "Who is able to break the seals?" The question has to do with someone being *worthy* to break the seals. The word "worthy" does not mean strength, but refers to moral competence. Charles says the phrase "who is worthy?" means "who is able?" and in the visions assumes that he who

143

opens the scroll also has power to execute what is written there. The answer is given in the next verse.

5:3 And no one in heaven or on the earth or under the earth was able to open the book or to look into it.

There was no one in either heaven or earth or under the earth to accomplish the task. Not a single person was capable (morally) to open the book. Heaven, earth, and under the earth is found also in Philippians 2:10, which seems to indicate a universal acknowledgment of the Lordship of Christ. Nonetheless, this threefold division encompasses the whole of creation. No one had the authority or virtue for such a task. Could this be an allusion to the acknowledgment of man's universal sinfulness (Rom. 3:10, 23)?

5:4 Then I *began* to weep greatly because no one was found worthy to open the book or to look into it;

John's response is understandable. If the scroll represents the plan of God for man and no one is to open it, then John knows that God's plan will remain unknown and unexecuted. The tears he sheds are not from frustration, but from disappointment and sorrow. John's sorrow is due to the fact that if the book is unopened, the divine plan contained in it would remain undisclosed. From one who had been promised to see, and now it seems like he might not see, John's response is understandable.

5:5 and one of the elders said to me, "Stop weeping; behold, the Lion that is from the tribe of Judah, the Root of David, has overcome so as to open the book and its seven seals."

The identity of which elder speaks is not important. But it is important to notice that the one who speaks is a representative of redeemed mankind. The fact is John is told that there is one who is able to open the scroll with the seven seals. He is described as a Lion of the tribe of Judah and the Root of David (cf. Isa. 11:1). Both of these are familiar Old Testament messianic titles. The tribe of Judah was the tribe through which the Messiah would come (2 Sam. 7:13-16). To speak of Him as of the "root of David" implies that He who would come after David was also before him. This gives testimony of the preexistence of the Son of God (cf. John 8:57-58).

5:6 And I saw between the throne (with the four living creatures) and the elders a Lamb standing, as if slain, having seven horns and seven eyes, which are the seven Spirits of God, sent out into all the earth.

John turns to see a Lion, but instead he sees a Lamb. This lion/lamb imagery is not the only double imagery found in the book of Revelation. Here Jesus is seen as the sacrificial Lamb of God (cf. Isa. 53; 1 Cor. 5:7; John 1:29), looking as if it had been slain. This symbolism is employed in the *Testament of Joseph* 19:8ff where a lion and a lamb appear together.

Two things are significant with this picture. One is that of sacrifice. The word "slain" refers not only to the historical event of the crucifixion, but the tense of the word indicates the continuous effect of a once-for-all past act. Second, the Lamb is standing, i.e., no longer dead, but alive; no longer entombed, but raised and victorious (cf. Rev. 1:18-19). This figure portrays the sacrificial death and links the Messiah to the Old Testament Passover lamb (cf. Exod. 12:5f; Isa. 53:7; John 1:29, 36; Acts 8:32; 1 Pet. 1:19). Throughout the rest of the book John uses the "lamb" picture to represent Jesus (6:1ff; 7:9ff; 12:11; 13:8; 21:9).

The Lamb had seven horns and seven eyes. In the Old Testament horns have represented strength or power (cf. Deut. 33:17; Ps. 18:2) and at times, royalty (cf. Dan. 7:7). In the book of Revelation horns symbolize the might of the persecuting power (12:3; 13:1; 17:3ff). The number seven is the divine number; hence we have a Lamb that has fullness of power or divine power (i.e., omnipotence). The seven eyes stand for divine knowledge (omniscience). The language here is from Zechariah 4:10. Jesus claims this knowledge on several occasions in the letters to the seven churches (cf. chs. 2-3, the phrase, "I know"). The seven spirits represent the Holy Spirit.

5:7 And He came and took the book out of the right hand of Him who sat on the throne.

The Lamb approaches the one on the throne and takes the scroll from the one seated on the throne, indicating His prerogative and right to perform this deed. Alan Johnson says the Greek language conveys a dramatic action in the tense of the verb and could be translated, "He went up and took it, and now has it."[1] This image could also be representative of the exaltation of Christ expressed in similar language in Matthew 28:18 and Philippians 2:9-11.

5:8 When He had taken the book, the four living creatures and the twenty-four elders fell down before the Lamb, each one holding a harp and golden bowls full of incense, which are the prayers of the saints.

Here is one of the greatest scenes recorded in Scripture of universal adoration. The Lamb's action results in the singing of three hymns of praise from the living creatures and the twenty-four elders. These three hymns (vv. 9,12,13) interpret the symbolism of the scroll and the Lamb. The prostration of all creation in adoration and gratitude to the Lamb in seen in the following verses. In their praise to the Lamb they offer "golden bowls of incense" which we are told "are the prayers of the saints." Prayers are said to be offered as an incense to God (cf. Ps. 141:2; Luke 1:10). These are prayers of petition and not of praise. More will be said about these prayers in chapter 6 in connection with a study of the opening of the fifth seal.

5:9 And they sang a new song, saying, "Worthy are You to take the book and to break its seals; for You were slain, and purchased for God with Your blood *men* **from every tribe and tongue and people and nation. 10 "You have made them** *to be* **a kingdom and priests to our God; and they will reign upon the earth."**

Songs of deliverance are familiar to us from the Old Testament (cf. Ps. 33:3; 40:3; 96:1; 144:9; 149:1), but this is described as a new song. It is the Song of Redemption. "You are Worthy" shows the identity with the song of 4:11. "The lamb is worthy to open the book for a threefold reason: He was slain (a historical fact), He purchased men unto God (the interpretation of that fact), and He made them a kingdom and priests (the result of the fact). That same ascription of worth is directed both to the One upon the throne (4:11) and to the Lamb (5:9) indicates the exalted Christology of the Apocalypse."[2] With the blood of the Lamb, men (i.e., people) have been purchased for God (cf. John 1:29; Acts 8:32; 1 Pet. 1:18-19; Exod. 12; Isa. 53). Here is a reference to the sacrificial death of Jesus on the Cross. During His earthly ministry Jesus taught that the Son of Man had come to give His life a ransom for many (Mark 10:45). Paul would later write that Christians were "bought with a price" (1 Cor. 6:20). It is a worldwide redemption embracing tribes, languages, peoples, and nations.

Singing a new song is mentioned again in 14:3 when we see the Lamb standing on Mt. Zion with the 144,000.

This motif of kingdom/priests and reigning/serving is found three times in the book (1:6; 5:10; 20:6). Corporately believers are a kingdom, and individually they are priests. In the kingdom, they reign with Christ. As priests, they give service to God.

The redeemed become a kingdom and priests to our God, not a kingdom consisting of priests. The redeemed ones are a part of the kingdom of God (cf. Col. 1:13-14) and serve, in that kingdom, as priests (cf. 1 Pet. 2:9). What was first promised at Mt. Sinai (Exod. 19:6) is fulfilled in the church (cf. Acts 2; Col. 1:13-14; et. al.). Isaiah foresaw the Lord's anointed would cheer the hearts of the mourners and said, "But you will be called priests of the LORD, you will be spoken of as ministers of our God" (Isa. 61:6).

5:11 Then I looked, and I heard the voice of many angels around the throne and the living creatures and the elders; and the number of them was myriads of myriads, and thousands of thousands, 12 saying with a loud voice, "Worthy is the Lamb that was slain to receive power and riches and wisdom and might and honor and glory and blessing." 13 And every created thing which is in heaven and on the earth and under the earth and on the sea, and all things in them, I heard saying, "To Him who sits on the throne, and to the Lamb, *be* blessing and honor and glory and dominion forever and ever." 14 And the four living creatures kept saying, "Amen." And the elders fell down and worshiped.

To the praise given to God by the created order (the four living creatures) and the redeemed of mankind (the twenty-four elders) is added a host of angels which cannot be numbered. They sing the Song of Assent (Agreement), as they encircle the throne of God. Their song consists of a sevenfold ascription: power, riches, wisdom, might, honor, glory and blessing. This is reminiscent of David's thanksgiving to the Lord for the gifts given for the building of the Temple (1 Chron. 29:10-13).

Song number 5 is the Song of All Creation in praise and adoration to God and the Lamb. This is the climax of the entire scene. The phrase "all things in them" reveals that no living creature is exempt from final praise to God (cf. Phil. 2:9-11). Three elements of the previous doxology (v. 12) are repeated here.

The praise of the entire created order is to the one who sits on the throne and to the Lamb. Their shared honor is seen throughout the book. As the book closes, the river of the water of life flows from the throne of God and the Lamb (22:1).

As the four living creatures start the praise to God (4:8), so they also bring it to a close in this picture (5:13-14). As the cherubim say "Amen," the elders fall down and worship.

NOTES

[1]Alan Johnson, *Book of Revelation*, The Expositor's Bible Commentary, Vol. 12, 468.

[2]Robert H. Mounce, *The Book of Revelation*, 148.

Revelation 6

V. THE LAMB OPENS THE SEALED BOOK, 6:1-8:5

A. The First Four Seals: The Four Horsemen, 6:1-8

[1]Then I saw when the Lamb broke one of the seven seals, and I heard one of the four living creatures saying as with a voice of thunder, "Come." [2]I looked, and behold, a white horse, and he who sat on it had a bow; and a crown was given to him, and he went out conquering and to conquer. [3]When He broke the second seal, I heard the second living creature saying, "Come." [4]And another, a red horse, went out; and to him who sat on it, it was granted to take peace from the earth, and that men would slay one another; and a great sword was given to him. [5]When He broke the third seal, I heard the third living creature saying, "Come." I looked, and behold, a black horse; and he who sat on it had a pair of scales in his hand. [6]And I heard something like a voice in the center of the four living creatures saying, "A quart of wheat for a denarius, and three quarts of barley for a denarius; and do

not damage the oil and the wine." ⁷When the Lamb broke the fourth seal, I heard the voice of the fourth living creature saying, "Come." ⁸I looked, and behold, an ashen horse; and he who sat on it had the name Death; and Hades was following with him. Authority was given to them over a fourth of the earth, to kill with sword and with famine and with pestilence and by the wild beasts of the earth.

Chapter 5 closes with the "Song of All Creation" and with the living creatures and the elders falling down and worshiping. The worship is "to Him who sits on the throne, and to the Lamb." As we begin this study, our concern now turns to the Lamb and the sealed book. The opening of the sealed book of chapters 4 and 5 continues as the scene shifts from heaven to events on earth. The opening of the book involves the rest of the book of Revelation and displays the future for all to see.

6:1 Then I saw when the Lamb broke one of the seven seals, and I heard one of the four living creatures saying as with a voice of thunder, "Come."

John sees the Lamb who has taken the sealed book from the one who is on the throne and begins to open the seals. As each seal is opened, one of the living creatures (which one is never identified) says in a thundering voice, "Come" (6:1, 3, 5, 7). We are not told to whom these words are addressed but when we see the following pictures of the horses and their riders, it implies that it is a command, not to John or to the readers, but to the horsemen in each case.

The horsemen seen here parallel visions given to Zechariah (1:8-11 and 6:1-9) who saw four colored horses, one group with riders and another pulling chariots. The responsibility given them was to patrol the earth. In Zechariah's vision the horsemen and chariots are used as divine instruments of God's judgments on the enemies of God's people.

6:2 I looked, and behold, a white horse, and he who sat on it had a bow; and a crown was given to him, and he went out conquering and to conquer.

When the first seal is broken John sees a rider sitting on a white horse holding a bow. The rider is given a crown and he rides out as a conqueror.

Who is this rider? Alan Johnson says the identity of the rider on the white horse is solved "depending on the presuppositions one brings to the passage."[1]

The question of identity is extensively discussed. Two answers given the most are: (1) the rider is Christ and the white horse represents the victorious progress of the gospel as it is preached throughout the world; and (2) the Antichrist and the evil forces of the world. The first sees a similarity between this rider and the portrayal of Christ in Revelation 19:11-16. There the rider is identified as the "Word (logos) of God." If this is the same rider then here we have a picture of the conquering, victorious Christ. In favor of the second position is that the rider of the white horse in 19:11-16 is called "Faithful and True" and of whom it is said that "in righteousness He judges and wages war." Here is, not a parallel, but a contrast to the rider of 6:2 who is not faithful or true and who wages war for unjust conquest. Since the Lamb is opening the seals He would not be one of the riders and it would seem inappropriate to have an angelic being call forth Christ or one of His servants.

What is the significance of this vision? White is used in the Scripture to represent purity, holiness, or victory. While there are some who take this rider to represent the Antichrist it does not seem likely since the word "white" is used sixteen times in the book and never represents evil (1:14; 2:17; 3:4-5, 18; 4:4; 7:9, 13-14; 20:11). It is therefore unlikely that in this instance the white horse represents something associated with the Devil. The bow indicates that this rider is a warrior (cf. Ps. 45:5-6; Heb. 1:8-9) and the crown he is given tells us that he is victorious in his conquests. The "crown" refers to victorious conquest (cf. 19:12). He is riding out as a "conqueror." The word "conquer" is the same word translated "overcome" in 3:21 and 5:5.

This interpretation — that the rider on the white horse is Christ conquering through the gospel — fits the context in that when the preaching of Christ went throughout the first century world, what followed was persecution. Thus, the red horse of the second seal.

6:3 When He broke the second seal, I heard the second living creature saying, "Come." 4 And another, a red horse, went out; and to him who sat on it, it was granted to take peace from the earth, and that *men* would slay one another; and a great sword was given to him.

When the second horse and rider are called, we see a fiery red horse. The rider is given power to take peace from the earth and to make men slay each other. He is also given a large sword.

The color red represents bloodshed. Here the indication is of severe persecution; i.e., persecution which causes pain and the loss of life (cf. 2 Kgs. 3:22-23). The word for "slay" could better be understood as slaughter or butcher. It is a word that is used in reference to offering a sacrifice. Here is a rider whose power is to cause men to butcher each other.

The sword he is given is a small Roman sword. This is a curved sword used generally for cutting and hacking, not one that is used for straightforward piercing as is commonly used in war. This would make us think that this is possibly persecution rather than war.

The color of the second horse corresponds to the mission of its rider; i.e., it symbolizes slaughter and bloodshed. The mission is to remove peace from the earth, and allow men to hurt each other (cf. Zech. 14:13; Isa. 19:2; 2 Thess. 2:6ff).

This picture would be well understood by the readers of John's day. Rebellion and disorder were all around them. In one year (A.D. 68-69) Rome had been ruled by four different emperors.

6:5 When He broke the third seal, I heard the third living creature saying, "Come." I looked, and behold, a black horse; and he who sat on it had a pair of scales in his hand. 6 And I heard *something* **like a voice in the center of the four living creatures saying, "A quart of wheat for a denarius, and three quarts of barley for a denarius; and do not damage the oil and the wine."**

As the third seal is open there comes a black horse and a rider with a pair of scales in his hand. Scales are used for measuring. The effects of war are now seen: sorrow, mourning, and desolation (Isa. 50:3; Jer. 4:28). The picture here is of economic discrimination. This discrimination is seen in that a quart of wheat or three quarts of barley represented a day's wages, but the oil and wine (reserved only for those wealthy enough to afford them) are not bothered.

In chapters two and three we were introduced to the trade guilds and the privileges that came from belonging to them. Here is further confirmation that the rich get richer and the poor are oppressed even more. Later in the book there will be a judgment from God because of this discrimination (cf. Rev. 13:16-17).

The scales indicate a scarcity in the basic commodities of life. In other words, there is a famine among the people. One day's work would allow a man to buy only enough wheat for himself or enough of the less nutritious barley for three. The price was ten times what it should have been (cf. Cicero *Verr.* iii.81).

6:7 When the Lamb broke the fourth seal, I heard the voice of the fourth living creature saying, "Come." 8 I looked, and behold, an ashen horse; and he who sat on it had the name Death; and Hades was following

with him. Authority was given to them over a fourth of the earth, to kill with sword and with famine and with pestilence and by the wild beasts of the earth.

When the fourth seal is opened, a pale horse comes and carries the rider named Death. Hades closely follows. Power is given over a fourth part of the earth to kill in four ways: by sword, famine, plague and wild beasts. This picture is related to the picture of judgment of Ezekiel 14:12-23.

John uses a different word for "sword" here than he used in 6:4. However, since both words are used synonymously in the LXX, it is likely that there is no significance in the change. Death by wild beasts is a natural result of plague by sword, famine, and plague.

Death identifies the rider and "Hades was following with him." But how? On foot? On the back of the same horse? On another horse? We are not told. But it seems evident that the appearance of Hades here shows the close association of Hades (see comments on 1:18) with Death.

B. The Fifth Seal: The Cry of Souls of Martyrs, 6:9-11

[9]When the Lamb broke the fifth seal, I saw underneath the altar the souls of those who had been slain because of the word of God, and because of the testimony which they had maintained; [10]and they cried out with a loud voice, saying, "How long, O Lord, holy and true, will You refrain from judging and avenging our blood on those who dwell on the earth?" [11]And there was given to each of them a white robe; and they were told that they should rest for a little while longer, until *the number of* their fellow servants and their brethren who were to be killed even as they had been, would be completed also.

The picture changes with the opening of the fifth

seal. Horses no longer appear but we see martyred souls under an altar. They were slain because of their faithfulness maintained to the word of God. They are crying out for vindication of their cause to come upon their oppressors.

Who are these martyrs? They appear again in 18:24 as "all who have been slain on the earth" and again in 20:4 as "those who had been beheaded." In 13:15 they are identified as those who would not worship the beast.

It is unclear if the altar is the altar of burnt offering or the altar of incense. Since sacrifice is a theme, it seems the former is the most valid. But, since prayers rise from the altar (v. 10) the latter seems appropriate. Perhaps it is both and serves as a double-image.

What John sees is described as "souls" (*psychē*) and stands for "persons" who were killed. Though they are now dead (physically) John sees them as very much alive in the presence of God. The location of the souls *under* the altar portrays their untimely deaths on earth as viewed by God as a sacrifice on the altar of heaven (cf. Paul in 2 Tim. 4:6). The cry of the martyrs for vindication (v. 10) is in contrast to Stephen's cry for forgiveness (Acts 7:60); as well as that of Jesus (Luke 23:24). How are we to understand this?

The background for this is Hebrew jurisprudence in which the plaintiff must plead his own case. Once condemned, the decision can only be reversed by a higher court. Condemned on earth, there is only condemnation in heaven as the martyrs cry for judgment against them to show the validity of their faith.

"Those who dwell on the earth" refers to the enemies of the Lord. They are seen in the Apocalypse in different ways: (1) Rejoicing over the death of the two witnesses, 11:10; (2) worshiping the beast, 13:8, 12; (3) drunk with the wine of fornicating with the great harlot, 17:2; (4) subject to the coming hour of trial, 3:10; 8:13.

White robes are symbols of purity and victory. Those who are before the throne are given white robes (7:11) and those who come out of the great tribulation wash their robes white in the blood of the Lamb (7:13-14). The church at Laodicea was counseled to buy white robes (3:18).

These martyrs are to rest for a while until others join them; i.e., their number is not yet complete. Others souls will follow.

C. The Sixth Seal: Terror of Judgment Announced, 6:12-17

[12]I looked when He broke the sixth seal, and there was a great earthquake; and the sun became black as sackcloth *made* of hair, and the whole moon became like blood; [13]and the stars of the sky fell to the earth, as a fig tree casts its unripe figs when shaken by a great wind. [14]The sky was split apart like a scroll when it is rolled up, and every mountain and island were moved out of their places. [15]Then the kings of the earth and the great men and the commanders and the rich and the strong and every slave and free man hid themselves in the caves and among the rocks of the mountains; [16]and they said to the mountains and to the rocks, "Fall on us and hide us from the presence of Him who sits on the throne, and from the wrath of the Lamb; [17]for the great day of their wrath has come, and who is able to stand?"

The opening of the sixth seal brings us to the announcement of a terrible judgment. The vision presents a great earthquake, the sun becomes blackened, stars fall from the sky, the sky recedes like a scroll and mountains and islands are removed from their place. In 2 Samuel 22:8 we read, "Then the earth shook and quaked, The foundations of heaven were trembling And were shaken, because He was angry." Joel 2:30-31 says, "I will display wonders in the sky and on the earth, Blood, fire and columns of smoke. The sun will be turned into darkness And the moon into blood Before the great and awesome day of the LORD comes." The prophet Haggai speaks of the shaking of the world, "For thus says the LORD of hosts, 'Once more in a little while, I am going to shake the heavens and the earth, the sea also and the dry land. 'I will shake all the nations; and they will come with the wealth of all nations, and I will fill this house with glory,' says the LORD of hosts" (Hag. 2:6-7; cf. Heb. 12:26).

The "earthquake" was a familiar figure to readers of the Old Testament (cf. Exod. 19:18; Isa. 2:19; Hag. 2:6). This earthquake is accompanied by the sun turning black as sackcloth made of goat hair (a reference to rough cloth from the hair of a goat which was worn during a time of mourning) and the moon turning blood red (cf. the same image is used on the day of Pentecost in Acts 2).

Using Old Testament imagery, John is shown a judgment of God. This is not the final judgment but rather a judgment in response to the cry of the souls under the altar for vindication of their cause. This is not the actual judgment, but an announcement of that judgment. *We will see this judgment carried out under the vision of chapter 16-17.*

As the picture continues to unfold, the outcome becomes evident. Everyone is hiding and seeking refuge from the wrath of God and the Lamb. The wrath of God is spoken of frequently in Scripture (Isa. 13:13; Jer. 50:13; Ezek. 7:7-8, 19; Hos. 5:10; Zeph. 1:14-15, 18; Zech. 7:12; John 3:36; Rom. 1:18; Eph. 5:6; Rev. 14:10, 19; 15:1, 7; 16:1, 19; 19:15).

The description of men seeking refuge in the caves and rocks and calling for mountains to fall on them, occurs three times in previous history and each time it refers to a national calamity. Hosea describes the destruction of Samaria by the Assyrians (Hos. 10:8);

Isaiah prophesies of Jerusalem's fall at the hands of Babylon (Isa. 2:19); and Jesus used the same imagery in describing the fall of Jerusalem by Rome (Luke 23:30).

The "wrath" of the lamb is a paradox. Lambs are usually gentle, but this Lamb shows "wrath" against ungodly men. In the book of Revelation the wrath of God and the Lamb is described under the figures of bowls and trumpets (11:18; 14:7, 10, 19; 15:1, 7; 16:1, 19; 19:15).

The opening of the sixth seal, then, anticipates the fear of wicked men when the time comes that God judges the power which was persecuting His people. The church might have stood in awe of the power and might of Rome, but as God has always stood with His people in times of trouble, He will now also stand with them in bring judgment upon this ungodly nation.

"And who is able to stand?" expresses the utter hopelessness of those who have rejected the gospel of God's marvelous grace. It is a damning question mark that robs every ungodly life of ultimate meaning. It is a question that has been asked before. "O LORD God of Israel, You are righteous, for we have been left an escaped remnant, as *it is* this day; behold, we are before You in our guilt, for no one can stand before You because of this" (Ezra 9:15). "Who can stand before His indignation? Who can endure the burning of His anger? His wrath is poured out like fire And the rocks are broken up by Him" (Nah. 1:6). "But who can endure the day of His coming? And who can stand when He appears? For He is like a refiner's fire and like fuller's soap" (Mal. 3:2).

NOTES

[1]Alan Johnson, *Book of Revelation*, The Expositor's Bible Commentary, vol. 12, 473.

Revelation 7

D. Interlude: 7:1-17

1. The Sealing of the 144,000, 7:1-8

[1]After this I saw four angels standing at the four corners of the earth, holding back the four winds of the earth, so that no wind would blow on the earth or on the sea or on any tree. [2]And I saw another angel ascending from the rising of the sun, having the seal of the living God; and he cried out with a loud voice to the four angels to whom it was granted to harm the earth and the sea, [3]saying, "Do not harm the earth or the sea or the trees until we have sealed the bond-servants of our God on their foreheads."

[4]And I heard the number of those who were sealed, one hundred and forty-four thousand sealed from every tribe of the sons of Israel: [5]from the tribe of Judah, twelve thousand were sealed, from the tribe of Reuben twelve thousand, from the tribe of Gad twelve thousand, [6]from the tribe of Asher twelve thousand, from the tribe of Naphtali twelve thousand, from the tribe of Manasseh twelve thousand, [7]from the tribe of Simeon twelve thousand, from the

tribe of Levi twelve thousand, from the tribe of Issachar twelve thousand, ⁸from the tribe of Zebulun twelve thousand, from the tribe of Joseph twelve thousand, from the tribe of Benjamin, twelve thousand were sealed.

In many respects this chapter is one of the most difficult and yet most important chapters in the book. The principal difficulty in chapter seven centers around the identification of the 144,000 sealed servants of God (vv. 1-8) and the great multitude which no one could count (vv. 9-17). Chapter Six closed with a cry from those who are judged by God and the question was asked, "Who can stand?" The implication is that no one would be able to stand against the wrath of the one that sits on the throne and the Lamb (6:16-17). But what kind of encouragement would that be for the Christian who is trying to stand firm in his faith by being a disciple of Jesus Christ?

Before the seals continue to be opened, and in response to the question with which chapter six ends, John is shown an interlude, a break in the scroll scenes, which gives both a response to the question and a word of encouragement to the Christian suffering under the oppression of the forces of evil.

7:1 After this I saw four angels standing at the four corners of the earth, holding back the four winds of the earth, so that no wind would blow on the earth or on the sea or on any tree.

Four angels are standing at the four corners of the earth holding back four winds that have been ordained to blow upon the earth. The imagery of wind is used elsewhere in Scripture as a power of destruction (cf. Jer. 49:34-36; 51:1). These angels, therefore, are holding back a destructive judgment of God. But why?

7:2 And I saw another angel ascending from the ris-

ing of the sun, having the seal of the living God; and he cried out with a loud voice to the four angels to whom it was granted to harm the earth and the sea, 3 saying, "Do not harm the earth or the sea or the trees until we have sealed the bond-servants of our God on their foreheads."

Another angel appears ascending from the rising of the sun (East-NIV) having the seal of the living God. He calls out to the four angels who have the four winds which are to blow upon the earth to withhold their judgment until he has sealed the servants of God on the foreheads.

The use of a seal could symbolize one of three things. First, sealing was used for protection against tampering (Matt. 27:66; Rev. 5:1). Second, sealing was used to show ownership or destination (Song of Songs 8:6; 2 Tim. 2:19). Third, sealing would often be used to certify genuineness (Esth. 3:12). Each of these could be significant for the Christian because a disciple lives under God's protection (Jude 24-25), Christ's redemption (1 Pet. 1:18-19), and the Spirit's sealing (Eph. 1:13-14).

The "sealing" (*sphragis*) of the servants of God here is seen in contrast to those who will receive the mark (*charagma*) of the beast (13:16-17). Those who receive the mark of the beast are identified as worshipers of the beast and become objects of the wrath of God (14:9, 11). They are also deceived by the beast (19:20), implying that the sealed of God are not deceived. A group of martyred saints is seen just prior to their resurrection and the thousand-year reign of Christ. They are described as "not having the mark of the beast or worshiping him" (20:4). The sealing here may not protect the sealed against harm inflicted by human agency (13:17; 20:4), but they are protected from the divine plagues (16:2).

Eugene Boring writes,

"sealing" not only evokes this powerful image from Scripture, it has particular overtones within the

Pauline stream of tradition to which John and his churches belong. Incorporation into the body of Christ by baptism (1 Cor. 12:13) was sometimes pictured in Pauline churches as the seal which stamped the new Christian as belonging to God (2 Cor. 1:22; Eph. 1:13; 4:30). In the midst of the Roman threat, baptism comes to have a new meaning: those who bear the mark of God are kept through (not from!) the coming great ordeal, whatever the beastly powers of evil may be able to do to them.[1]

7:4 And I heard the number of those who were sealed, one hundred and forty-four thousand sealed from every tribe of the sons of Israel: 5 From the tribe of Judah, twelve thousand *were* sealed, from the tribe of Reuben twelve thousand, from the tribe of Gad twelve thousand, 6 from the tribe of Asher twelve thousand, from the tribe of Naphtali twelve thousand, from the tribe of Manasseh twelve thousand, 7 from the tribe of Simeon twelve thousand, from the tribe of Levi twelve thousand, from the tribe of Issachar twelve thousand, 8 from the tribe of Zebulun twelve thousand, from the tribe of Joseph twelve thousand, from the tribe of Benjamin, twelve thousand *were* sealed.

The sealing results in the name of the Lord being placed upon the head of each of the sealed servants of God (cf the significance in 9:4; 14:1; and 22:4).

"And I heard the number of those who were sealed" — The number sealed is 144,000. From each of the twelve tribes of the sons of Israel (with the exception that Dan and Ephraim are omitted and Manasseh and Joseph are included) are numbered 12,000 (vv. 5-8). Levi, who received no land inheritance, appears among the twelve, although his name does not appear in some of the Old Testament lists; e.g., Numbers one and two. The significance of this omission is unknown. One possible explanation is that through Jeroboam I, a descendant (1 Kgs. 11:26), Ephraim led Israel into idolatry (1 Kgs. 12:25-33) and Dan left his inheritance and moved north to Laish (later called Dan) where he settled and practiced idolatry (Judg. 18).[2]

Perhaps this is to indicate that the 144,000 are not to be *interpreted* as literal Jews. But to say this, does not answer all the questions. How many servants of God were sealed? Answer: all of them. There was no partial sealing. All the servants of God were sealed, not part of them, or some of them, or a few of them, but *all of them*.

But how are they numbered? They are numbered as 144,000. The number 12 has always had an association with the people of God. There were 12 patriarchs, 12 apostles, 12 tribes of Israel, 12 gates, 12 foundations which support the city of God's people. The number twelve speaks of the completeness of God's people. All the servants (i.e., the complete people of God) who are to undergo this period of trial and tribulation are assured of God's protection. The number 144,000 is derived by 12×12×1000 = 144,000. To this can also be added the idea that the number 12 is derived by taking 3 (the number for the Triune God) and multiplying it times 4 (the number for the world) and thus 12 represents God at work in His world. That is to say, 12 represents not just the saints of Old Testament days, but the redeemed of both the Old and New Testaments; or, the redeemed of all the ages. Since the number 144,000 is based on the number 12, then this number represents (in the figure) all the redeemed. In chapter 14, the 144,000 are standing with the Lamb on Mt. Zion. They have the name of the Father written on their foreheads, and they sing a new song which no one could learn except the 144,000 who had been purchased out of the earth (14:1, 3).

What is intended by John is not to be taken as literal mathematics. In the ears of John's readers this number is intended to convey a rather large number. The number

1,000, along with "myriad" (10,000), is the largest numerical unit used in the Bible. When used it the Bible, it is not to be taken literally, but rather to convey a very large number. For example, in Exodus 20:6, God says He would show "lovingkindness to thousands, to those who love Me and keep My commandments." In Deuteronomy 7:9, Moses writes that God "keeps His covenant and His lovingkindness to a thousandth generation with those who love Him and keep His commandments." In each of these instances, the number thousand is not to be taken literally, but merely to convey the idea of a very large number. (Cf. also 1 Sam. 18:7; 21:11; Ps. 3:6; 68:17; Dan. 7:10).

But these are described as 144,000 Jews. But the fact that it says Jews does not answer the question completely, because if the picture is literally of physical Israel, then why does it exclude Dan and Ephraim? Some think that the 144,000 of vv. 1-8 represents Jewish Christians in contrast to the great multitude from every nation of vv. 9-17. But John later identifies this same group with the same number in 14:1-5 which cannot be limited to Jewish Christians. It seems that the 144,000 represent the active faithful church on earth at any time; i.e., they are the "militant church on earth."

Boring writes, "'Thousand' also has military connotation, a division of the army. The 'thousands of Israel' is used of Israel's army and has the same ring to it as 'the battalions of Israel' (cf. Num. 31:14, 48; Deut. 1:15; 1 Sam. 8:12; 22:7; 2 Sam. 18:1, 4). John uses much battle imagery, transformed by the paradigmatic symbol of the Lion who has become the Lamb. He here pictures the church in its aspect of earthly struggle, the 'church militant.'"[3]

2. The Innumerable Company, 7:9-17

[9]After these things I looked, and behold, a great multitude which no one could count, from every

nation and all tribes and peoples and tongues, standing before the throne and before the Lamb, clothed in white robes, and palm branches were in their hands; [10]and they cry out with a loud voice, saying,

"Salvation to our God who sits on the throne, and to the Lamb."

[11]And all the angels were standing around the throne and around the elders and the four living creatures; and they fell on their faces before the throne and worshiped God, [12]saying,

"Amen, blessing and glory and wisdom and thanksgiving and honor and power and might, be to our God forever and ever. Amen."

[13]Then one of the elders answered, saying to me, "These who are clothed in the white robes, who are they, and where have they come from?"

[14]I said to him, "My lord, you know."

And he said to me, "These are the ones who come out of the great tribulation, and they have washed their robes and made them white in the blood of the Lamb.

[15]"For this reason, they are before the throne of God; and they serve Him day and night in His temple; and He who sits on the throne will spread His tabernacle over them. [16]"They will hunger no longer, nor thirst anymore; nor will the sun beat down on them, nor any heat; [17]for the Lamb in the center of the throne will be their shepherd, and will guide them to springs of the water of life; and God will wipe every tear from their eyes."

7:9 After these things I looked, and behold, a great multitude which no one could count, from every nation and *all* tribes and peoples and tongues, standing before the throne and before the Lamb, clothed in white robes, and palm branches *were* in their hands;

John is then shown "a great multitude, which no one could count," from every nation, and all tribes and peoples and tongues. They are standing in front of the Lamb, wearing white robes and holding palm branches. They sing a song of salvation to God and the Lamb (v. 10). They are identified in verse 14 as "the ones who come out of the great tribulation, and . . . have washed their robes and made them white in the blood of the Lamb. White should be connected with the white robes given to the martyrs under the altar found in opening of the fifth seal (6:11). They are standing before the throne and before the Lamb with palm branches in their hands. Palm branches were associated with the annual feast of Tabernacles under the Old Covenant which was the most joyous of all Jewish festivals (cf. Lev. 23:26-44).

7:10 and they cry out with a loud voice, saying, "Salvation to our God who sits on the throne, and to the Lamb." 11 And all the angels were standing around the throne and *around* the elders and the four living creatures; and they fell on their faces before the throne and worshiped God, 12 saying, "Amen, blessing and glory and wisdom and thanksgiving and honor and power and might, *be* to our God forever and ever. Amen."

When this occurs, all the angels standing around the throne, in the presence of the elders and the four living creatures, sing a song of Agreement, saying, "Amen, blessing and glory and wisdom and thanksgiving and honor and power and might, *be* to our God forever and ever. Amen."

7:13 Then one of the elders answered, saying to me, "These who are clothed in the white robes, who are they, and where have they come from?" 14 I said to him, "My lord, you know." And he said to me, "These are the ones who come out of the great tribulation, and they have washed their robes and made them white in the blood of the Lamb. 15 "For this reason,

they are before the throne of God; and they serve Him day and night in His temple; and He who sits on the throne will spread His tabernacle over them. 16 "They will hunger no longer, nor thirst anymore; nor will the sun beat down on them, nor any heat; 17 for the Lamb in the center of the throne will be their shepherd, and will guide them to springs of the water of life; and God will wipe every tear from their eyes."

At this point our concern is over the great multitude, the ones in white robes. One of the elders asks, "Who are they, and where did they come from?" After urging from John, the elder answers his own question. They are the one who were victorious through persecution and are blessed because of their faithfulness.

They serve God both day and night and receive the blessings of (1) perfect communion — "they are before the throne of God"; (2) perfect service — "they serve Him day and night in His temple"; (3) perfect protection — "He who sits on the throne will spread His tabernacle over them"; (4) perfect provision — "they will hunger no longer, nor thirst anymore"; (5) perfect life — "the lamb . . . will guide them to springs of the water of life"; (6) perfect joy — "and God shall wipe away every tear from their eyes."

NOTES

[1]M. Eugene Boring, *Revelation*, Interpretation: A Bible Commentary for Teaching and Preaching (Louisville: John Knox Press, 1989), 129.

[2]Homer Hailey, *Revelation: An Introduction and Commentary*, 205-206.

[3]M. Eugene Boring, *Revelation*, Interpretation: A Bible Commentary for Teaching and Preaching, 131.

Revelation 8

E. The Seventh Seal: Introduction to Seven Trumpets, 8:1-5

¹When the Lamb broke the seventh seal, there was silence in heaven for about half an hour. ²And I saw the seven angels who stand before God, and seven trumpets were given to them.

³Another angel came and stood at the altar, holding a golden censer; and much incense was given to him, so that he might add it to the prayers of all the saints on the golden altar which was before the throne. ⁴And the smoke of the incense, with the prayers of the saints, went up before God out of the angel's hand. ⁵Then the angel took the censer and filled it with the fire of the altar, and threw it to the earth; and there followed peals of thunder and sounds and flashes of lightning and an earthquake.

As the final seal is opened there is silence in heaven for half an hour. The "silence" here is similar to the restraining of the four winds (7:1-3) and the sealing up of the utterance of the seven thunders (10:4). Keeping silence in the Old Testament refers to coming judgment, much like we would think of the quietness before a storm hits (cf. Zech. 2:8-13; Zeph. 1:7-12; Hab. 2:6, 9, 12, 20).

Here are seven angels standing in the presence of God prepared for service. They are each given a trumpet which they will blow. Trumpets are used in different ways in the Bible. According to Numbers 10:1-10 there are four ways in which a trumpet was used: (1) To call the congregation together, (2) to set out the children of Israel on their journey, (3) to call the people to prepare for war, and (4) to sound an alarm.

The scene of vv. 3-5 is to prepare us for the seven trumpets which are about to sound. This angel (v. 3) is not identified but performs priestly functions. He is called "another angel" to distinguish him from the seven angels of verse 2 who are about to sound the seven trumpets. This angel stands before the altar and is pictured offering the prayers of the saints in much the same way a priest would do in the temple (cf. Luke 1:9; also Exod. 30:1-10; 2 Kgs. 6:22; Heb. 9:4).

The smoke of the incense together with the prayers of the saints go up before God and indicates that there is something significant about genuine prayers.

The scene suddenly turns to one of judgment. The angel takes the censer, fills it with fire from the altar and hurls it to the earth (cf. Ezek. 10:2-7). It is here that we *begin* to see the answer to the cry for vindication from the souls under the altar (6:10).

VI. THE ANGELS BLOW THE SEVEN TRUMPETS, 8:6-11:19

[6]And the seven angels who had the seven trumpets prepared themselves to sound them.

[7]The first sounded, and there came hail and fire, mixed with blood, and they were thrown to the earth; and a third of the earth was burned up, and a third of

the trees were burned up, and all the green grass was burned up.

⁸The second angel sounded, and something like a great mountain burning with fire was thrown into the sea; and a third of the sea became blood, ⁹and a third of the creatures which were in the sea and had life, died; and a third of the ships were destroyed.

¹⁰The third angel sounded, and a great star fell from heaven, burning like a torch, and it fell on a third of the rivers and on the springs of waters. ¹¹The name of the star is called Wormwood; and a third of the waters became wormwood, and many men died from the waters, because they were made bitter.

¹²The fourth angel sounded, and a third of the sun and a third of the moon and a third of the stars were struck, so that a third of them would be darkened and the day would not shine for a third of it, and the night in the same way.

¹³Then I looked, and I heard an eagle flying in mid-heaven, saying with a loud voice, "Woe, woe, woe to those who dwell on the earth, because of the remaining blasts of the trumpet of the three angels who are about to sound!"

As we came to the close of chapter six and the sixth seal was opened it pronounced judgment on the earth. Those in fear of this righteous judgment asked the question, "Who is able to stand?" The response came in chapter seven. The answer is, the 144,000 will stand. Two pictures are seen of the same thing — the victorious church. In 7:1-8, the vision is of the church militant. Numbered at 144,000 they are the sealed servants of God. In 7:9-17, the vision is of the church triumphant, numbered as a "great multitude which no one could count" (v. 9). These are the ones who came out of the great tribulation and have washed their robes white in the blood of the Lamb. The seventh seal is opened and it contains seven trumpets which are about to sound.

As we study these trumpets, observe two significant things: First, the trumpets serve only as warnings. That is one of the uses of a trumpet (cf. Num. 10). Second, while it announces a judgment from God, it is not full and final judgment. In fact, it is a judgment tempered with mercy for only one-third of everything is affected in these judgments. So the judgments here are only partial judgments.

A. The First Trumpet: Land Disasters, 8:6-7

8:6 And the seven angels who had the seven trumpets prepared themselves to sound them. 7 The first sounded, and there came hail and fire, mixed with blood, and they were thrown to the earth; and a third of the earth was burned up, and a third of the trees were burned up, and all the green grass was burned up.

When the first angel sounds his trumpet, the judgment comes upon the earth. Hail symbolized the implement of war (Ezek. 13:11-16). It is hail and fire mixed with blood and affects one-third of the earth, trees, and all the green grass. This does not mean that all the green grass was burned up for that would contradict chapter 9:4 where the locusts are told not to hurt the green grass on the earth. What is mentioned here has reference to the green grass where the judgment is coming, namely, upon ungodly Rome. (Not literally Rome, but Rome in the figure). This judgment resembles the Egyptian plague recorded in Exodus 9:23ff, only this is accompanied with a shower of blood. The same imagery is found in Ezekiel 38:22ff in the retribution pronounced against Gog for her wickedness. The fact that only one-third is affected reveals that the judgment is only partial and not full and complete.

B. The Second Trumpet: Maritime (Salt Water) Disasters, 8:8-9

8:8 The second angel sounded, and *something* like a great mountain burning with fire was thrown into the sea; and a third of the sea became blood, **9** and a third of the creatures which were in the sea and had life, died; and a third of the ships were destroyed.

As the second angel sounds his trumpet John sees a huge fiery mountain thrown into the sea. Which sea? We do not know. There are only four seas of significance mentioned in the Bible: the Red Sea, the Sea of Galilee, the Mediterranean Sea; and the Dead Sea.

The sea is turned into blood and a third of everything connected with the sea either dies or is destroyed. This vision speaks of God's power and wrath.

In the Old Testament, the removing of mountains signified the overthrowing of a government. Jeremiah 51:25 reads, "'Behold, I am against you, O destroying mountain, Who destroys the whole earth,' declares the LORD, 'And I will stretch out My hand against you, And roll you down from the crags And I will make you a burnt out mountain.'" Notice, once again, the affinity between this judgment of God and the Egyptian plague where the Nile and other waterways of Egypt were turned into blood (cf. Exod. 7:20ff).

C. The Third Trumpet: Land (Fresh Water) Disasters, 8:10-11

8:10 The third angel sounded, and a great star fell from heaven, burning like a torch, and it fell on a third of the rivers and on the springs of waters. **11** The name of the star is called Wormwood; and a third of the waters became wormwood, and many men died from the waters, because they were made bitter.

The waters of the land rivers and springs are affected by a great star that falls from heaven. Similar imagery is found in Isaiah 24:21-22; 34:4; where the removal of a heavenly star signified the overthrow of his earthly counterpart (viz., a king, dignitary, authority or some notable one). This star fell on the waters. In the book of Revelation, water sometimes means people (cf. 17:5).

The name of the star (Wormwood) indicates the judgment; the waters become bitter. The word "wormwood" refers to a bitter herb *Artemesia absinthium* found in the Near East and mentioned elsewhere in the Bible in Jeremiah 9:15; 23:15; Lamentations 3:15,19; Amos 5:7. In this plague we have the first mention of the loss of human life (cf. 9:15, 20).

D. The Fourth Trumpet: Heavenly Body Disasters, 8:12

8:12 The fourth angel sounded, and a third of the sun and a third of the moon and a third of the stars were struck, so that a third of them would be darkened and the day would not shine for a third of it, and the night in the same way.

When the fourth trumpet is sounded the heavenly bodies (sun, moon, stars) are darkened. The sun, moon, and stars are the source of light upon the earth. In the Old Testament the removal of these means God's light is going out upon a nation. Joel declares, "Before them the earth quakes, The heavens tremble, The sun and moon grow dark, And the stars lose their brightness. The LORD utters His voice before His army; Surely His camp is very great, For strong is he who carries out His word. The day of the LORD is indeed great and very awesome, And who can endure it?" (2:10-11). And again, "Multitudes, multitudes in the valley of decision! For the day of the LORD is near in the valley of decision. The sun and moon grow dark, And the stars lose their brightness" (3:14-15). Amos, the great prophet of God declares, "'It will come about in that day,' declares the Lord GOD, 'That I will make the sun go down at noon And make the earth dark in broad daylight'" (8:9). This plague is comparable to the plague of darkness in Egypt (Exod. 10:21ff) except that the Egyptian darkness was total darkness; a darkness that could be felt over the whole land. By turning away from God, who is the source of light, man finds himself in darkness. John writes elsewhere, "This is the judgment, that the Light is come into the world, and men loved the darkness rather than the light; for their deeds were evil" (John 3:19).

The effect is for one-third part of the day and one-third part of the night. Similar to the ninth plague in Egypt (cf. Exod. 10:21ff) the world will be living in darkness.

E. Interlude: Eagle Flying in Midair, 8:13

8:13 Then I looked, and I heard an eagle flying in midheaven, saying with a loud voice, "Woe, woe, woe to those who dwell on the earth, because of the remaining blasts of the trumpet of the three angels who are about to sound!"

As this chapter closes there is an interlude (pause) between the sounding of the fourth and fifth trumpets. An eagle (KJV-Angel) flying in midair and crying out with three woes, not because of what has happened, but because of what is about to happen. The judgment to this point has been mild compared to the judgment about to come. The next three trumpets will also each be seen as a woe. The fifth trumpet will be the first woe; the sixth trumpet, the second woe; and the seventh trumpet, the third woe. Each with increasing intensity; for after the seventh trumpet (third woe) the next judgment will be more severe (the seven bowls of God's wrath, ch. 16).

Revelation 9

F. The Fifth Trumpet: The First Woe, 9:1-12

[1]Then the fifth angel sounded, and I saw a star from heaven which had fallen to the earth; and the key of the bottomless pit was given to him. [2]He opened the bottomless pit, and smoke went up out of the pit, like the smoke of a great furnace; and the sun and the air were darkened by the smoke of the pit. [3]Then out of the smoke came locusts upon the earth, and power was given them, as the scorpions of the earth have power. [4]They were told not to hurt the grass of the earth, nor any green thing, nor any tree, but only the men who do not have the seal of God on their foreheads. [5]And they were not permitted to kill anyone, but to torment for five months; and their torment was like the torment of a scorpion when it stings a man. [6]And in those days men will seek death and will not find it; they will long to die, and death flees from them.

[7]The appearance of the locusts was like horses prepared for battle; and on their heads appeared to be crowns like gold, and their faces were like the faces of

men. [8]They had hair like the hair of women, and their teeth were like the teeth of lions. [9]They had breastplates like breastplates of iron; and the sound of their wings was like the sound of chariots, of many horses rushing to battle. [10]They have tails like scorpions, and stings; and in their tails is their power to hurt men for five months. [11]They have as king over them, the angel of the abyss; his name in Hebrew is Abaddon, and in the Greek he has the name Apollyon.

[12]The first woe is past; behold, two woes are still coming after these things.

John now focuses attention to the fifth and sixth trumpets (the first and second woes). Chapter nine presents two pictures: (1) a locust plague that affects the non-Christian, and (2) a great army that invades the land. The fifth and sixth trumpets are also the first and second woes.

9:1 Then the fifth angel sounded, and I saw a star from heaven which had fallen to the earth; and the key of the bottomless pit was given to him.

A fifth angel sounds a trumpet and John sees a star which had fallen to the earth. If this star represents an angel, there is all the difference between this fallen angel to whom was given the key to the bottomless pit and the angel of 20:1, whom John sees descending from heaven with the key of the abyss in his hand. The difference is not just that the one releases the destroyers and the other locks them up. One is an evil agent acting on divine permission and the other is a good agent voluntarily carrying out the benevolent purpose of God.

This angel is given the key to the pit of the abyss (i.e., the dwelling place of demons, cf. Luke 8:31). The "abyss" ("bottomless pit," KJV) is referred to in 17:11 and 17:8 as the place from where the beast arises, and was ruled over by "the Destroyer" (v. 11). It is also the place into which Satan is finally cast (20:1, 3). Of the nine references to the abyss in the New Testament, seven are found in the book of Revelation.

The key is a symbol of power given to him and implies that Satan was permitted to open the pit of the abyss. The permissive power of Satan is also seen in such passages as Job 1:12; 2:6. God is in control, and even Satan cannot move without the Lord God's permission.

9:2 He opened the bottomless pit, and smoke went up out of the pit, like the smoke of a great furnace; and the sun and the air were darkened by the smoke of the pit.

As he opens the abyss, a smoke arises that darkens the sun and the sky from a gigantic furnace. Smoke is a symbol of judgment on the ungodly. Smoke went up from the destruction of Sodom and Gomorrah (Gen. 19:28). Smoke signified the power of God's presence at Mt. Sinai (Exod. 19:18). The smoke of divine judgment goes up forever and ever (Isa. 34:10; Rev. 14:11; 19:3).

The darkness caused by the smoke from the abyss permeates the air and obscures the sun. The truth which directs men's lives is darkened by the deceptions of Satan. This darkness is the way by which "the god of this world" blinds the minds of the unbelievers (2 Cor. 4:3-4). The "god of this world" is Satan, "the prince of the power of the air," who rules over this world and perverts the "sons of disobedience" (Eph. 2:2).

9:3 Then out of the smoke came locusts upon the earth, and power was given them, as the scorpions of the earth have power. 4 They were told not to hurt the grass of the earth, nor any green thing, nor any tree, but only the men who do not have the seal of God on their foreheads. 5 And they were not permitted to kill anyone, but to torment for five months;

and their torment was like the torment of a scorpion when it stings a man. 6 And in those days men will seek death and will not find it; they will long to die, and death flees from them.

Out of the smoke there come locusts. Locusts are mentioned in Exodus when God said He would bring them in judgment upon Pharaoh's land because of his rebellion against God (Exod. 10:4-20; Ps. 105:34-35). A large locust invasion occurred in the days of Joel when God brought upon the land His army as a means of bringing the people back to Him. They come upon the earth with the power of scorpions to hurt, not the grass, plants, or trees, but only those people who do not have the seal of God on their forehead. Those who have the seal of God belong to God (cf. 7:3, 22:4). Their sting is so severe that those struck will seek death but will not be able to find it. Job mentions the misery of one who longs for death but cannot find it (Job 3:21). This thought illustrates the severity of the judgment God is bringing upon Rome. Locusts are yet another symbol of judgment (cf. Joel 1:4; 2:25; Nahum 3:15).

The locusts appear with the sting of scorpions. Scorpions are mentioned in the Old Testament as dwelling in the wilderness of Sinai (Deut. 8:15), and as symbolizing the people among whom Ezekiel dwelt in Chaldea (Ezek. 2:6). When Rehoboam indicated that he would chastise the people more severely than his father, Solomon, he said, "my father disciplined you with whips, but I will discipline you with scorpions"' (1 Kgs. 12:11). The scorpion is mentioned in the New Testament only here (vv. 3,5,10) and in Luke 10:19; 11:12. Jesus assured His disciples saying, "Behold, I have given you authority to tread on serpents and scorpions, and over all the power of the enemy, and nothing will injure you" (Luke 10:19). These serpents, scorpions, and enemies symbolize the forces of spiritual evil in the world which disciples would overcome and tread under foot.

The "five months" has been explained by some as the normal time of the life span of a locust from birth, through the larva stage, to death. Thus, John is indicating that one generation of demonic locusts is being unleashed upon the earth. However, there is no evidence that such is the case. We have no evidence for a locust plague lasting that long.

9:7 The appearance of the locusts was like horses prepared for battle; and on their heads appeared to be crowns like gold, and their faces were like the faces of men. 8 They had hair like the hair of women, and their teeth were like *the teeth* of lions. 9 They had breastplates like breastplates of iron; and the sound of their wings was like the sound of chariots, of many horses rushing to battle. 10 They have tails like scorpions, and stings; and in their tails is their power to hurt men for five months.

After describing the origin and mission of the locusts, John now turns to describe what these locusts look like. They are described as "horses prepared for battle." This is certainly reminiscent of Joel's day, "Their appearance is like the appearance of horses; And like war horses, so they run. With a noise as of chariots They leap on the tops of the mountains, Like the crackling of a flame of fire consuming the stubble, Like a mighty people arranged for battle" (2:4-5). This army of locusts represent sin's own destructive force.

On their heads appears to be "crowns like gold." While one would not want to make too much out of it there is one observation which could be important. The crown mentioned here is the *stephanos*, the victory crown. This is the word normally used to describe Christ and the saints of God. Here, the wicked are seen receiving the *stephanos*. But it is not a genuine *stephanos*. It is a "*stephanos*" that is "like" (*homoios*) gold. It is interesting to note that John does not describe the crown as "a crown *of* gold," but merely "a crown *like* gold." This would indicate that the victory of wickedness is not permanent, but only temporary. Their victory is not the genuine thing, if it were, it would be a crown of God, not a crown like gold.

Their human faces indicate intelligence and shows that this affliction was brought about by a deceived mankind whose intelligent wills are in rebellion against God. This also illustrates the human dimension of evil. Evil is the result of human rebellion against God.

Their protection was that of a "breastplate of iron" indicating there is no possible way of striking back with any success. In flight, they sound like chariots drawn by horses rushing to battle. The significance of this seems to be the indication that they are of sufficient number; it sounds just like an army that is going to war.

9:11 They have as king over them, the angel of the abyss; his name in Hebrew is Abaddon, and in the Greek he has the name Apollyon.

They have a king over them, the angel of the abyss; his name is "The Destroyer." In the Hebrew it is *Abbadon*; in the Greek it is *Apollyon*. In the Hebrew this term means "destruction, or ruin" (Job 26:6 mg; Prov. 27:20 mg); and more often "the place of ruin" in Sheol (Job 26:6 mg; Prov. 15:11 mg), or "death" (Job 28:22 mg). In the Greek the term means "exterminator, or destroyer" and occurs nowhere else in the Bible.

Specific identification of all the details of this picture is not necessary to understand the message. What John sees is destructive power that will bring hurt upon all those who are not the redeemed. Only those who are sealed servants of God (cf. Chapter 7) will escape the horror of this plague.

This is not a final judgment. We know this for several reasons. First, the plague is only to hurt, not to kill. Second, the plague lasts only five months, which means that even though it is a complete plague (which serves as a warning), it is not final for verse 20 indicates that the purpose of this plague was to get men to "repent of the works of their hands." At the final judgment, no one will be given the opportunity to repent.

9:12 The first woe is past; behold, two woes are still coming after these things.

This verse is transitional. It tells us the first Woe is over, but there are still two more to come. It is implied that the first woe was bad enough, but there are two more woes to come. Are they more severe? We shall see.

G. The Sixth Trumpet: The Second Woe, 9:13-21

[13]Then the sixth angel sounded, and I heard a voice from the four horns of the golden altar which is before God, [14]one saying to the sixth angel who had the trumpet, "Release the four angels who are bound at the great river Euphrates." [15]And the four angels, who had been prepared for the hour and day and month and year, were released, so that they would kill a third of mankind. [16]The number of the armies of the horsemen was two hundred million; I heard the number of them.

[17]And this is how I saw in the vision the horses and those who sat on them: the riders had breastplates the color of fire and of hyacinth and of brimstone; and the heads of the horses are like the heads of lions; and out of their mouths proceed fire and smoke and brimstone. [18]A third of mankind was killed by these three plagues, by the fire and the smoke and the brimstone which proceeded out of their mouths. [19]For the power of the horses is in their mouths and in their tails; for their tails are like serpents and have heads, and with them they do harm.

[20]And the rest of mankind, who were not killed by these plagues, did not repent of the works of their

hands, so as not to worship demons, and the idols of gold and of silver and of brass and of stone and of wood, which can neither see nor hear nor walk; [21]and they did not repent of their murders nor of their sorceries nor of their immorality nor of their thefts.

9:13 Then the sixth angel sounded, and I heard a voice from the four horns of the golden altar which is before God,

As the sixth angel sounds there is a voice from the horns of the golden altar in heaven. This is the golden altar before the throne of God upon which the saints' prayers ascend (8:3-5). It is not the altar under which souls were seen earlier (6:9). The speaker is never identified. Is this the voice of the prayers of the righteous saints? Is it the voice an angel? Or could this be the voice of God himself?

In the previous picture the army from the Abyss was to bring pain; this army is allowed to kill men on the earth. To indicate that this is not final destruction, however, note that only one-third part of men will be killed.

9:14 one saying to the sixth angel who had the trumpet, "Release the four angels who are bound at the great river Euphrates."

The voice says that it is time to release the four angels which have been held in check at the River Euphrates. Who are these angels? Attempts to identify them have not been satisfactory. Some suggest a connection between these angels and the four restraining angels of 7:1. But the angels of 7:1 are stationed at the four corners of the earth. Their job is to hold back the winds of destruction. The angels here (9:15) are to bring about the destruction. These angels are in charge of the two hundred million horsemen (v. 16). The angels are loosed for the purpose of killing one third of the earth's population. Under the fourth seal, one-fourth part of mankind was killed. Now, a third more are killed by this demonic army that sweeps across the earth.

The Euphrates River is one of the four branches of the river that flowed out of Eden in the account of creation (Gen. 2:10ff). It becomes the eastern boundary of the promised land (Exod. 23:31) and marks the boundary between Israel and her enemies. In Isaiah 8:5-8 the invading armies of Assyria are pictured as a mighty flood in which the great river overflows its banks and sweeps over Judah. Being the eastern boundary of Israel's land, it was also the western boundary of the Assyrian Empire. In ancient times, God's enemies came from the River Euphrates (cf. Jer. 2:18 mg; 13:4f. mg; 51:63; Rev. 16:12). It is a geographical term used to depict the fearful character of the coming judgment of God.

9:15 And the four angels, who had been prepared for the hour and day and month and year, were released, so that they would kill a third of mankind.

The phrase "for the hour and day and month and year" is biblical terminology which shows that what is to happen is under the direction of divine judgment. God's judgments always occur according to His timetable, not man's. Similar "timetables" are found elsewhere. In Acts 1:7, the Lord speaks of "times or epochs (dates — NIV) which the Father has fixed by His own authority." Paul speaks of the "fulness of the time" when Jesus was born (Gal. 4:4); and that God's plans are "suitable to the fulness of the times" (Eph. 1:10) in summing up all things in Christ.

9:16 The number of the armies of the horsemen was two hundred million; I heard the number of them.

When this happens judgment once again comes when an army of two hundred million is released by these angels. Older versions number "twice ten thousand times ten thousand" (10,000 X 10,000). To reduce this to a literal number is to miss the point. A regular formation of this size army would make a column one mile wide and eighty-five miles long. Here is a symbol of a mighty host, perhaps take from Psalm 68:17, "The chariots of God are myriads, thousands upon thousands."

9:17 And this is how I saw in the vision the horses and those who sat on them: *the riders* **had breastplates** *the color* **of fire and of hyacinth and of brimstone; and the heads of the horses are like the heads of lions; and out of their mouths proceed fire and smoke and brimstone.**

The description of the breastplates as "the color of fire and of hyacinth and of brimstone" is familiar imagery from both the Old and New Testaments. They signify the wrath of God and are always used with reference to judgment and punishment upon the wicked (Gen. 19:24; Ps. 11:6; Ezek. 38:22; Luke 17:29; Rev. 14:10; 19:20; 20:10; 21:8).

9:18 A third of mankind was killed by these three plagues, by the fire and the smoke and the brimstone which proceeded out of their mouths. 19 For the power of the horses is in their mouths and in their tails; for their tails are like serpents and have heads, and with them they do harm.

The power of the horses is from their lion-like heads which give our fire, smoke, and brimstone; and from their serpent-like tails that inflict great hurt (cf. 9:10). The power in their tails may refer to the scorpion sting of 19:10. Some commentators see this as a reference to the Parthian calvary's rearward archery.

9:20 The rest of mankind, who were not killed by these plagues, did not repent of the works of their hands, so as not to worship demons, and the idols of

gold and of silver and of brass and of stone and of wood, which can neither see nor hear nor walk; 21 and they did not repent of their murders nor of their sorceries nor of their immorality nor of their thefts.

The purpose of the plagues is to call men to repentance (cf. 20-21). But, they still do not repent of their false worship and worldliness. While one-third of the ungodly were killed, the remaining two-thirds, described as "the rest of mankind" did not repent. They continued in their ungodliness.

There are two things mentioned about the remaining two-thirds of the population of the wicked. First is their worship of demons, described here as the "works of their hands, . . . the idols of gold and of silver and of brass and of stone and of wood, which can neither see nor hear nor walk." The demons may refer either to pagan deities (Deut. 32:17; Ps. 106:37) or to evil spirits (1 Cor. 10:20-21; 1 Tim. 4:1). Forsaking God and substituting a god of his own desires, is the greatest folly of man (Deut. 4:28; 2 Kgs. 19:18; Ps. 115:4; 135:15; Isa. 2:8; 37:19; Jer. 1:16; 10:3-5; 25:6-7; Acts 7:41; 19:26).

Second is their immoral conduct (murder, sorceries, immorality, and thefts). *Murder* is the disdain for human life and taking of it unjustly. It shows a contempt, not only for God, but also for man, who is made in the image of God (Gen. 1:26-27). In other words, there is a loss of the sanctity of human life. *Sorcery* (*pharmakōn*) occurs here (9:21), in Revelation 18:23, and in Galatians 5:20. The word indicates the use of drugs and generally is understood to represent the use of occult power. All forms of sorcery, witchcraft, and satanic ritual are forbidden practices among the people of God. *Immorality* (*porneia*) refers to sexual immorality and includes all forms of sexual perversion and moral uncleanness which grows out of unbridled lust (cf. Rom. 1:18ff). *Thefts* describes one who has a total disregard for the property of others.

Revelation 10

H. Interlude: Four Pictures, 10:1-11:13

Before the last trumpet sounds there is a break (an interlude) in the sounding of the trumpets. This prophetic interlude corresponds to the break between the sixth and seventh seals being opened. We have heard the Second Woe, but before we hear the final Woe (contained in the blowing of the final trumpet) there is an interlude.

Three visions have "sevens" in them: the seals (ch. 6), the trumpets (chs. 8-9), and the bowls of wrath (ch. 16). Between the sixth and seventh seals there was an interlude consisting of two visions (the 144,000 and the great multitude). These visions were given to respond to the question raised by those fleeing from the wrath of God and the Lamb, when they asked, "who is able to stand?" The answer is seen in the visions and, put succinctly, is the redeemed of God. They are the ones who are able to stand in the day of God's great and terrible wrath.

Now, before the blowing of the seventh trumpet (which is also the last Woe, 11:14), there is another interlude. There is no such interlude between the sixth and seven bowls of wrath for all warning is gone and nothing can suspend the final and furious judgment of God at that time.

In this interlude there are four pictures: (1) The Seven Unrecorded Thunders, 10:1-7; (2) The Little Bitter-Sweet Book, 10:8-11; (3) The Measuring of the Temple, 11:1-2; and (4) The Two Witnesses, 11:3-13. The Seven Unrecorded Thunders means there will be no more warning. The Little Bitter-Sweet Book represents the fact that John must continue to prophesy, though it will be pleasant in delivery, it will be unpleasant in reception. The Measuring of the Temple means that God knows those who belong to Him (His people) and the Two Witnesses portray that God's servants will be victorious.

1. Seven Unrecorded Thunders, 10:1-7

[1]I saw another strong angel coming down out of heaven, clothed with a cloud; and the rainbow was upon his head, and his face was like the sun, and his feet like pillars of fire; [2]and he had in his hand a little book which was open. He placed his right foot on the sea and his left on the land; [3]and he cried out with a loud voice, as when a lion roars; and when he had cried out, the seven peals of thunder uttered their voices. [4]When the seven peals of thunder had spoken, I was about to write; and I heard a voice from heaven saying, "Seal up the things which the seven peals of thunder have spoken and do not write them."

[5]Then the angel whom I saw standing on the sea and on the land lifted up his right hand to heaven, [6]and swore by Him who lives forever and ever, WHO CREATED HEAVEN AND THE THINGS IN IT, AND THE EARTH AND THE THINGS IN IT, AND THE SEA AND THE THINGS IN IT, that there will be delay no longer, [7]but in the days of the voice of the seventh angel, when he is about to sound, then the mystery of God is finished, as He preached to His servants the prophets.

In chapters 4-9 John has seen the visions unfold from heaven. Now, he is evidently on earth, for the strong angel is "coming down out of heaven." In 9:1 we saw a star falling from heaven, in 10:1 we see an angel descending out of heaven. The phrase "another strong angel" simply means, another angel — a strong one. There are three strong angels we meet in the Revelation. One speaks with a loud voice asking who is worthy to open the sealed book (5:2). In Revelation 18:21, we meet a strong angel who casts a great millstone in the sea. Here (10:2) the strong angel is connected with holding a bitter-sweet book which John will soon be told to take and eat (10:8).

10:1 I saw another strong angel coming down out of heaven, clothed with a cloud; and the rainbow was upon his head, and his face was like the sun, and his feet like pillars of fire;

Who is this strong angel? Some have identified him with the Christ. There are certain characteristics which seem to make this connection; e.g., he is dressed in a cloud (Ps. 104:3; Rev. 1:7); there is a rainbow upon his head (4:3); his face is as the sun (Rev. 1:16); and his feet are as pillars of fire (Exod. 13:21f). But, similarity does not guarantee identity. There are at least two reasons for rejecting such identification: (1) elsewhere in the Apocalypse Christ never appears as an angel; and (2) the oath of verse six would be in appropriate for Christ. It could possibly have reference, however, to the angel Gabriel (cf. Dan. 8:16).

This angel is arrayed "with a cloud" (*nephelē*). This word is used twenty- five times in the New Testament and in all but three occurrences (Luke 12:54; 2 Pet. 2:17; Jude 12) it refers to deity or some divine appearance (often in judgment).

10:2 and he had in his hand a little book which was open. He placed his right foot on the sea and his left on the land;

In his hand the angel holds a book. There is a contrast here with what is found in chapter five. This book is a smaller scroll ("booklet"), it is opened, not sealed; and its contents are consumed by the seer (vv. 8-10). The significance of this book is revealed later (vv. 9-11). The angel places one foot on the sea and another on the land to indicate his authority over both the entire world and the inclusiveness of his mission; i.e., it was for the entire world.

10:3 and he cried out with a loud voice, as when a lion roars; and when he had cried out, the seven peals of thunder uttered their voices.

The roaring of a lion is imagery from the Old Testament of God bringing judgment upon wicked (cf. Isa. 31:4; Jer. 25:30f; Hos. 11:10; Joel 3:16; Amos 1:2). As the lion roars, seven peals (voices — NIV) of thunder utter their voices. Thunder may be significant in that it serves as a warning of an impending storm. When a storm is brewing, the thunder begins to roar and warns us to make preparation for what is on the way. Thunder generally serves as a warning. Elsewhere in the Revelation thunders form a warning of the judgment of divine wrath (cf. 8:5; 11:19; 16:18).

These thunders, however, are not just audible sounds, but are linked with intelligent utterances as is indicated in the next verse. While we are told that these seven peals of thunder had spoken, we are never told what they said.

10:4 When the seven peals of thunder had spoken, I was about to write; and I heard a voice from heaven saying, "Seal up the things which the seven peals of thunder have spoken and do not write them."

John was about to write, presumably to tell us what the thunders had spoken, but is told "seal up the things . . . and do not write them." The fact that the voice John hears is from heaven indicates that the commission not to write comes from either God or Christ (cf. 14:13; 18:4). This prohibition is in contrast with 1:19 ("Therefore write the things which you have seen, and the things which are, and the things which will take place after these things.") and 22:10 (And he said to me, "Do not seal up the words of the prophecy of this book, for the time is near."). It seems likely that the seven thunders formed another series of warnings for man like the seven seals and the seven trumpets. But since "they did not repent" (9:21) there would be no more warning. The fact that the thunder sounds, but is never heard (i.e., written down) indicates that God has given His last warning. If man refuses to repent, he will be judged. If men will not repent after the judgments God has sent that have been tempered with mercy (seals and trumpets), then they will reap the destruction of the final wrath of God (cf. the bowls of wrath).

10:5 Then the angel whom I saw standing on the sea and on the land lifted up his right hand to heaven, 6 and swore by Him who lives forever and ever, WHO CREATED HEAVEN AND THE THINGS IN IT, AND THE EARTH AND THE THINGS IN IT, AND THE SEA AND THE THINGS IN IT, that there will be delay no longer,

The angel lifts his hand toward heaven, a gesture which usually accompanies a solemn oath or swearing, indicating an appeal to God as witness to an oath (cf. Gen. 14:22; Deut. 32:40; Ezek. 20:5ff; Dan. 12:7; Judg. 8:19). Lifting his hand toward heaven is significant because heaven is the place of God's abode (Isa. 57:15). The angel, as a representative for God, also calls on God to witness the things which are about to be done.

The phrase "that there will be delay no longer" implies that there had been delay. In Daniel's day (12:7) there was to be a delay before the three and one-half years of persecution began. In John's day, there would be no delay; the crisis was upon the church. To make this refer to the Second Coming is to miss the point. John is writing about "the things which must soon take place" (1:1).

The souls under the altar had cried, "How long?" (6:9-10); saints had offered prayers (8:3-4); the trumpets had sounded (8:7-9:21); now, there shall be no more delay before the fulfillment of the divine purpose for the church on earth. It is time for the promise of God for the vindication of His saints to be fulfilled.

10:7 but in the days of the voice of the seventh angel, when he is about to sound, then the mystery of God is finished, as He preached to His servants the prophets.

What is "the mystery of God" which is finished? It is hard to tell. This is especially difficult since Amos 3:7 says, "Surely the Lord GOD does nothing Unless He reveals His secret counsel To His servants the prophets." But His revealing is sometimes now clear. Some think it may refer to the overthrow of Satan (cf. 12:8-9). Others think it refers to God's plan for human redemption, conceived in His mind, and summed up in Christ (Eph. 1:9-11; 3:8-11). In its context the reference seems like to the subject matter of the revelation; viz., when the persecution would come and why it was necessary. God's servants had the gospel preached to them and in the gospel the certainty and purpose of suffering had been made known (cf. Acts 14:22). What has already been revealed, is now emphasized in this book. The message John is revealing in this book is the conflict of the church with Rome. There are terrors still ahead which the church must face. But, the church will ultimately triumph over Rome.

2. The Little "Bitter-Sweet" book, 10:8-11

[8]And the voice which I heard from heaven, I heard again speaking with me, and saying, "Go, take the book which is open in the hand of the angel who stands on the sea and on the land."

⁹So I went to the angel, telling him to give me the little book. And he said to me, "Take it and eat it; it will make your stomach bitter, but in your mouth it will be sweet as honey." ¹⁰I took the little book out of the angel's hand and ate it, and in my mouth it was sweet as honey; and when I had eaten it, my stomach was made bitter. ¹¹And they said to me, "You must prophesy again concerning many peoples and nations and tongues and kings."

10:8 And the voice which I heard from heaven, *I heard* again speaking with me, and saying, "Go, take the book which is open in the hand of the angel who stands on the sea and on the land."

The voice John hears again refers to the voice which told John to seal up the seven thunders (v. 4). This time, the voice tells him to go and take the little book which lies open in the hand of the angel. This angel is standing on the sea and on the land; i.e., his message is universal.

10:9 So I went to the angel, telling him to give me the little book. And he said to me, "Take it and eat it; it will make your stomach bitter, but in your mouth it will be sweet as honey." 10 I took the little book out of the angel's hand and ate it, and in my mouth it was sweet as honey; and when I had eaten it, my stomach was made bitter.

As John goes to the angel (is he now on earth?) asking for the book, the angel instructs him to "take it and eat it." Eating the book here is used in the sense of consuming its contents. But the angel foretells, and it follows as true (v. 10), that it will be "sweet as honey" in his mouth, but when he had eaten it, his stomach "was made bitter."

The emphasis is on the sweetness of God's Word. The Psalmist says the judgment of the Lord "are more desirable than gold, yes, than much fine gold; Sweeter also than honey and the drippings of the honeycomb" (Ps. 19:10). Also, "How sweet are Your words to my taste! *Yes, sweeter* than honey to my mouth!" (Ps. 119:103).

The prophet Jeremiah writes, "Your words were found and I ate them, And Your words became for me a joy and the delight of my heart; For I have been called by Your name, O LORD God of hosts" (15:16). But the sweetness of God's Word also had a bitter after effect: "I have become a laughingstock all day long; Everyone mocks me. For each time I speak, I cry aloud; . . . the word of the LORD has resulted In reproach and derision all day long. But if I say, 'I will not remember Him Or speak anymore in His name,' Then in my heart it becomes like a burning fire Shut up in my bones; And I am weary of holding *it* in, And I cannot endure it" (Jer. 20:7-9). The obvious parallel for this vision is the commission of the prophet Ezekiel (2:8-3:11).

The identity of the little book is uncertain. While some might think this refers to the entire New Testament, it seems more plausible that the little book is a message for the church found in the following verses (11:1-13). As the larger book (ch. 5) contained the message of chapters six — nine, so the smaller book (ch. 10) contains a smaller message (ch. 11:1-13).

10:11 And they said to me, "You must prophesy again concerning many peoples and nations and tongues and kings."

After John has eaten the book, he is told that he must prophesy again to many "peoples and nations and tongues and kings." This prophesy begins with chapter twelve; i.e., after the sounding of the seventh trumpet.

The word "kings" is used here rather than "tribes" (5:9; 7:9; 13:7; 14:6). This suggests that God's Word through His prophets takes precedence over the

authority of kings. It may also be that John here anticipates the seven kings of 17:10 and the ten kings of
17:12.

Revelation 11

3. Measuring the Temple, 11:1-2

[1]Then there was given me a measuring rod like a staff; and someone said, "Get up and measure the temple of God and the altar, and those who worship in it. [2]"Leave out the court which is outside the temple and do not measure it, for it has been given to the nations; and they will tread under foot the holy city for forty-two months.

The third picture is short, contained in two verses. One cannot help but notice how John's participation in the vision has changed. Until John had been given the little book and told to eat it, he was confined to writing what he saw and heard, i.e., he has been more of a spectator. Now John becomes active in the Revelation. After eating the little book, John is given a measuring rod and told to measure three things: (1) the temple of God, (2) the altar, and (3) the worshipers.

John is given a "reed" (*kalamos*) or "cane." In Ezekiel 40:5 the measuring rod was ten feet long. This would make it suitable for measuring a building or large area. In the ancient world, measuring was accomplished by the reed cane (Ezek. 40:2ff) or with a rope (1 Kgs. 7:23; Isa. 44:13). Exactly who told John to do the measuring is uncertain. It is likely, however, that it is either God or Christ since later the voice refers to "my two witnesses" (11:3).

Some people believe that since John is told to measure the temple, it implies that the temple is still standing. This would in turn imply that the Revelation was written prior to A.D. 70. The conclusion is not necessary. John is seeing a vision, and he participates in the vision. But an object can be seen in a vision whether it actually exists or not.

The first thing John measures is the temple of God. There are two Greek words for temple. One is *hieron* which is a broad term used to refer to the whole structure of Herod's temple, including its building, courts, and porches (Matt. 4:5; John 2:14). The other word is *naos* which is narrower and refers to the sanctuary or inner court where only the priests were allowed (Matt. 23:35; 27:51). It is possible that John has in his mind the Old Testament tabernacle. Its sanctuary had only one court with the altar and ark of the covenant within. In the book of Hebrews the tabernacle serves as a type of the church. The church is identified as the temple of God elsewhere (cf. 1 Cor. 3:16-17; 2 Cor. 6:16; Eph. 2:19-22). It is made up of living stones (2 Pet. 2:5), and is made up of priests who offer spiritual sacrifices unto God (2 Pet. 2:9).

John then measures the altar (a huge stone altar) and its worshipers. These symbolically represent the true servants of God, who are worshiping Him.

The symbolic action of measuring the temple reminds us of other prophets whose actions were dramatized. Isaiah walked about naked and barefoot (Isa. 20:2-5) to symbolize Egypt's impending captivity to Assyria. Ezekiel dug through the wall and carried out his baggage as a symbol to Israel of their coming exile (Ezek. 12:1-7). The New Testament prophet, Agabus, bound his hands and feet with Paul's girdle to illustrate how Paul would be bound by the Jews at Jerusalem (Acts 21:10-11). John is dramatizing the message by measuring the temple.

If this picture takes its significance from Ezekiel 40:20 then the measuring is for both separation and protection. Measuring was done to separate the holy from the common; the clean from the unclean. Therefore, two groups are here separated from each other. One will be separated for destruction, the other for protection. The temple represents the church (cf. 1 Cor. 3:16-17; Eph. 2:19-22), the altar represents their place of worship, and the worshipers represent the redeemed.

Thus the measuring of the temple is a way of declaring its preservation and protection. This preservation was not security against physical suffering or even death, but against spiritual danger. It corresponds to the sealing of 7:1-8, which did not protect anyone from physical death, but served to assure those who suffered, that God knows who they are and will claim them as His own.

11:2 "Leave out the court which is outside the temple and do not measure it, for it has been given to the nations; and they will tread under foot the holy city for forty-two months.

The court which is outside the temple would be the court of the Gentiles. The ancient tabernacle had one court (Exod. 27:9), Solomon's temple had an inner court (1 Kgs. 6:36), and outer court (1 Kgs. 7:21), a court for the priests (1 Chron. 4:9), and an upper court (Jer. 36:10). Herod's court was divided into three courts (the courts of the women, of the Israelites, and of the priests). There was an inscription between these three courts from the court of the Gentiles which threatened death to any Gentile who would pass beyond the court of the Gentiles into the other court (Josephus, *Bell.* v. 2).

Opinions vary regarding what this court represents. The word for "nations" is the word *ethnē* and is used throughout the book of Revelation to refer either to all the peoples on earth who are in rebellion against God (11:18; 14:8; 19:15; 20:3), or, those who are redeemed and under the rule of Christ (2:26; 21:24, 26; 22:2). The former use seems to best fit the context of the vision and the purpose for which John writes. That is to say, this court, symbolized by those left out of or cast out (*ekballō*) from God's protection, is given to those who live in rebellion of God. The reason for this is that they are separated (measured) because they are to be judged.

The faithful will be protected during this period of judgment (42 months). The forty-two months is a time figure used in the Apocalypse for (1) the time of the authority of the beast, 13:5; (2) the time the holy city is trodden under foot, 11:2; (3) the period of time during which two witnesses prophesy, 11:3; (4) the equivalent to "time, times, and half a time" [i.e., three and one half], 12:6; 12:14; and (5) the period of time in which the woman is nourished, 12:6, 14.

4. The Two Witnesses, 11:3-13

[3]"And I will grant authority to my two witnesses, and they will prophesy for twelve hundred and sixty days, clothed in sackcloth." [4]These are the two olive trees and the two lampstands that stand before the Lord of the earth. [5]And if anyone wants to harm them, fire flows out of their mouth and devours their enemies; so if anyone wants to harm them, he must be killed in this way. [6]These have the power to shut up the sky, so that rain will not fall during the days of their prophesying; and they have power over the waters to turn them into blood, and to strike the earth with every plague, as often as they desire.

[7]When they have finished their testimony, the beast that comes up out of the abyss will make war with them, and overcome them and kill them. [8]And

their dead bodies will lie in the street of the great city which mystically is called Sodom and Egypt, where also their Lord was crucified.⁹Those from the peoples and tribes and tongues and nations will look at their dead bodies for three and a half days, and will not permit their dead bodies to be laid in a tomb. ¹⁰And those who dwell on the earth will rejoice over them and celebrate; and they will send gifts to one another, because these two prophets tormented those who dwell on the earth.

¹¹But after the three and a half days, the breath of life from God came into them, and they stood on their feet; and great fear fell upon those who were watching them. ¹²And they heard a loud voice from heaven saying to them, "Come up here." Then they went up into heaven in the cloud, and their enemies watched them. ¹³And in that hour there was a great earthquake, and a tenth of the city fell; seven thousand people were killed in the earthquake, and the rest were terrified and gave glory to the God of heaven.

11:3 "And I will grant *authority* to my two witnesses, and they will prophesy for twelve hundred and sixty days, clothed in sackcloth."

The fourth, and final, picture in the interlude presents two witnesses, clothed in sackcloth, who are empowered to prophesy. Their prophecy will last for 1,260 days (equivalent to the 42 months already mentioned). During their period of prophecy they will receive divine protection. However, after their testimony is finished, the beast comes up out of the abyss and kills them. The witnesses lay dead in the street for three and one-half days, without compassion even for burial, while the people of the city gloat and celebrate over their death. But after the three and a half days God breathes the breath of life into them and they stand on their feet. As God calls them up to heaven to his presence, an earthquake occurs and a tenth of the city collapses causing seven thousand people to be killed. The result is that the survivors are terrified and give glory to the God of heaven.

Who are these two witnesses and what do they symbolize in John's vision? There are various answers given: (1) Moses and Elijah, (2) Enoch and Elijah, (3) two different groups, (4) two different principles, e.g., the law and the prophets, and (5) two great prophets of God, coming in the spirit of Elijah and Moses, who will yet rise up in the future to prophesy for God.

It is unlikely that two individuals are referred to here but rather that this figure (of two witnesses) represents the faithful church who stands against the powers of evil in a time of great persecution. Her faithfulness is related to their imagery being taken from the two great prophets, Moses and Elijah, as is seen in verse 5-6.

The number "two" suggests the number of required legal witnesses (Num. 35:30; Deut. 17:6; 19:15). It is also interesting to note that the Lord said "two" witnesses would be needed in practicing church discipline (Matt. 18:10) and that when he sent out the disciples on the limited commission, he sent them out two by two (Luke 10:1-23). Paul appeals to two or three witnesses to validate a judgment (2 Cor. 13:1; 1 Tim. 5:19). Some would suggest that the number "two" represents the priestly and kingly aspects of the church; others, the Jewish and Gentile aspects of the church.

11:4 These are the two olive trees and the two lampstands that stand before the Lord of the earth. 5 And if anyone wants to harm them, fire flows out of their mouth and devours their enemies; so if anyone wants to harm them, he must be killed in this way.

Fire is understood to symbolically represent a judgment from God (Gen. 19:23-25; 2 Sam. 22:7-9; Ps. 97:3). In this vision, these two witnesses are seen as having divine protection from their enemies described in terms familiar with former prophets' protection from God. Elijah had called down fire from heaven to devour two groups of soldiers sent against him (2 Kgs. 1:10-14). Daniel's three friends were cast into a fiery furnace, but the furnace, in turn, slew those who cast them into it (Dan. 3:22). The Lord spoke through the prophet Jeremiah and said, "Because you have spoken this word, Behold, I am making My words in your mouth fire And this people wood, and it will consume them" (5:14). Later the prophet himself said, "But if I say, 'I will not remember Him Or speak anymore in His name,' Then in my heart it becomes like a burning fire Shut up in my bones; and I am weary of holding *it* in, And I cannot endure it" (20:9). In much the same way these witnesses had the promise that in the midst of persecution, God would provide for them the power they need to be victorious.

The explanation of these witnesses as two olive trees and two lampstands is taken from Zechariah four except that in Zechariah's vision there is a single lampstand with seven lamps ("the eyes of the LORD," v. 10) and it is flanked by two olive trees. The Lord encourages the governor, Zerubbabel, by saying that the temple would be built "'Not by might nor by power, but by My Spirit,' says the LORD of hosts" (Zech. 4:6). God will preserve His church by the same power today.

11:6 These have the power to shut up the sky, so that rain will not fall during the days of their prophesying; and they have power over the waters to turn them into blood, and to strike the earth with every plague, as often as they desire.

The powers mentioned in this verse, "to shut up the sky, so that rain will not fall" and "power over the waters to turn them into blood" are clear references to the ministries of Elijah and Moses (1 Kgs. 17 and Exod. 7:17-21). The fact that these two witnesses possess the same powers as Moses and Elijah indicate there is no need to make this refer to the literal prophets themselves. According to Luke 4:25 and James 5:17, Elijah's prophecy shut up the heavens and it did not rain for three and a half years, an interesting foreshadowing of the span of time that these two witnesses prophesy (i.e., 1,260 days, v. 3).

11:7 When they have finished their testimony, the beast that comes up out of the abyss will make war with them, and overcome them and kill them.

This verse implies that when their time of testimony is complete, they lose their protective power. John then mentions "the" beast coming up out of the abyss. Not "a" beast, but "the beast," which implies that even though this is John's first mention of the beast, he was already known to his readers. The beast, which comes up out of the abyss, makes war with them and kills them. The introduction of the beast here prepares us for chapters thirteen and seventeen. He is described as coming up "out of the abyss" (here and in 9:1) which shows his demonic origin.

11:8 And their dead bodies *will lie* in the street of the great city which mystically is called Sodom and Egypt, where also their Lord was crucified.

Adding to the indignity of their death is the fact that "their dead bodies will lie in the street of the great city." There is no ceremony of sorrow over the death of these witnesses for God, rather for three and a half days they are left open to public exposure. The three and a half days of public exposure corresponds to the 1260 days of their prophetic ministry. Refusing to bury the dead was like adding insult to injury (cf. Isa. 5:25; Jer. 8:1-2). Their bodies lie on public display, not for mourning, but rather for merry-making and celebration (v. 10).

The identity of "the great city" is described mystically or symbolically as "Sodom and Egypt, where also their Lord was crucified." The "great city" is a description given to Babylon throughout the rest of the book (14:8; 16:19; 17:5,18; 18:2,10,16,18,19,21). She represents the ungodly power of the Roman Empire. The descriptions given to her in this verse have special significance. She is called Egypt, because she is the oppressor of God's people as was ancient Egypt (cf. Exodus). She is called Sodom, because she is immoral as was the ancient city of Sodom (Gen. 19:4-11). She is called the place where "their Lord was crucified" because Rome is a city of perverse and vile religion.

11:9 Those from the peoples and tribes and tongues and nations *will* look at their dead bodies for three and a half days, and will not permit their dead bodies to be laid in a tomb. 10 And those who dwell on the earth *will* rejoice over them and celebrate; and they will send gifts to one another, because these two prophets tormented those who dwell on the earth.

The phrase "peoples and tribes and tongues and nations" corresponds to "those who dwell on the earth" in verse 10. As the Lord said the ungodly would rejoice over His death (John 16:20), so it now rejoices over the death of His two witnesses. Their rejoicing is minimal, only three and a half days, in comparison to the time of the testimony of the witnesses. The three and a half days represents a broken seven, which means this is a relatively small, indefinite period of time. The number is analogous to the forty-two months and the twelve hundred sixty days of verses 2-3, but by comparison it is much shorter.

Mounce sees the celebration here as a perverse counterpart to the Jewish feast of Purim.[1] During the feast of Purim the people of God rejoice and are festive. But in this vision, the people of God are represented by these two witnesses who lay dead in the street while the ungodly celebrate what they believe to be their victory. Others have suggested that this is a parallel between the crucifixion and the resurrection.

11:11 But after the three and a half days, the breath of life from God came into them, and they stood on their feet; and great fear fell upon those who were watching them. 12 And they heard a loud voice from heaven saying to them, "Come up here." Then they went up into heaven in the cloud, and their enemies watched them.

The rejoicing of the unrighteous is short lived. After three and a half days, God breathes the breath of life into them and they stand on their feet. The celebration of the wicked, regardless of how long it may seem, is always but for a moment. As the dry bones of the house of Israel had life infused into them and they rose to their feet (Ezek. 37:10), so also God now revives His witnesses and they stand on their feet. Great fear fell upon those who were watching when this reveling was cut short. It is no wonder that they fear. The vision continues and reveals that in response to a voice from heaven, these witnesses "went up into heaven in the cloud" (v. 12) as the ungodly watched. Not only were they revived, they were translated. The background for this would be the ascension of Jesus (Acts 1:9-10). No man saw the resurrection, only a few witnessed the ascension, but in this vision the enemies of God witness both the resurrection and ascension of the two witnesses. Even the enemies of God will stand in awe at His majesty and power manifested in the life of His people.

11:13 And in that hour there was a great earthquake, and a tenth of the city fell; seven thousand people were killed in the earthquake, and the rest were terrified and gave glory to the God of heaven.

An earthquake is a further sign of God's vindication. The prophets used earthquakes to illustrate God's judgments on mankind. Isaiah announced such a judgment in Isaiah 29:5-6, "But the multitude of your enemies will become like fine dust, And the multitude of the ruthless ones like the chaff which blows away; And it will happen instantly, suddenly. From the LORD of hosts you will be punished with thunder and earthquake and loud noise, *With* whirlwind and tempest and the flame of a consuming fire." Jeremiah said, "But the LORD is the true God; He is the living God and the everlasting King. At His wrath the earth quakes, And the nations cannot endure His indignation" (10:10; cf. also Job 9:4-6; Ps. 97:3-4; Isa. 24:18f).

Only one-tenth part of the city and seven thousand were killed thus indicating the judgment is only partial. The city here means the symbolic city of Jerusalem of verse eight. This city symbolizes Rome. The description of that judgment will be given in chapters 17-19.

Unlike the earthquake under the sixth seal, this one produces what appears to be repentance. To fear and give glory to God means to repent and worship God in John's language (cf. 14:7; 15:4; 16:9).

The vision represents the church being under persecution and seemingly the world being victorious over the church. The witnesses represent the apostles and prophets of the New Testament. As the two witnesses are killed and lay dead in the street, we visualize the church being defeated by the worldly powers. However, that is only the physical picture, the divine picture is that God's church will be victorious. God will revive his people and they will stand vindicated for His cause after the period of persecution.

This concludes the interlude. We have seen a message of divine retribution, there is to be no more delay (10:1-7); God's message of judgment is to be proclaimed in all its bitterness (10:8-11); God's people are known and protected by Him (11:1-2); and there will be a strong witness of the gospel during the period of distress just ahead. When it is over, Christianity will have been thoroughly vindicated in the sight of men (11:3-13).

I. The Seventh Trumpet: The Third Woe, 11:14-19

[14]The second woe is past; behold, the third woe is coming quickly.

[15]Then the seventh angel sounded; and there were loud voices in heaven, saying,

"The kingdom of the world has become the kingdom of our Lord and of His Christ; and He will reign forever and ever."

[16]And the twenty-four elders, who sit on their thrones before God, fell on their faces and worshiped God, [17]saying,

"We give You thanks, O Lord God, the Almighty, who are and who were, because You have taken Your great power and have begun to reign. [18]"And the nations were enraged, and Your wrath came, and the time came for the dead to be judged, and the time to reward Your bond-servants the prophets and the saints and those who fear Your name, the small and the great, and to destroy those who destroy the earth."

[19]And the temple of God which is in heaven was opened; and the ark of His covenant appeared in His temple, and there were flashes of lightning and sounds and peals of thunder and an earthquake and a great hailstorm.

11:14 The second woe is past; behold, the third woe is coming quickly.

The interlude then closes with these words, "The second woe is past; behold, the third woe is coming quickly." This statement serves as a transition between the second and third woes. The events of 9:13 to 11:14 fall under the sixth trumpet and are called the second woe. Further judgments are mentioned in this chapter and it is only natural that the third woe would take place under the seventh judgment (11:15-19).

The woes were introduced by an eagle crying, "Woe, woe, woe to those who dwell on the earth, because of the remaining blasts of the trumpet of the three angels who are about to sound" (8:13). When the judgments of God are on the earth, the righteous are given assurance that truth will reign victorious over evil. God is in control and His cause will prevail. The third woe, in which "the mystery of God . . . will be fulfilled" is about to sound.

11:15 Then the seventh angel sounded; and there were loud voices in heaven, saying, "The kingdom of the world has become *the kingdom* of our Lord and of His Christ; and He will reign forever and ever." 16 And the twenty-four elders, who sit on their thrones before God, fell on their faces and worshiped God, 17 saying, "We give You thanks, O Lord God, the Almighty, who are and who were, because You have taken Your great power and have begun to reign. 18 "And the nations were enraged, and Your wrath came, and the time *came* for the dead to be judged, and *the time* to reward Your bond-servants the prophets and the saints and those who fear Your name, the small and the great, and to destroy those who destroy the earth." 19 And the temple of God which is in heaven was opened; and the ark of His covenant appeared in His temple, and there were flashes of lightning and sounds and peals of thunder and an earthquake and a great hailstorm.

The Third Woe is the Seventh Trumpet. With the sounding of this trumpet we will see the answer to the cry from the souls under the altar (6:9-10). The judgment is one brought upon Rome because of her ungodliness. It is not the final judgment but signals the completion of God's mystery which was looked for and sought for by God's prophets.

A song is sung as the seventh angel sounds. This is a song of victory of the kingdom. The voices cry, "The kingdom of the world has become the kingdom of our Lord and of His Christ, and He will reign forever and ever" (v. 15). This victory song indicates that we know the outcome of the battle before it is ever fought. God's purposes will be accomplished. Evil will not win; good will be victorious. God can call things that are not as though they were (cf. Rom. 4:17b). In response to these voices, the twenty-four elders fall on their faces from their thrones and worship God in a song of praise for God's righteous judgment.

When the song is completed, God's temple in heaven was opened and John sees the sacred chest of God's covenant, indicating God is a covenant God and will keep His covenants.

NOTES

[1]Robert H. Mounce, *The Book of Revelation*, 227.

Revelation 12

VII. THE CONFLICT BETWEEN GOD AND SATAN, 12:1-13:18

With chapter twelve our study begins to unfold the last half of the book of Revelation. Beginning with chapter four, we have been seeing in vision after vision a struggle between the church and the Roman Empire. It is the struggle between the anti-Christian forces (i.e., the Roman government and the false religions) and the church. We will now see the same theme presented with a deeper meaning. That is to say, the real struggle is not between the church and Rome, but between Christ and Satan. It is a struggle between good and evil.

In this lesson there will be seen four different characters which represent the anti-Christian forces at work: the dragon, the beast which comes up out of the sea, the beast which comes up out of the earth, and Babylon.

In this section there are five battles. We will observe each battle as it occurs and try to find its significance. Chapter twelve has three major figures: the woman, the child, and the dragon. There are also three scenes; the birth of the child (vv. 1-6), the expulsion of the dragon (vv. 7-12), and the attack of the dragon on the woman and the rest of her seed (vv. 13-17).

A. Battle One: The Woman and Her Child, 12:1-6

[1]A great sign appeared in heaven: a woman clothed with the sun, and the moon under her feet, and on her head a crown of twelve stars; [2]and she was with child; and she cried out, being in labor and in pain to give birth. [3]Then another sign appeared in heaven: and behold, a great red dragon having seven heads and ten horns, and on his heads *were* seven diadems. [4]And his tail swept away a third of the stars of heaven and threw them to the earth. And the dragon stood before the woman who was about to give birth, so that when she gave birth he might devour her child. [5]And she gave birth to a son, a male *child*, who is to rule all the nations with a rod of iron; and her child was caught up to God and to His throne. [6]Then the woman fled into the wilderness where she had a place prepared by God, so that there she would be nourished for one thousand two hundred and sixty days.

This section begins with the words "A great sign appeared in heaven" (i.e., from heaven's viewpoint). The word for "sign" is the word *sēmeion* and occurs seven times in this book. Three times it refers to special revelations from God (12:1, 3, 15:1), and four times to deceptions imposed by Satan's helpers (13:13, 14; 16:14; 19:20).

This battle pictures the birth and glory of Christ and the eternal struggle which continues with the people of God. There are four main characters in this chapter: the woman, who symbolizes the people of God under both covenants (cf. Isa. 50:1; 54:1; Hos. 2:1; Eph. 5:32);

the Dragon, who symbolizes Satan (v. 9); the male child represents the Christ (v. 5, the one who is to rule the nations with a rod of iron); and, finally, there are those described as "the rest of her children" (v. 17) who represent the children of God on earth (i.e., the church).

The first thing we see is a radiant woman who is pregnant and crying out in pain for she is about to give birth. The woman is clothed with the sun to indicate her brightness and glory (cf. Ps. 89:36), and the moon is at her feet, to indicate the relationship she sustained to the moon (cf. Ezra 3:5; Neh. 10:33; Ps. 81:3). She has a crown of twelve stars on her head (Gen. 37:9-11) and she is about to give birth. The crown is a victor's crown (*stephanos*, cf. 2:10; 3:11; 4:4, 10; 6:2; 9:7; 14:14).

The woman represents the faithful of Israel in the Old Testament; i.e., the spiritual remnant of God's people who have kept covenant with him. Micah prophesied of this when he wrote, "Be in pain, and labor to bring forth, O daughter of Zion, like a woman in travail; for now shalt thou go forth out of the city, and shalt dwell in the field, and shalt come even unto Babylon: there shalt thou be rescued; there will Jehovah redeem thee from the hand of thine enemies" (Micah 4:10, ASV). According to Micah, the nation would be given up until the time that the remnant, the daughter of Zion, brought forth one who would be ruler in Israel; i.e., the Messiah-King, for whom the people looked (Micah 5:2). That is to say, God used the nation of Israel (i.e., the remnant) to bring the Christ in to the world. But the imagery also changes and the woman comes to represent all of God's people; her children are those "who keep the commandments of God, and hold to the testimony of Jesus" (v. 17).

Next, we see an enormous red dragon that has seven heads and ten horns and seven crowns upon his head. The dragon is identified in verse nine as, "the serpent of old who is called the devil and Satan, who deceives the whole world."

Why is the dragon chosen as a symbol? In the Old Testament there are numerous passages which speak of the serpent or dragon under various names: Leviathan or Lotan or Rahab (a variant of *Tiamat*, an allied form of which *tehom*, is the Hebrew word for "deep" or abyss). Among the Hebrews what had been seen as myth among the Semitic culture has become a reality. This figure is then used in typological language to identify historical enemies of Israel with the ancient enemy which the Lord had "slain and cut to pieces at creation." Thus Jeremiah had compared Nebuchadnezzar to the monster (*tannin*) who had swallowed Israel (Jer. 51:34,44), and Ezekiel had identified Pharaoh, king of Egypt, as "the great sea monster (*tannin*) that lies in the midst of his rivers" (Ezek. 29:3), and as the dragon *Rahab* (Isa. 30:7). The slaying of the dragon was repeated as God overcame Babylon once more and prepared a way in the waters for Israel's return to Zion (Isa. 27:1; 51:9-11).

The seven heads refers either to his intelligence, or to the fact that he has authority in this realm. The crowns which the dragon wears are not to be confused with the crowns worn by the redeemed. The victory crown, which belongs to the overcomer (cf. Revelation 2-3) is the *stephanos*; this crown is *diadēma*, that is "diadem." The word "diadema" occurs three times in the book of Revelation (12:3; 13:1; 19:12) and nowhere else in the New Testament. The diadem originated with the Persians and signified royalty. In two of these instances it is used to designate Satan or those associated with him (12:1; 13:1). The last reference is to Christ, exercising royal rule as "King of kings and Lord of lords" (19:12-16). In time it came to designate the royal headdress of a monarch, ornamented with gold and jewels. These seven diadems are the adornment of royalty or kingship (cf. Isa. 62:3). These are indeed royal crowns to illustrate his complete authority as one who is king (cf. 9:11, "they have as king over them..."). He is the "ruler of demons" (Matt. 12:24). Satan is in control of his wicked kingdom and has servants who obey him (cf. Matt. 25:41; 1 Cor. 6:3; 2 Cor. 11:4-15; 2 Pet. 2:4; Jude 6, 13).

He has ten horns on his head. Horns are consistently used in Scripture to refer to power (Deut. 33:17; Ps. 18:2; 1 Kgs. 22:11). As this figure is developed later in the book, the ten horns are identified as ten kings (cf. 17:7, 12) which have the power of the beast.

The great red dragon is so enormous that with one swoop of his tail he knocks out one-third of the stars out of the sky and hurls them to the earth. Reminiscent of the first four trumpets, one-third of the stars of heaven are cast out of the sky and hurled to the earth. This indicates the power and might of the dragon.

He is standing in front of the woman. His concern, however, is not with the woman, but with her child. He wants to devour the child when he is born. The woman gives birth to a male child but the child is snatched up to God and his throne, and the woman flees into the desert where she is nourished for 1,260 days.

The thought brought to mind is not of Mary giving birth to Jesus, but the entire period of time from the child's birth until He ascended to heaven (cf. Matt. 26:64; Acts 2:33-34; Eph. 1:20-23; Heb. 1:3, 13; 8:1; 10:12; 12:2; 1 Pet. 3:22). The whole experience of his being caught up was not simply for his protection, but for his rule (cf. Ps. 2:6-9; 45:6; Heb. 1:8).

The wilderness to which the woman flees is a place of hiding, an uninhabited area. This is a place of safety, discipline, and testing. There she is fed 1,260 days (which corresponds to forty-two months [11:2], or time, times, and half a time [12:14]). While all these expressions are similar in length, it is not to be thought that they are identical. The 42 months refers to the period of oppression of the Holy City and the time of the authority of the beast (11:2; 13:5). A time and times and half a time" seems to be synonymous with 1,260 days during which the woman will be protected in the desert (12:4). The woman's flight into the wilderness reminds us of the nation of Israel in the wilderness wanderings where the people were protected by God; and would naturally recall the prophet Elijah who was sustained by God in the wilderness when his life was sought by Jezebel (cf. 1 Kgs. 17:2ff; 19:4ff). First century readers, familiar with these events, would be reminded that they are "strangers and exiles on the earth" whose true home is in heaven (Heb. 11:13-16). While here, they are nurtured by God as He supplies their every need "according to his riches in glory in Christ Jesus" (Phil. 4:19).

B. Battle Two: The War in Heaven, 12:7-9

[7]And there was war in heaven, Michael and his angels waging war with the dragon. The dragon and his angels waged war, [8]and they were not strong enough, and there was no longer a place found for them in heaven. [9]And the great dragon was thrown down, the serpent of old who is called the devil and Satan, who deceives the whole world; he was thrown down to the earth, and his angels were thrown down with him.

The scene now changes. Satan and his angels do battle with Michael and his angels. It is not a real battle in heaven, but a real battle seen in a vision to teach us some spiritual truth.

Michael, the one who leads the army of God in the vision is called Michael. His name means "Who is like God?" He is mentioned three times in the book of Daniel as "one of the chief princes" (10:13), "your [Israel's] prince" (10:21), and "the great prince" (12:1), who stood for the people of God against their enemies. In the New Testament (Jude 6) he is called "the archangel" and contends with the devil over the body of Moses (Jude 9). Some also think he is the archangel mentioned in 1 Thessalonians 4:16.

Dragon — Satan is no longer seen as a dragon, slashing and sweeping stars out of the heaven; he is now seen as a warrior. The fivefold description of Satan in verse nine is: Devil, Satan, Great Dragon, that Ancient Serpent, and the one "who leads the whole world astray" (ASV, the deceiver of the whole world).

The battle is not a specific battle but represents the long and continuous battle between good and evil. The casting down of the dragon to the earth does not mean that there had been no evil influence on earth prior to that time. The influence of evil began in the Garden of Eden and can be traced throughout biblical history. The climactic moment arrives as the devil is defeated and cast out of heaven. An event of crucial importance had taken place in history, namely the death of Christ on the cross. He and his followers had been dealt a severe setback.

This expulsion from heaven is directly associated with and follows after the completion of the mission of redemption of the male child on earth (cf. v. 5). The purpose of the incarnation was to make an attack on Satan's kingdom. When Christ spoke of the casting out of demons by himself and his disciples, he viewed it as Satan falling from heaven (Luke 10:17f). His dying for the sins of the world brought judgment upon this world and the ruler of this world was cast out (cf. John 12:31). Christ came into the world (1) to destroy him who has the power of death, that is, the devil; and (2) to deliver all those who through fear of death were subject to lifelong bondage (Heb. 2:14). "When He had disarmed the rulers and authorities, He made a public display of them, having triumphed over them through Him" (Col. 2:15). This disbarment of Satan is reflected in language in the Gospel of John. Jesus was innocent but had no illusions about who his real accuser was. He said, "I will not speak much more with you, for the ruler of this world is coming, and he has nothing in me" (John 14:30, cf. also John 16:11).

While the battle is announced, we never see the fight. We are only told the outcome and that is that Satan and his angels are hurled to the earth, i.e., they are defeated.

C. Interlude: Battle Song of Triumph, 12:10-12

[10]Then I heard a loud voice in heaven, saying, "Now the salvation, and the power, and the kingdom of our God and the authority of His Christ have come, for the accuser of our brethren has been thrown down, he who accuses them before our God day and night. [11]"And they overcame him because of the blood of the Lamb and because of the word of their testimony, and they did not love their life even when faced with death. [12]"For this reason, rejoice, O heavens and you who dwell in them. Woe to the earth and the sea, because the devil has come down to you, having great wrath, knowing that he has *only* a short time."

A voice from heaven speaks with a loud voice the cry of triumph. Satan is overcome. "Now the salvation, and the power, and the kingdom of our God and the authority of His Christ have come." The fulfillment of the coming of Christ is found in his death, burial, and resurrection. This victory song presents the fact that the work of Christ has been conclusively demonstrated. He is victorious and has established his power as the Anointed One. The one who has been accusing our brethren, day and night, "has been cast down."

Instead of overcoming the ones he slanders, the ones he slanders overcome him. His accusations rebound against him. The victory, however, is not of their own doing. The reasons for their overcoming are given as: 1) because of the blood of the Lamb (1 Pet. 1:18-19; Acts 20:28), 2) the word of their testimony (Acts 5:3) and they did not love their lives so much as to shrink from death (Rev. 2:10; 1 Cor. 15).

Defeated but not destroyed, the devil and his forces now turn to the earth to wreak havoc upon the people of God. This is seen in the woe pronounced on the earth and sea, because the devil knows that he only has a short time; a time related to the 1,260 days of verse 6. Paul's triumphant words of Romans 8:31-34 are appropriate here.

D. Battle Three: The War on Earth against the Woman and Her Seed, 12:13-17

[13]And when the dragon saw that he was thrown down to the earth, he persecuted the woman who gave birth to the male child. [14]But the two wings of the great eagle were given to the woman, so that she could fly into the wilderness to her place, where she was nourished for a time and times and half a time, from the presence of the serpent. [15]And the serpent poured water like a river out of his mouth after the woman, so that he might cause her to be swept away with the flood. [16]But the earth helped the woman, and the earth opened its mouth and drank up the river which the dragon poured out of his mouth. [17]So the dragon was enraged with the woman, and went off to make war with the rest of her children, who keep the commandments of God and hold to the testimony of Jesus.

12:13 And when the dragon saw that he was thrown down to the earth, he persecuted the woman who gave birth to the male *child.*

The following picture helps us understand a little

more about how the woman was cared for in the first battle. Having missed the male child he was waiting to destroy, the devil now turns toward the woman and begins to pursue her. He intends to destroy her. But, she is given two wings of a great eagle so she could fly to the desert to be cared for and be out of the serpent's reach. It is here that the identity of the woman changes to that of the church, whose members endure the dragon's persecution.

12:14 But the two wings of the great eagle were given to the woman, so that she could fly into the wilderness to her place, where she was nourished for a time and times and half a time, from the presence of the serpent.

When God delivered the children of Israel from Pharaoh's threats, He said, "I bore you on eagles' wings, and brought you to Myself" (Exod. 19:4; cf. Deut. 32:11). The psalmist asserted, "And children of men take refuge in the shadow of Your wings" (Ps. 36:7). Later, the prophet Isaiah captured this significance when he wrote, "Yet those who wait for the LORD will gain new strength; they will mount up with wings like eagles" (Isa. 40:31).

12:15 And the serpent poured water like a river out of his mouth after the woman, so that he might cause her to be swept away with the flood.

As the woman flees, out of the mouth of the serpent comes water like a river to overtake the woman and drown her. The idea of floods threatening to engulf God's people was not new. It is found repeatedly throughout the prophets and Psalms (cf. Isa. 8:5-8; 34:2; Ps. 32:6; 69:1-2; 124:2-5). The river by which the dragon tries to sweep the woman away is said to be "delusions in the form of lies, false impressions of invincible power, false religious teachings, false philosophies, false charges, and malicious reports intended to destroy the church."[1] But, whatever we take this to be, we can be assured that its significance would not be exhausted to events in John's day.

12:16 But the earth helped the woman, and the earth opened its mouth and drank up the river which the dragon poured out of his mouth. 17 So the dragon was enraged with the woman, and went off to make war with the rest of her children, who keep the commandments of God and hold to the testimony of Jesus.

But the earth swallows up the water and the woman is saved. The dragon then is enraged and goes off to make war with the rest of the woman's offspring. These offspring are identified as those who keep God's commandments and hold to the testimony of Jesus. Paul writes of this when he speaks of our warfare against the dragon in Ephesians 6:10ff. Consequently, the dragon's rage extends to "the rest of her children." As the power of the gospel spreads from Jerusalem, Judea, Samaria, and to the ends of the earth (Acts 1:8), the hostility between the woman's seed and the dragon and his followers become more and more apparent. The age-old hostility, then, continues even to this day between Satan and those "who keep the commandments of God and hold to the testimony of Jesus."

In chapter twelve there were two main figures: the woman and the dragon. They demonstrate to us the deeper, inner struggle against good and evil; against the Lord and Satan. The battle was mentioned and the victor was announced — Christ and his followers. The devil is defeated more than once in the scenes in chapter twelve: once in heaven, and once on earth. This should be comforting to the children of God. They can know, and rest assured, that their enemy is defeated. The dragon was unsuccessful in devouring the baby of the woman, in defeating the woman, and when he wars with Michael and his angels, he is also defeated.

Again and again, he loses. This angers him greatly and, instead of accepting his defeat, he turns to wage war against the "rest of her children" (i.e., the community of believers — the church). In the following chapter John introduces two allies of the dragon who assist in his warfare. They are formidable foes and present a strength that must be reckoned with.

NOTES

[1]Homer Hailey, *Revelation: An Introduction and Commentary*, 279.

Revelation 13

E. Battle Four: The Sea Beast, 13:1-10

[1]And the dragon stood on the sand of the seashore. Then I saw a beast coming up out of the sea, having ten horns and seven heads, and on his horns were ten diadems, and on his heads were blasphemous names.

[2]And the beast which I saw was like a leopard, and his feet were like those of a bear, and his mouth like the mouth of a lion. And the dragon gave him his power and his throne and great authority. [3]I saw one of his heads as if it had been slain, and his fatal wound was healed. And the whole earth was amazed and followed after the beast; [4]they worshiped the dragon because he gave his authority to the beast; and they worshiped the beast, saying, "Who is like the beast, and who is able to wage war with him?"

[5]There was given to him a mouth speaking arrogant words and blasphemies, and authority to act for forty-two months was given to him. [6]And he opened his mouth in blasphemies against God, to blaspheme His name and His tabernacle, that is, those who dwell in heaven. [7]It was also given to him to make war with the saints and to overcome them, and authority over

every tribe and people and tongue and nation was given to him. [8]All who dwell on the earth will worship him, everyone whose name has not been written from the foundation of the world in the book of life of the Lamb who has been slain.

[9]If anyone has an ear, let him hear.

[10]If anyone is destined for captivity, to captivity he goes; if anyone kills with the sword, with the sword he must be killed. Here is the perseverance and the faith of the saints.

13:1 And the dragon stood on the sand of the seashore. Then I saw a beast coming up out of the sea, having ten horns and seven heads, and on his horns *were* ten diadems, and on his heads *were* blasphemous names. 2 And the beast which I saw was like a leopard, and his feet were like *those* of a bear, and his mouth like the mouth of a lion. And the dragon gave him his power and his throne and great authority.

John sees a beast coming out of the sea. The ancient Hebrews were an agricultural people, not sea people. They viewed the sea as an awesome and fearful part of creation where storms and destructive forces came from. The voice of the Lord is seen in a storm by the psalmist David (Ps. 29). Isaiah compares the sea to the turbulence of the nations (cf. Isa. 60:5). Jeremiah describes the many people over which Babylon ruled "you who dwell by many waters" (Jer. 51:13). "The sea has come up over Babylon; She has been engulfed with its tumultuous waves" (Jer. 51:42). Ezekiel compares many nations to the sea and its waves as they came up against Tyre (Ezek. 26:3).

In the book of Revelation, the sea: (1) refers to a part of creation (5:13; 10:6; 14:7); (2) describes the limits of the angel's voice (7:1-3); (3) represents the transcendence of God [i.e., separation of God from others]; and, (4) symbolizes the whole of society known at the time (8:8f; 10:2, 8; 12:12; 31:1; 20:13; 21:1).

To better understand this vision one must go to Daniel 7. Daniel sees four winds of heaven "stirring up the great sea" (v. 2). From out of this sea arises four beasts, different from one another. The beasts are identified as four kings [kingdoms] (Dan. 7:17, 23). This would indicate that the sea represents human societies or nations from which these kings (kingdoms) come.

The composite of the sea beast of Revelation 13 with its seven heads, ten horns, blasphemous names, and features of the leopard, bear, and lion are like that of Daniel 7:1-8. In Daniel 7 the beast represents a "kingdom" (i.e., "historical empire"). The word "beast" occurs several times in the book of Revelation (11:7; 14:9, 11; 15:2; 16:2, 10, 13; 19:19-20; 20:4, 10 [excluding the references to the scarlet colored beast in chapter 17]). In 11:7 the beast rises from the abyss. Revelation 19:19 refers to a coalition of the beast with the "kings of the earth" and 19:20 describes his final end in the lake of fire.

John wants the picture of the beast to evoke images of Rome and her emperors in the imaginations of his readers, especially Nero, the first emperor to persecute the church. This will be more clearly identified in chapter 17 when we see the picture of a woman (great harlot) who is sitting on the beast. The woman is identified as "the great city, which reigns over the kings of the earth" (17:18). The dragon had seven heads and ten horns, but the diadems were on his head; here, the diadems are on the beast's horns. The seven heads are the seven hills of Rome, as well as the seven "kings." Plainly stated, they are Augustus, Tiberius, Caligula (Gaius), Claudius, Nero, Vespasian and Titus. In 17:10, five are fallen (Augustus, Tiberius, Caligula, Claudius and Nero). One is, that would be Vespasian, and one is yet to come, and would be Titus. When he comes, he must continue for a little while; Titus ruled two years. Jim McGuiggan charts it in this manner:[1]

In Daniel	In Revelation	
1. Augustus	1. Augustus	These would
2. Tiberius	2. Tiberius	be the five
3. Caligula	3. Caligula	that are
4. Claudius	4. Claudius	fallen,
5. Nero	5. Nero	17:10
6. Galba*		
7. Otho*		
8. Vitellius*		
9. Vespasian	6. Vespasian	
10. Titus	7. Titus	
11. Domitian	8. Domitian	

[Vespasian would be the one that "is," 17:10. Titus, the other is to come and abide a little, 17:10]

[*the three uprooted **and** the three ignored by John]

John presents the heads as kings (Rev. 17:10). Daniel presents the horns as kings (Dan. 7:24). In Daniel, three kings are uprooted by the eleventh king now become an eighth (Dan. 7:24). John takes the vision from Daniel as he finds it with three missing (17:11). In other words, the three uprooted in Daniel are ignored by John (Galba, Otho, and Vitellius). Who is the fourth beast in Daniel? It is Rome, and if our parallel is correct, so is the beast of Revelation 13.

The "heads of blasphemy" indicates the irreverent attitude toward God and all that is sacred. This image is repeated in 17:3. Arrogance and blasphemy also characterize the "little horn" in Daniel's fourth beast (Dan. 7:8, 11, 20, 25) and the willful king of Daniel 11:36.

The power, throne, and authority which this beast exercises are given to him by the dragon. Though seen as defeated and cast down (ch. 12) Satan continues to rule in his evil kingdom. As the Lamb received power, throne, and authority to carry out the purpose of God, so also the sea beast is given power, throne, and authority by which to wage his war.

13:3 *I saw* one of his heads as if it had been slain, and his fatal wound was healed. And the whole earth was amazed *and followed* after the beast;

The beast has a fatal wound, but the wound is healed. This wounded "head" is referred to elsewhere in the chapter as a wound of the whole beast (cf. vv. 12, 14). The slain head possibly refers to Nero. With him the beast lived, and in his death the beast died. But, the death stroke was healed.

The head being "wounded" and then healed is often referred to as the legend of *Nero redivivus*. Nero died in A.D. 68 but many people refused to believe that he was actually dead. The legend was that he had gone to live among the Parthians and would soon return as the head of the Parthian army to destroy Rome. Some of the Jews took comfort in the fact that Nero's return would be the way Rome would be punished for the fall of Jerusalem (*Sibylline Oracles* 4:119, 138; 5:143ff., 362ff). Whether the legend had merit or not, John seems to expect the persecuting policy of Nero to be revived under another emperor as it was under Domitian. Tertullian writes, "Consult your histories; you will there find that Nero was the first who assailed with the imperial sword the Christian sect . . . Domitian, too, a man of Nero's type in cruelty, tried his hand at persecution" (*Apology*, ch. 5).

The word for "wound" is the Greek word *plēgē* and means "plague." The word is used in the book of Revelation to refer to a divinely inflicted judgment (9:18,20; 11:6; 15:1ff; 16:9,21; 18:4,8; 21:9; 22:18). In 13:14 the beast has the plague of the "sword." In the book of Revelation the "sword" (*machaira*, or *rhomphaia*) refers: (1) symbolically to the divine judgment, 1:16; 2:12, 16; 19:15, 21; (2) is the sword of the rider on the red horse and equals divine judgment, 6:4, 8; (3) is used as a weapon against the saints of God, 13:10. The sword is the symbol of God's wrath that in some event had struck a death blow to the authority of the beast (and the dragon), yet which had been deceptively covered up or restored.

There are many as ten different interpretations that have been given to this passage. What is this "death stroke" or "fatal wound" to which John refers? Homer Hailey says there are only three that are worthy of consideration. (1) The death stroke administered to one of the heads was the resurrection, ascension, and coronation of Christ, which stunned the beast until the church had gained a sound foothold in the world; (2) the seven heads are seven heathen or anti-God powers which had arisen and would arise in opposition to God and His people; (3) the death stroke is the death of Nero, the first emperor to persecute the church, whose policy of persecution was revived by Domitian, in whom "the death-stroke was healed."

He then writes,

> . . . the third is preferable. The death of Nero dealt a severe blow to the empire, which was immediately thrown into a two-year state of anarchy and confusion. Order was restored by Vespasian of the Flavian family. But to the church, which is John's interest, the healing of the death-stroke came with the revival of persecution under Domitian. Tacitus points out that after Nero's death there were various rumors that the return of the tyrant was at hand, whereupon pretenders arose claiming to be the deceased emperor (*His. II.8*). Suetonius, another early Roman historian, writes that after Nero's death friends circulated his edicts, "Presenting he was still alive and would soon return to confound his enemies"; he tells of one in particular who came forward claiming to be Nero (*Nero, 57*).[2]

There is a parallel here in some respects to what has already been seen in chapter twelve. In chapter twelve the dragon is defeated and cast out of heaven. On the other hand, he still has time and ability to wage a relentless war against the people of God. In chapter thirteen the sea beast is dealt a "fatal wound" but still has full use of his abilities to wage war (v. 7).

13:4 they worshiped the dragon because he gave his authority to the beast; and they worshiped the beast, saying, "Who is like the beast, and who is able to wage war with him?"

The beast seems so invincible that the people worship the beast and the dragon who had invested the beast with his authority. The point is that whoever worships the beast, is really worshiping the dragon. Since the beast represents the Roman Empire, the worship paid to him is directed to the empire's great strength. In rendering homage to the emperor the world was worshiping the one who had given his authority to the Roman power. This worship is the counterpart to the worship of the one true and living God. Rome was now displaying unbelievable power and was giving the people what the gods had failed to give — worldly wealth, glory, and influence.

13:5 There was given to him a mouth speaking arrogant words and blasphemies, and authority to act for forty-two months was given to him.

The similarity of this creature with the one of Daniel 7:1-8, helps us in our identification. Without losing sight of the vision one important point is that this beast is given power, throne, and great authority from the dragon. Whatever else may puzzle us we need to remember that whoever this sea beast represents, it is in cooperation with the dragon. The power the beast exercises astonishes the whole world and men worship both the dragon and the beast asking, "Who is like the beast? Who can make war against him?" (vv. 4, 8).

The beast speaks blasphemies and exercises authority for forty-two months and slanders the name of God and those who live in heaven. The arrogance of the beast in speaking blasphemies is not that difficult to document. Suetonius[3] mentions how Domitian was known for his arrogance and claims to be deity. This is arrogance and blasphemy with a vengeance. You would think from what John says that the beast would last a long time. Instead, we read that he was given authority to act for only forty-two months. The period of forty-two months is mentioned four times in the book of Revelation and once in the book of Daniel. The passages are as follows:

1. The period of the holy city being trodden under foot, 11:2.
2. The period during which the witnesses prophesy, 11:3.
3. The period the Woman is nourished in the wilderness, 12:6, 14.
4. The period of the beast's authority, 13:5.
5. The period the "little horn" persecutes the saints, Dan. 7:25.

The forty-two months (1,260 days, three and one-half years, or in Daniel's case, the "time, times, and half a time") is not a period of time, but a state of affairs in which the saints are persecuted but also protected. They are subject to suffering but are sustained. This is the time of the beast's authority and blasphemies. It is a time of Roman persecution, a period of oppression and trials for the children of God.

He makes war against the saints and conquers them and is given authority over every tribe, people, language and nation. Such an overpowering picture calls for patient endurance and faithfulness on the part of the saints (cf. 13:10b).

13:6 And he opened his mouth in blasphemies against God, to blaspheme His name and His tabernacle, *that is*, those who dwell in heaven.

To blaspheme God also implies the blasphemy of His tabernacle and those who dwell in heaven. This is a way of referring to the church of the living God. Christians are those whose citizenship is in heaven (Phil. 3:20) and who sit with Christ in the heavenly places (Eph. 2:6). The idea of God dwelling in His people and His people in Him is confirmed throughout the Scriptures (cf. 1 John 1:1-2; 2:24, 27; 3:6, 24).

13:7 It was also given to him to make war with the saints and to overcome them, and authority over every tribe and people and tongue and nation was given to him.

The beast is given authority to make war with the saints and overcome them, but only for the time that God permitted. The outward impression is that the beast will be victorious, but the victory is short lived. Remember, the beast made war against the two witnesses, but that was only for a moment (11:7, 12). Of the little horn, Daniel says, "I kept looking, and that horn was waging war with the saints and overpowering them until the Ancient of Days came, and judgment was passed in favor of the saints of the Highest One, and the time arrived when the saints took possession of the kingdom" (Dan. 7:21-22). The "little horn" of Daniel's vision represents the persecuting element of the Roman emperors.

The beast in John's vision is the fourth of Daniel's vision. He is brought to an end through the judgment executed by the Lamb, in which the beast is cast into the lake of fire (19:19ff). The authority was over all the earth (i.e., "every tribe and people and tongue and nation"). They were from among whose from whom the redeemed had been purchased (5:9) and out of which came the great multitude standing before the throne of God (7:9). They were the ones who looked upon the dead bodies of the two witnesses and did not allow them to be buried (11:9).

13:8 All who dwell on the earth will worship him, *everyone* whose name has not been written from the foundation of the world in the book of life of the Lamb who has been slain. 9 If anyone has an ear, let

him hear. 10 If anyone *is destined* for captivity, to captivity he goes; if anyone kills with the sword, with the sword he must be killed. Here is the perseverance and the faith of the saints.

The contrast is between "all who dwell on the earth" (i.e., unbelievers) with "those who dwell in heaven" (i.e., believers). Saints are known because their names are written in the Lamb's book of life. This simply refers to a list of the saved. Those whose names are not written in the Lamb's book of life give worship to the beast; those whose names are written there do not.

Whether the reference is to the "names written in the Lamb's book of life" modifies "from the foundation of the world" or "the Lamb who has been slain" refers to "from the foundation of the world," makes no practical difference. In either case the reference is to God's simple foreknowledge.

"If anyone has ears to hear" reminds us of similar words through the letters to the seven churches of Asia (chs. 2-3).

"If anyone is destined for captivity" seems pointless in one sense, but in fact it conveys a message of profound significance for the Lord's people. Jeremiah declared, "And it shall be that when they say to you, 'Where should we go?' then you are to tell them, 'Thus says the LORD: "Those destined for death, to death; And those destined for the sword, to the sword; And those destined for famine, to famine; And those destined for captivity, to captivity"'" (Jer. 15:2). The context of this passage is one of judgment for which an apostate people and a godless nation are destined and from which there will be no escape. In John's passage, the reference is to the people of God, giving them assurance that through all their suffering, they have nothing to fear. Those who face captivity or sword may be sure that it is in accord with his plan. Trust in God. Allow Him to work things out for his good pleasure.

John closes this part of the vision with words of encouragement in referring to the "perseverance and faith of the saints."

F. Battle Five: The Earth Beast, 13:11-18

[11]Then I saw another beast coming up out of the earth; and he had two horns like a lamb and he spoke as a dragon. [12]He exercises all the authority of the first beast in his presence. And he makes the earth and those who dwell in it to worship the first beast, whose fatal wound was healed. [13]He performs great signs, so that he even makes fire come down out of heaven to the earth in the presence of men. [14]And he deceives those who dwell on the earth because of the signs which it was given him to perform in the presence of the beast, telling those who dwell on the earth to make an image to the beast who had the wound of the sword and has come to life. [15]And it was given to him to give breath to the image of the beast, so that the image of the beast would even speak and cause as many as do not worship the image of the beast to be killed. [16]And he causes all, the small and the great, and the rich and the poor, and the free men and the slaves, to be given a mark on their right hand or on their forehead, [17]and he provides that no one will be able to buy or to sell, except the one who has the mark, either the name of the beast or the number of his name.

[18]Here is wisdom. Let him who has understanding calculate the number of the beast, for the number is that of a man; and his number is six hundred and sixty-six.

Another beast is seen coming out of the earth. He exercises the same authority as the first beast. This beast represents the false religion of the Roman Empire found in the form of emperor worship. He has two horns like a lamb (i.e., he appears or looks innocent) but speaks like a dragon (i.e., devilish). He makes the earth and its inhabitants worship the first beast; that is to say, emperor worship demanded not only a religious obedience, but a civil obedience as well. Commitment to the earth beast (worship of the Emperor) also involved commitment to the sea beast (the civil power of the Roman Empire).

13:11 Then I saw another beast coming up out of the earth; and he had two horns like a lamb and he spoke as a dragon.

The second of these beasts arises to serve the same purpose as the first; viz., to serve the dragon. But they are not of the same source. The first beast "stood on the sand of the seashore"(13:1), this beast comes "up out of the earth" (13:11). The outward appearance of this beast would make one think that he is a cute and innocent creature. He has two horns and looks like a lamb. No one would think of anything fierce when thinking of a lamb. They would think of innocence. But when he speaks, he exposes his true character for he speaks with the voice of the dragon. This awful sound would strike fear in the heart of anyone who heard. But there is probably more involved here than this. The earth beast serves the dragon, the devil, and the devil is a liar from the beginning (cf. John 8:44). The fact that this beast comes up out of the earth indicates that he is fully imbibed with the spirit of the river — lies, false charges, deceits and so forth — which had come out of the dragon's mouth and been swallowed up by the earth (12:16). There will be references to him later as a false prophet (16:13; 19:20; 20:10). This means that this beast is one used by the devil as a means of deceiving and seducing the people. The reference to his looking like a lamb indicates the religious nature of this beast and horns represent power; therefore, here we have the power of the false religion of the Roman Empire. Or, to say it another way, this beast represents the religions of the Roman Empire which are used by the empire to subject the people of its domain to Roman rule. Pagan religions served the empire in an effort to subject the world to the worship of Rome. Images of the Caesar were set up in the pagan temples, and the worshipers of the gods were directed to worship the empire and the emperors. Jesus spoke of false prophets who were inwardly ravenous wolves (Matt. 7:15) and Paul warned of Satan's ministers who "disguise themselves as servants of righteousness" (2 Cor. 11:15).

13:12 He exercises all the authority of the first beast in his presence. And he makes the earth and those who dwell in it to worship the first beast, whose fatal wound was healed.

Notice that this beast is inferior to the first. He is acting under the authority of the first beast. In other words, there is a cooperation between both beasts as they are allies of the dragon. Whatever the second beast wants to do; he is backed up by the first beast. Here we have emperor worship enforced by the imperial power of the sea beast (Rome). Enforcement is carried out by the second beast for earth dwellers to worship the first beast, whose fatal wound was healed. This worship was emphasized under Domitian, in whom the death-stroke was healed.

Here is a picture of Rome in religious clothes. The first beast, the civil persecuting power of Rome is now accompanied by a religious pervert. A Rome whose idea of worship was not to the one true and living God, but to the god of Rome, i.e., the emperor.

13:13 He performs great signs, so that he even makes fire come down out of heaven to the earth in the presence of men.

It is difficult to discern whether the signs (*semeion*) mentioned here are actual miracles that the beast performs or if these are pseudo-signs; i.e., imitations of the real thing. One way the devil works is to imitate the original or the real. The ability of Satan to inspire prophets to perform deceiving miracles is found not only in the book of Revelation but elsewhere in Scripture (Rev. 16:14; 19:20; Deut. 13:1-5; Matt. 7:22; 24:24; Mark 13:22; 2 Thess. 2:9). The challenge before the people of God has always been to distinguish carefully between the true and false spirits (cf. 1 John 4:1-3).

The fire from heaven could have reference to the prophet Elijah calling down fire from heaven (1 Kgs 18:38), or the fire coming down out of the mouths of the two witnesses (Rev. 11:5). John may be intending to present a deliberate contrast between the two witnesses' use of fire and the fire used by the false prophets.

One other theory about this "fire" connects the fire of God with the true word of God and the Holy Spirit's witness at Pentecost (Acts 2). The false fire is seen as a reference to pseudo-charismatic gifts today that create a counterfeit within the community of believers. Much like the magicians who faced Moses in Egypt, duplicating the first three plagues (Exodus 7-8), these pagan priests were magicians who deceived the people with their magical tricks (cf. Acts 8:9-10). The tremendous power of deception is certainly known in the magicians' use of illusions even today. We should also be reminded of Nadab and Abihu (Lev. 10) who offered "unauthorized fire" upon the altar and received as their judgment "fire coming from the presence of the Lord." One thing is certain, the reference to fire being from heaven indicates no mighty deed from God is too hard for these false prophets to mimic as they receive their power from the beast and the dragon.

13:14 And he deceives those who dwell on the earth because of the signs which it was given him to perform in the presence of the beast, telling those who

dwell on the earth to make an image to the beast who had the wound of the sword and has come to life.

The deception of the earth beast is seen in the false signs which he is allowed to do ("given him to perform"). The signs are false signs used by false prophets and should be seen in contrast with the true signs which come from God. A good example of this is seen in Simon's response to the signs of Philip (Acts 8:5-13). When a Roman dignitary and provincial governor within the religious hierarchy met to dedicate a new image of a Caesar in the temple, there would be signs and wonders performed to impress the people. It was a spirit of delusion and deception which continues even to this day.

The people were told, by the second beast, to make an (image) *eikōn* of the first beast. The worship of the first beast, his "image" and his "mark" are inseparable (14:9, 11; 15:2; 16:2; 19:20; 20:4). An *eikōn* was not just a copy but a real representation which took on the reality of the thing represented. In this instance the reference is probably to Domitian; the one who received the death-stroke and lived (vv. 3,12,14).

13:15 And it was given to him to give breath to the image of the beast, so that the image of the beast would even speak and cause as many as do not worship the image of the beast to be killed.

The responsibility of the earth-beast was to give breath (spirit, life) to the image of the emperor. This means that it was the function and obligation of the community to make the Caesar-worship live and speak the mind of the empire. The power of death rested with the religious hierarchy for those who refused to pay homage to "Augustus and Rome." This placed the Christian in a perilous position. A Christian could not say "Caesar is Lord" for to him there was only one Lord, and that was Christ.

This idolatrous satanic system has the power of

death over those who worship the true God and the Lamb. The same "image" tried to kill Daniel and his friends (Daniel 1-7), killed many of the prophets, crucified the Lord, put to death Stephen (Acts 7:60), James (Acts 12:1-2), and Antipas (Rev. 2:13). In doing this, the beast demonstrated the healing of his wound.

13:16 And he causes all, the small and the great, and the rich and the poor, and the free men and the slaves, to be given a mark on their right hand or on their forehead,

God had sealed his people unto himself by impressing His own name and the name of the Lamb upon their foreheads (cf. 7:3; 9:4; 14:1). He has also promised to write His name upon the foreheads of the victors (3:12; 22:4). The beast, then, imitates this with his followers by requiring that all who are loyal to him have etched, engraved or impressed upon their right hand, or upon their forehead, a mark (*charagma*). His "causing" this to be done, means there would be no exceptions. Indeed, "the rich and the poor, the free men and the slaves" alike must receive the mark on their right hand or foreheads.

The question is asked: "What is this mark?" When you compare the passages where the beast, image, mark, and name of the beast are mentioned you will notice that the "mark" is an equivalent expression of the "name of the beast" (13:17; 14:11; also 14:9; 15:2; 16:2; 19:20; 20:4), which is also the "number of his name" (13:17; 15:2).

The Greek word *charagma* is used to refer to a work of art such as a carved image of a god (Acts 17:29) and sometimes to any written inscription or document. It also is used with reference to a snake bite or to a red "seal" of the emperor or other official documents. It was used also used in describing the branding on camels to indicate ownership. But with all this background, there is no evidence of a *charagma* being put on a person, either placed on the right hand or the forehead. Slaves and soldiers received a mark (*sphragis*). But there is no concrete evidence of a person ever receiving a *charagma*. This means we must reject any notion that the emperors placed a mark of any kind on their subjects to indicate their faithfulness. Since the servants of God are said to receive an impress (7:3; 14:1), so the servants of the beast are marked with the stamp of the beast. In other words, the *charagma* is not a literal seal or mark of any kind. It is John's way of symbolically describing authentic ownership and loyalty. In this case, the loyalty is to the beast and Satan.

13:17 and *he provides* that no one will be able to buy or to sell, except the one who has the mark, *either* the name of the beast or the number of his name.

Those who have the *charagma* are able to buy and sell while those without it cannot. No doubt this refers to the economic sanctions which would effect the Christian in the first century world. John had earlier referred to such conditions in the letters to the seven churches when he said of Smyrna that she was "poor" (2:9), and the church in Philadelphia had only a "little strength" (3:8).

13:18 Here is wisdom. Let him who has understanding calculate the number of the beast, for the number is that of a man; and his number is six hundred and sixty-six.

John begins this passage by saying "here is wisdom" and "let him who has understanding . . ." Though difficult, it seems that John wants us to understand. The *charagma* is the name of the beast or the number of his name. He now reveals the number of the beast: his number is 666. There are many scholars who think John's reference here is to an early Hebrew game called *Gematria* which was common among the

Hebrews. The Greeks called it *isopsēphia*. This refers to the use of standard letters corresponding with the alphabet as numerical signs. For example, *alpha* in Greek would represent the number one; *beta* the number two; etc. Through the years commentators have assigned this number (666) to either Nero or Domitian. I would agree with Johnson when he writes,

> . . . none of the key words of v. 18 — name, number, man, 666 — requires the effort to find an emperor (or future political dictator) with a name whose letters will add up to 666. The sheer disagreement and confusion created through the years by the *gematria* method should have long ago warned the church that it was on the wrong track. If John was seeking to illumine believers so that they could penetrate the deception of the beast as well as to contrast the beast and his followers with the Lamb and his followers (14:1ff), he has clearly failed — that is, if he intends for us to play the gematria game. How Nero could fit these requirements is, on closer examination, difficult to see. If some Christians of John's time did succumb to Caesar worship, it was due less to their being deceived than to their fear of death.[4]

NOTES

[1]Jim McGuiggan, *The Book of Revelation* (West Monroe, LA: William C. Johnson, Inc., 1976), 184.

[2]Homer Hailey, *Revelation: An Introduction and Commentary*, 286.

[3]Suetonius, *Lives of the Twelve Caesars*, 354-355.

[4]Alan Johnson, *Book of Revelation*, The Expositor's Bible Commentary, vol. 12, 534.

Revelation 14

VIII. THE FORCES OF THE LAMB, 14:1-20

In chapter 13 we saw two beasts backed by the power of the dragon who formed a great, cruel opposition, against the people of God. From there the scene shifts to a scene of triumphant victory in chapter 14.

The transition takes place from earth to Mt. Zion, as is characteristic of the book. The vision shifts from opposition and persecution to victory and triumph. Chapter 14 is a significant chapter because it shows the forces for righteousness.

In chapter twelve we saw a war against Michael and his angels and the Dragon and his angels. But the forces for the Dragon increased in chapter thirteen with two additions; viz., the sea beast and the earth beast.

The question of significance for us is this: What about the Lamb? Does he stand alone? Is there anyone who fights with him? Chapter 14 is going to provide us with an answer.

A. The Lamb and the Saints, 14:1-5

[1]Then I looked, and behold, the Lamb *was* standing on Mount Zion, and with Him one hundred and forty-four thousand, having His name and the name of His Father written on their foreheads. [2]And I heard a voice from heaven, like the sound of many waters and like the sound of loud thunder, and the voice which I heard *was* like *the sound* of harpists playing on their harps. [3]And they sang a new song before the throne and before the four living creatures and the elders; and no one could learn the song except the one hundred and forty-four thousand who had been purchased from the earth. [4]These are the ones who have not been defiled with women, for they have kept themselves chaste. These *are* the ones who follow the Lamb wherever He goes. These have been purchased from among men as first fruits to God and to the Lamb. [5]And no lie was found in their mouth; they are blameless.

There are three significant divisions in this chapter, each one beginning with the phrase, "and I saw," (found in verses 1, 6, and 14). Over and over and over again John is stating he saw something.

Two questions of importance for us are: (1) What is mount Zion? It is important for us to answer this because it is here the Lamb is standing. (2) Who are the 144,000? Since they are standing with the Lamb, who are they and what is their significance?

Mt. Zion — John sees a Lamb standing, not lying, but standing. Where is he standing? On Mt. Zion. In the Old Testament, Zion is the place from which the Savior and salvation come (cf. Ps. 14:7; Isa. 59:20 and Rom. 11:26). In 2 Samuel 5:7 and 1 Chronicles 11:5 Zion was introduced as a stronghold of the city of David. Psalm 9:11; 135:21; Isaiah 8:18 and Joel 3:17 are passages that indicate that Mount Zion came to represent the dwelling place of Jehovah among His people. The Lamb is seen here in His glory and the place of His glory is Mt. Zion.

There are seven occurrences of Mt. Zion in the New Testament. Matthew and John quote Zechariah 9:9, where Zion is called upon to rejoice at the coming of her king. The reference there is to Jesus' entrance into the city of Jerusalem as fulfilling this prophecy. Both Paul and Peter quote Isaiah 28:16, where God says, "Behold, I am laying in Zion a stone, a tested stone, A costly cornerstone for the foundation, firmly placed. He who believes in it will not be disturbed" (cf. also Rom. 9:33; 1 Pet. 2:6). Paul also quotes Isaiah 59:20 (Rom. 11:26) and says the deliverer will come out of Mt. Zion. In this instance he applies the prophecy to redemption found in Christ. The Hebrews writer sums up the prophecies of Isaiah 2:2-4 and Micah 4:1-8 when he says, "But you have come to mount Zion, and to the city of the living God, the heavenly Jerusalem, and to myriads of angels, to the general assembly and church of the firstborn who are enrolled in heaven, and to God, the Judge of all, and to the spirits of the righteous made perfect, and to Jesus, the mediator of a new covenant, and to the sprinkled blood which speaks better than the blood of Abel" (12:22-24). Here is a picture of the redeemed standing in the presence of Christ; perfected by the blood of the Lamb. The final occurrence of Mt. Zion is in our passage under consideration, Revelation 14:1.

Homer Hailey writes,

As Westcott observes in commenting on Hebrews 12:22, "In a sense the heavenly Jerusalem is already reached: in another sense it is still sought for (13:14)." Here in John's vision, the redeemed have, in one sense, reached Zion, the heavenly Jerusalem pointed to by the prophets. In another sense Zion still lies ahead (21:2). From the relationship of Zion to God in the Old Testament and the prophecies of the Messiah and Zion found there, and from the application of Old Testament prophecies quoted in the New Testament as being fulfilled in Jesus, we conclude that John is not describing a final scene in heaven, but the Zion of the Messiah to which the saints of this dispensation have come. John's use of the definite article *the* Mount Zion, further confirms this view. The scene symbolizes security, permanence, and a victorious spirit of rejoicing enjoyed by the church on earth at any time, because the Lamb is in their midst.[1]

The 144,000. With the Lamb are the 144,000. We have already been introduced to 144,000 before in chapter 7. The 144,000 needed to be sealed by God before four angels were given the authority or permission to exercise their power of destruction that was going to take place on the earth. There is no reason why the 144,000 that are identified in chapter 7 are not similar, if not the same ones that John is seeing here. Who do these 144,000 represent? They represent the victorious and triumphant church on earth.

There are seven characteristics that we know from the book of Revelation about the 144,000. Our purpose here is to see what those characteristics are and use that to assist in identifying who the 144,000 represent. We begin by noticing a characteristic mention earlier in chapter seven. (1) They are sealed by God, 7:1-8. (2) They are purchased out of the earth, 14:3. (3) They sing a new song, 13:3. (4) They are not defiled/virgins, 14:4. (5) They follow the Lamb, 14:4. (6) They are the first fruits unto God and unto the Lamb, 14:4. (7) They are without blemish, 14:5.

Identity for these characteristics is helped with a look at some New Testament passages to help us to see who the 144,000 are: (1) They are sealed by God. In Ephesians 1:13-14 and 2 Corinthians 1:21-23 Paul writes that the Holy Spirit is given to those who are children of God as our seal. (2) Purchased out of the earth. 1 Peter 1:18-19, Revelation 5:9-10, and Acts 20:28

are passages that indicate that the church is composed of those which have been purchased by the precious blood of Jesus Christ. (3) For they are not defiled. Paul writes in 2 Corinthians 11:2 that Christians are presented as pure virgins to Christ. In Ephesians 5:25-32 the church is pictured as the beautiful bride of Christ. (4) Follow the Lamb. In 1 Peter 2:20-21 we are instructed to "follow in His steps" and in John 21 those who are Jesus' disciples are described as lambs following the good shepherd. (5) First fruits. It is said of Christians in James 1:18, "In the exercise of His will He brought us forth by the word of truth, so that we would be a kind of first fruits among His creatures." Hebrews 12:22-23 reads, "But you have come to Mount Zion and to the city of the living God, the heavenly Jerusalem, and to myriads of angels, to the general assembly and church of the firstborn who are enrolled in heaven, and to God, the Judge of all, and to the spirits of the righteous made perfect." (6) Without blemish. In Ephesians 5:27 it is said of the church, "that He might present to Himself the church in all her glory, having no spot or wrinkle or any such thing; but that she should be holy and blameless" (cf. also Col. 1:22-23). (7) Sing a new song. In Revelation 5:9-10 we read, "And they sang a new song, saying, "Worthy are You to take the book and to break its seals; for You were slain, and purchased for God with Your blood men from every tribe and tongue and people and nation. You have made them to be a kingdom and priests to our God; and they will reign upon the earth."

When one puts all of those together with those verses, the 144,000 are the redeemed, they are Christians. The 144,000 are not to be taken literally at all. What you have is twelve times twelve, times one thousand and that is where you get your number, but as this represents the redeemed, chapter 7 also says along with this 144,000 there is a great multitude which no man can number. I think the purpose of this is to lead us in understanding that the 144,000 represent the redeemed, but it is not to be taken as a literal, specific number. One of the greatest forces that the Lamb of God has standing with him is you and me, Christians fighting the battle together with him as he goes to war. He does not go all alone but carries us with him. That is why we are to always be ready to fight the battle that we are to fight.

B. Four Headline Banners, 14:6-13

[6]And I saw another angel flying in midheaven, having an eternal gospel to preach to those who live on the earth, and to every nation and tribe and tongue and people; [7]and he said with a loud voice, "Fear God, and give Him glory, because the hour of His judgment has come; worship Him who made the heaven and the earth and sea and springs of waters."

[8]And another angel, a second one, followed, saying, "Fallen, fallen is Babylon the great, she who has made all the nations drink of the wine of the passion of her immorality."

[9]Then another angel, a third one, followed them, saying with a loud voice, "If anyone worships the beast and his image, and receives a mark on his forehead or on his hand, [10]he also will drink of the wine of the wrath of God, which is mixed in full strength in the cup of His anger; and he will be tormented with fire and brimstone in the presence of the holy angels and in the presence of the Lamb. [11]"And the smoke of their torment goes up forever and ever; they have no rest day and night, those who worship the beast and his image, and whoever receives the mark of his name." [12]Here is the perseverance of the saints who keep the commandments of God and their faith in Jesus.

[13]And I heard a voice from heaven, saying, "Write, 'Blessed are the dead who die in the Lord from now

on!'" "Yes," says the Spirit, "so that they may rest from their labors, for their deeds follow with them."

Beginning in verse 6, there are four headline banners that are presented and these will announce what is going to happen in the rest of the book. The headlines serve in much the same way a headline would assist in a newspaper. These headlines give us a glimpse of the story that is to follow. The details are a part of the story which will be found later in the book.

(1) Banner #1 — The Triumph of the Righteousness of God, 14:6-7

14:6 And I saw another angel flying in midheaven, having an eternal gospel to preach to those who live on the earth, and to every nation and tribe and tongue and people; 7 and he said with a loud voice, "Fear God, and give Him glory, because the hour of His judgment has come; worship Him who made the heaven and the earth and sea and springs of waters."

The story in this headline banner is found in chapters fifteen and sixteen. "And I saw" introduces a second section of this chapter. The angel mentioned here is conspicuous as the eagle of 8:13. He gains attention. This angel is flying in midheaven, indicating that his mission is one of urgency. His message is referred to as an "eternal gospel" to present to those who live on the earth; viz., "every nation and tribe and tongue and people." These are the earth-dwellers from among whom the redeemed had been purchased (5:9), over whom the beast exercises authority (13:7), and the waters upon which the harlot sits (17:1, 15). The message is to be proclaimed to the entire world.

The word "gospel" (*euangelion*) occurs only here in John's writings. Is this the gospel as revealed in the New Testament, or is it a special gospel revealed or announced just before the end of time? It is doubtful that it is the latter because the gospel has already been revealed and preached (Matt. 28:18-20; Mark 16:15-16) and once for all delivered to the saints (Jude 3). Paul said the gospel was entrusted to "earthen vessels" (2 Cor. 4:7), and if anyone, even an angel, preaches any other gospel, he is accursed (*anathēma*, Gal. 1:6-9). This, then, is the everlasting gospel of salvation that is preached to every creature under heaven. The message announced by the angel can be summed up in three phrases: "fear God," "give Him glory," and "worship Him." The judgment preached should motivate and bring men to repentance (Acts 17:30-31). The judgment under consideration is not the final judgment for he says "the hour of His judgment has come" — a probable reference to the judgment brought upon Babylon announced in v. 8.

(2) Banner #2 — Judgment on Wicked Rome, 14:8

14:8 And another angel, a second one, followed, saying, "Fallen, fallen is Babylon the great, she who has made all the nations drink of the wine of the passion of her immorality."

The headline banner is in verse 8, but the story is given in chapters 17 and 18. This second angel announced the judgment upon Babylon the great. She is fallen. The actual fall is not seen until 16:19 with the final bowl of judgment. But in anticipation of the sure and certain judgment from God, Babylon is announced as if she has already fallen. The words here are adopted from Isaiah 21:9, "Fallen, fallen is Babylon," said Isaiah, "and all the images of her gods are shattered on the ground" (21:9). "Suddenly Babylon," said Jeremiah, "has fallen and been broken" (Jer. 51:8, cf. Jer. 51:6-10; Isa. 51:21-23; Rev. 17:2). Each time Babylon is referred to in Revelation she is identified as "great" (14:8; 16:19; 17:5; 18:2, 10, 21), or as "the great city." Many see Babylon identified as Rome, not of the world power which was represented by the beast out of the sea, but of the world of lust and seduction (cf. chs. 17-18). Philip Edgcumbe Hughes says,

> Babylon the great denotes not some particular earthly city or empire (such as Rome, which has been widely supposed) but the concentration of all ungodly arrogance and dissoluteness in all the world and throughout the course of history. Thus Babylon is personified as the whore who has corrupted all the nations with her whoredom (cf. 16:19; 17:5; 18:2).[2]

Babylon is said to have made all the nations to drink of the wine of the wrath of her fornication. Two Old Testament pictures have been melded into one. Jeremiah 51:7 says of Babylon, "Babylon has been a golden cup in the hand of the LORD, Intoxicating all the earth. The nations have drunk of her wine; Therefore the nations are going mad." Babylon's power and influence lured and corrupted the nations into a kind of insane immorality. The picture is of a prostitute seducing and persuading a man into immorality, adultery, and fornication by filling him full of wine and making him drunk so that he could no longer resist her wiles. The second picture is of the cup of the wrath of God, which the sinner must drink to its bitter dregs. The second naturally follows the first. Once a nation is guilty of such corruption described as "drunk on the wrath of fornication," it follows that she must then, eventually, "drink of the cup of the wrath of God."

(3) Banner #3 — Judgment Announced on Emperor Worshipers, 14:9-12

14:9 Then another angel, a third one, followed them, saying with a loud voice, "If anyone worships the beast and his image, and receives a mark on his forehead or on his hand, 10 he also will drink of the wine of the wrath of God, which is mixed in full strength in the cup of His anger; and he will be tormented with fire and brimstone in the presence of the holy angels and in the presence of the Lamb. 11 "And the smoke of their torment goes up forever and ever; they have no rest day and night, those who worship the beast and his image, and whoever receives the mark of his name." 12 Here is the perseverance of the saints who keep the commandments of God and their faith in Jesus.

Here is the headline banner, but we will read the story in chapters nineteen and twenty. Warning has already been given to the beast and those who receive his mark (ch. 13). Now there is warning to those who fall in time of trial. In the time that John is writing, the church is fighting for its very existence. The individual Christian must be prepared for suffering, trial, tribulation, and persecution. If the individual Christian yielded, the church died. The church's existence is dependent on the individual Christian remaining faithful unto death.

The judgment is pictured in the most awful image of a judgment that fell on the earth — the judgment of Sodom and Gomorrah (cf. Gen. 19). This is reminiscent also of Isaiah's words describing the Lord's vengeance: "For the LORD has a day of vengeance, A year of recompense for the cause of Zion. Its streams will be turned into pitch, And its loose earth into brimstone, And its land will become burning pitch. It will not be quenched night or day; Its smoke will go up forever; From generation to generation it will be desolate; None will pass through it forever and ever" (34:8-10). Also in Isaiah 66:24, we read, "Then they will go forth and look on the corpses of the men Who have transgressed against Me. For their worm will not die, And their fire will not be quenched; And they will be an abhorrence to all mankind."

(4) Banner #4 — The Righteous Dead Will Rest, 14:13

14:13 And I heard a voice from heaven, saying, "Write, 'Blessed are the dead who die in the Lord from now on!'" "Yes," says the Spirit, "so that they may rest from their labors, for their deeds follow with them."

A distinction is seen between those who worship the beast and those who do not. Here is the headline banner but the story will be read in chapter 21 and 22. The fourth headline banner announces the final blessedness of the saints.

The second beatitude in the book of Revelation is found in this verse. After the terrible prophecies of terrors to come there follows the gracious promise of blessedness to those who die in the Lord. The idea of dying in the Lord is familiar in the New Testament. Paul speaks of the dead in Christ (1 Thess. 4:16) and of those who have fallen asleep in Jesus (1 Cor. 15:18). The obvious meaning is that it refers to those whose life comes to an end but who are still one with Christ. Trials, tribulations, heartaches, heartbreaks, and persecutions have not been successful in breaking these faithful from their commitment to Jesus Christ. The phrase "from now on" can be understood in two ways. First, from the time John is writing this book onward. Second, from the time of the fulfillment of the vision onward (i.e., the judgment of the idolaters and the 144,000 with the Lord on Mt. Zion). Either could be grammatically correct but the context favors the latter. John is expecting an immediate intensification of persecution associated with the beast, and the beatitude indicates that those who remain faithful to Christ will indeed be blessed. The blessedness consists of their "resting from their labors, for their deeds follow with them." The deeds mentioned here are not to be understood as meritorious deeds which the Christian has performed which thereby earn salvation. When John speaks of deeds of the Ephesians he speaks of their "toil and perseverance" (2:2); to the Thyatirans it was their "love and faith and service" (2:19). By deeds, John never means a legalistic deed of the law, but rather their "character." When a person comes to the end of their life, it is their character that follows them, even into eternity.

C. The Sickles of Judgment, 14:14-20

[14]Then I looked, and behold, a white cloud, and sitting on the cloud *was* one like a son of man, having a golden crown on His head and a sharp sickle in His hand. [15]And another angel came out of the temple, crying out with a loud voice to Him who sat on the cloud, "Put in your sickle and reap, for the hour to reap has come, because the harvest of the earth is ripe." [16]Then He who sat on the cloud swung His sickle over the earth, and the earth was reaped.

[17]And another angel came out of the temple which is in heaven, and he also had a sharp sickle. [18]Then another angel, the one who has power over fire, came out from the altar; and he called with a loud voice to him who had the sharp sickle, saying, "Put in your sharp sickle and gather the clusters from the vine of the earth, because her grapes are ripe." [19]So the angel swung his sickle to the earth and gathered *the clusters from* the vine of the earth, and threw them into the great wine press of the wrath of God. [20]And the wine press was trodden outside the city, and blood came out from the wine press, up to the horses' bridles, for a distance of two hundred miles.

A picture of judgment is presented following this in the remaining verses of chapter 14 that is seen from two perspectives. First, judgment as is viewed by the righteous, 14:14-16. The second perspective is judgment viewed by the unrighteous, 14:17-20.

The scene opens with the picture of the son of man from Daniel 7:13-14. Daniel writes, "I kept looking in the night visions, And behold, with the clouds of heaven One like a Son of Man was coming, And He came up to the Ancient of Days And was presented before Him. And to Him was given dominion, Glory and a kingdom, That all the peoples, nations, and *men of every* language Might serve Him. His dominion is an everlasting dominion Which will not pass away; And His kingdom is one Which will not be destroyed." In Revelation we have the victorious Christ coming to judgment.

John uses two familiar metaphors in describing the judgment to come. In the first section is the picture of a harvest (vv. 14-16). When Joel spoke of the nearness of judgment he said, "Put in the sickle, for the harvest is ripe. Come, tread, for the wine press is full; The vats overflow, for their wickedness is great" (3:13). Jesus said, "But when the crop permits, he immediately puts in the sickle, because the harvest has come" (Mark 4:29). Also, in the parable of the wheat and tares Jesus uses the picture of the harvest to symbolize judgment (Matt. 13:24-30; 37-43). Harvesting is a good picture for judgment; the good are gathered together and the useless are cast away. Here is judgment that has to do with the harvest. Harvest is an ingathering. As viewed by the righteous then, judgment simply is like going out and gathering all the grain and bringing it into the store house. The picture changes with verse 17 for the opposite.

Judgment is viewed by the righteous as a harvest time where everybody is gathered in and brought home. Judgment is viewed by the unrighteous as a harvest time of the gathering the grapes where they are placed in the winepress and trampled upon. The classic Biblical figure of judgment upon the wicked is a winepress. The fully ripe grapes are mature.

In Palestine the winepress consisted of an upper and lower trough connected by a channel. The troughs might be hollowed out in the rock or they might be built of brick. Grapes were put in the upper trough which was on a slightly higher level. They were then trampled with the feet, and so the juice was pressed out. The juice then flowed down the connecting channel and was collected in the lower trough. God's judgments are sometimes pictured as the trampling of the grapes. Lamentations 1:15 says, "The Lord has rejected all my strong men In my midst; He has called an appointed time against me To crush my young men; The Lord has trodden *as in* a wine press The virgin daughter of Judah." Joel 3:2 says, "I will gather all the nations And bring them down to the valley of Jehoshaphat. Then I will enter into judgment with them there On behalf of My people and My inheritance, Israel, Whom they have scattered among the nations; And they have divided up My land."

The idea of the grapes being ripe means they are ready for harvesting. The same type of imagery is used in Genesis 15:16 in describing the iniquity of the Amorites being full. Judgment of the unrighteous is viewed as God has said, You have filled up with your unrighteousness, now you are going to be squashed. A figure of grapes being crushed representing judgment is also found in Isaiah 63:3, "I have trodden the wine trough alone, And from the peoples there was no man with Me. I also trod them in My anger And trampled them in My wrath; And their lifeblood is sprinkled on My garments, And I stained all My raiment."

In chapter 14 we have noticed the Lamb has standing with Him the 144,000 which represents the redeemed of God. We are quickly given a preview of what is to come with four headline banners of what is to take place. These headline banners prepare us for the revelation of the rest of the book. Then finally, we are made to understand what happens in the judgment of both the righteous and the unrighteous.

NOTES

[1]Homer Hailey, *Revelation: An Introduction and Commentary*, 302.
[2]Philip Edgcumbe Hughes, *The Book of Revelation: A Commentary*, 161.

Revelation 15

IX. THE WAR WITH THE BEAST, 15:1-16:21

Chapter 15 announces of the coming judgment and the seven bowls of wrath. There is a very close connection between the trumpets found in chapters 8 through 11 and the bowls of wrath we will find in chapters 15 and 16.

The trumpets were blown to warn. The bowls of wrath on the other hand, are completely poured out. With God's wrath in the trumpets that were blown in chapters 8 through 11, there was mercy. Now, there is no mercy.

In the history of the world there is always a definite, ever occurring order of events that is clearly evident. This seems to come across over and over and over again and it is something that can almost be outlined with the first 14 chapters we have studied so far of the book of Revelation. For instance, through the preaching of the gospel, churches are established and they stand as light bearers shining light in this sin darkened world in which we live. That is the essence of chapters 1-3 of the book of Revelation. Again and again as they shine forth that light breaking into the world of darkness, God's people suffer persecution with many trials and afflictions. This is found in chapters 4, 5, 6, and 7. Then the judgments of God are visited upon the persecuting world but they fail to bring about repentance, chapters 8, 9, 10, and 11. After this comes the conflict between the church and the world points to a deeper struggle, a fundamental warfare that is between the seed of the woman and the dragon, chapters, 12, 13, and 14. The question "what then" arises, when the wicked fail to repent as a result of God's judgments. Chapter 15 announces and chapter 16 tells us the answer.

If there was one verse in the Scripture that could summarize chapter 15 and 16 it would be Hebrews 12:29, "our God is a consuming fire." This section answers the question of what happens when judgments from God fail to bring about repentance.

A. The Song of Moses and the Lamb, 15:1-8

[1]Then I saw another sign in heaven, great and marvelous, seven angels who had seven plagues, which are the last, because in them the wrath of God is finished. [2]And I saw something like a sea of glass mixed with fire, and those who had been victorious over the beast and his image and the number of his name, standing on the sea of glass, holding harps of God. [3]And they sang the song of Moses, the bond-servant of God, and the song of the Lamb, saying,

"Great and marvelous are Your works, O Lord God, the Almighty; Righteous and true are Your ways, King of the nations! [4]"Who will not fear, O Lord, and glorify Your name? For You alone are holy; For ALL THE NATIONS WILL COME AND WORSHIP BEFORE YOU, FOR YOUR RIGHTEOUS ACTS HAVE BEEN REVEALED."

[5]After these things I looked, and the temple of the tabernacle of testimony in heaven was opened, [6]and

the seven angels who had the seven plagues came out of the temple, clothed in linen, clean and bright, and girded around their chests with golden sashes. [7]Then one of the four living creatures gave to the seven angels seven golden bowls full of the wrath of God, who lives forever and ever. [8]And the temple was filled with smoke from the glory of God and from His power; and no one was able to enter the temple until the seven plagues of the seven angels were finished.

This is the third sign (*sēmeion*) specifically identified in the book, the woman and the dragon being the others (cf. 12:1, 3). It is the final manifestation of the wrath of God which takes form in seven angels of judgment. These angels are given seven bowls of wrath.

Before the seals were opened in chapter six, we were shown a scene in heaven. God is on the throne and all living creatures fall down and worship God and the Lamb, thus indicating that the one who rules the world sits on a throne in heaven, not in Rome. Before the trumpets were blown in chapters 8 and 9, there was a period of silence in which the angels were offering up the prayers of the saints, indicating the acceptance of such prayers. Now, the bowls of wrath are about to be poured out. But we are first shown a picture of the angels of God who are given the bowls of wrath and are told that in them is the work of God made complete. Here is the victory over the beast and the saints of God are there to witness it.

15:1 Then I saw another sign in heaven, great and marvelous, seven angels who had seven plagues, *which are* the last, because in them the wrath of God is finished.

The seven angels represent the completion of God's wrath; viz., the last plagues. In them John understands God's judgment is made complete. The word "completed" (NIV) is from the word *teleō* which means to "finish," "to bring to an end," "to accomplish," "to perform" (BAG, p. 818). The same word is used in Revelation 10:7 which refers to the blowing of the trumpets "fulfilling" the mystery of God (cf. 11:7; 15:8; 17:17; 20:3, 5, 7).

15:2 And I saw something like a sea of glass mixed with fire, and those who had been victorious over the beast and his image and the number of his name, standing on the sea of glass, holding harps of God.

The things mentioned here have already been observed in chapter 14:14-16 and refer to the righteous view of judgment. We will see later the sea of glass that is mingled with fire, but keep in mind that in the presence of the righteous stands a sea of glass. We were introduced to this sea of glass in chapter 4, the throne scene, verse 6, before the throne as it were a sea of glass like unto crystal. The sea of glass is the approach to God. This is modeled after the laver (Solomon's "brazen sea"). The priest had to go through the laver in order to enter the sanctuary to serve God. Therefore the sea of glass in one sense speaks of the holiness of God; i.e., His unapproachableness or separation from others. The sea of glass is said here to be mingled with fire.

Standing on the sea of glass are those who were "victorious over the beast." These are the same ones who have been victorious throughout the book of Revelation. They have won out over the idolatrous beast. They are victorious because of their testimony to Christ and their willingness to face death with that testimony (cf. 2:7, 10, 11, 26; 12:11; 21:7; also 3:5; 5:5). They are pictured as 144,000 (7:4; 14:1); a great multitude (7:7); and a company of martyrs (6:11).

15:3 And they sang the song of Moses, the bond-servant of God, and the song of the Lamb, saying, "Great and marvelous are Your works, O Lord God, the

Almighty; Righteous and true are Your ways, King of the nations! 4 "Who will not fear, O Lord, and glorify Your name? For You alone are holy; For ALL THE NATIONS WILL COME AND WORSHIP BEFORE YOU, FOR YOUR RIGHTEOUS ACTS HAVE BEEN REVEALED."

Here the faithful are singing the song of praise for God's judgments. It is called the "song of Moses and the Lamb." The Song of Moses is found in Exodus 15:1-18. It is a song sung in celebration of the victory of the Lord in defeating the Egyptians at the Red Sea. This song was often sung at the Sabbath evening service in the synagogue. At every Jewish service the recital of the *Shema*, the creed of Israel, was followed by two prayers. One of these prayers refers to this song: "True it is that Thou art Jehovah our God, and the God of our fathers, our Saviour, and the Saviour of our fathers, our Creator, the Rock of our Salvation, our Help and our Deliverer. Thy name is from everlasting, and there is no God beside Thee. A new song did they that were delivered sing to Thy name by the sea-shore; together did all praise and own Thee King, and say, Jehovah shall reign, world without end! Blessed be the Lord who saveth Israel."[1] This song of Moses commemorated their deliverance from bondage, the greatest event in the life of Israel. The victorious martyrs, brought through the sea of persecution to the promised land of heaven, sing that song. The song is made up almost entirely of Old Testament quotations. Various authors provide the similarities. Using Barclay's list as a foundation, we will add to it. First will be the quotation from the Revelation, then verses which remind us of the truthfulness stated.

Great and marvelous are Your works. "How great are Your works, O LORD! Your thoughts are very deep" (Ps. 92:5). "Great are the works of the LORD; *They are* studied by all who delight in them" (Ps. 111:2). "O sing to the LORD a new song, For He has done wonderful things, His right hand and His holy arm have gained the victory for Him" (Ps. 98:1). "I will give thanks to You, for I am fearfully and wonderfully made; Wonderful are Your works, And my soul knows it very well" (Ps. 139:14).

O Lord God, the Almighty. "For behold, He who forms mountains and creates the wind And declares to man what are His thoughts, He who makes dawn into darkness And treads on the high places of the earth, The LORD God of hosts is His name" (Amos 4:13).

Righteous and true are Your ways. "The LORD is righteous in all His ways And kind in all His deeds" (Ps. 145:17).

Who will not fear, O Lord, and glorify Your name? "All nations whom You have made shall come and worship before You, O Lord, And they shall glorify Your name" (Ps. 86:9).

For You alone are holy. "There is no one holy like the LORD, Indeed, there is no one besides You, Nor is there any rock like our God" (1 Sam. 2:2). "Let them praise Your great and awesome name; Holy is He" (Ps. 99:3). "He has sent redemption to His people; He has ordained His covenant forever; Holy and awesome is His name" (Ps. 111:9).

For all the nations will come and worship before You. "All nations whom You have made shall come and worship before You, O Lord, And they shall glorify Your name" (Ps. 86:9).

For Your righteous acts have been revealed. "The LORD has made known His salvation; He has revealed His righteousness in the sight of the nations" (Ps. 98:2).

One noticeable characteristic about this song is that nothing is said by the triumphant martyrs about their own victory. All the words, from beginning to end, are about the greatness of God. Barclay says this is because heaven is a place where men forget themselves, forget their own achievements, and remember only God. H.B. Swete has written,

In the Presence of God the martyrs forget themselves; their thoughts are absorbed by the new wonders that surround them; they glory of God and the mighty scheme of things in which their own sufferings form an infinitesimal part are opening before them; they begin to see the great issue of the world-drama, and we hear the doxology with which they greet their first unclouded vision of God and his works.[2]

15:5 After these things I looked, and the temple of the tabernacle of testimony in heaven was opened, 6 and the seven angels who had the seven plagues came out of the temple, clothed in linen, clean *and* bright, and girded around their chests with golden sashes. 7 Then one of the four living creatures gave to the seven angels seven golden bowls full of the wrath of God, who lives forever and ever.

Now we turn our attention to a very impressive scene. The door to the temple of heaven is opened for a second time (cf. 11:19). Seven angels dressed in white and gold come out of the temple. One of the four living creatures gives a bowl to each of the seven messengers. The bowl was a vessel used in the temple for the ministry of offerings and incense (5:8). This might have been a large banquet bowl often used for wine (Amos 6:6) or a ritual bowl used for collecting the blood of the sacrifices (Exod. 27:3). Golden bowls were often associated with the temple services (cf. 1 Kgs 7:50; 2 Kgs 12:13; 25:15).

15:8 And the temple was filled with smoke from the glory of God and from His power; and no one was able to enter the temple until the seven plagues of the seven angels were finished.

The "smoke" which fills the temple refers to the shekinah cloud first associated with the tabernacle and then the temple. It shows the solemnity of the occasion. In the Old Testament we read of this happening a

267

number of times (cf. Exod. 40:34ff; 1 Kgs. 8:10-11; 2 Chron. 5:13-14; Ezek. 11:23; 44:4). This indicates God's special presence and that He is the source of the judgments. His presence in the temple allows for the presence of no one else (Isa. 6:4; Hab. 2:20).

NOTES

[1]William Barclay, *The Revelation of John, Vol. 2* (Philadelphia: The Westminster Press, 1960), 156.

[2]H.B. Swete, *Commentary on Revelation*, 196.

Revelation 16

B. The Seven Bowls of Wrath, 16:1-21

[1]Then I heard a loud voice from the temple, saying to the seven angels, "Go and pour out on the earth the seven bowls of the wrath of God."

[2]So the first angel went and poured out his bowl on the earth; and it became a loathsome and malignant sore on the people who had the mark of the beast and who worshiped his image.

[3]The second angel poured out his bowl into the sea, and it became blood like that of a dead man; and every living thing in the sea died.

[4]Then the third angel poured out his bowl into the rivers and the springs of waters; and they became blood. [5]And I heard the angel of the waters saying, "Righteous are You, who are and who were, O Holy One, because You judged these things; [6]for they poured out the blood of saints and prophets, and You have given them blood to drink. They deserve it."

[7]And I heard the altar saying, "Yes, O Lord God, the Almighty, true and righteous are Your judgments."

[8]The fourth angel poured out his bowl upon the sun, and it was given to it to scorch men with fire. [9]Men were scorched with fierce heat; and they blasphemed the name of God who has the power over these plagues, and they did not repent so as to give Him glory.

[10]Then the fifth angel poured out his bowl on the throne of the beast, and his kingdom became darkened; and they gnawed their tongues because of pain, [11]and they blasphemed the God of heaven because of their pains and their sores; and they did not repent of their deeds.

[12]The sixth angel poured out his bowl on the great river, the Euphrates; and its water was dried up, so that the way would be prepared for the kings from the east. [13]And I saw coming out of the mouth of the dragon and out of the mouth of the beast and out of the mouth of the false prophet, three unclean spirits like frogs; [14]for they are spirits of demons, performing signs, which go out to the kings of the whole world, to gather them together for the war of the great day of God, the Almighty.

[15]("Behold, I am coming like a thief. Blessed is the one who stays awake and keeps his clothes, so that he will not walk about naked and men will not see his shame.")

[16]And they gathered them together to the place which in Hebrew is called Har-Magedon.

[17]Then the seventh angel poured out his bowl upon the air, and a loud voice came out of the temple from the throne, saying, "It is done." [18]And there were flashes of lightning and sounds and peals of thunder; and there was a great earthquake, such as there had not been since man came to be upon the earth, so great an earthquake was it, and so mighty. [19]The great city was split into three parts, and the cities of the nations fell. Babylon the great was remembered before God, to give her the cup of the wine of His

fierce wrath. ²⁰And every island fled away, and the mountains were not found. ²¹And huge hailstones, about one hundred pounds each, came down from heaven upon men; and men blasphemed God because of the plague of the hail, because its plague was extremely severe.

"Then I heard a loud voice from the temple saying to the seven angels, 'Go, pour out the seven bowls of God's wrath on the earth'." Notice a voice at this point in verse 1. It does not say the voice of an angel as we are told on other occasions. We are simply told he hears a voice. The voice has to be the voice of God himself for verse 8 of chapter 15 says the temple was filled with smoke from the glory of God and from his power and no one was able to enter the temple until the seven angels finished their seven plagues. No one is in the temple but God, and when John hears this great voice come out of the temple it can only be God's voice. God pronounces the final judgment. God may use other means, methods, and sources to bring a judgment upon people to cause them to repent, but when it gets to the final judgment, God's voice is the voice that will be heard. This is the final judgment on Rome.

The description of the bowls of wrath have a connection with two things: first, they have a connection with the ten plagues in Egypt; and, second, with the seven trumpets of Revelation 8-11. To help us see the resemblances we will set out the three lists:

The Ten Plagues (Exod. 7-12)
i.	The water made into blood, 7:20-25
ii.	The frogs, 8:5-14
iii.	The lice, 8:16-18
iv.	The flies, 8:20-24
v.	The murrain on the cattle, 9:3-6
vi.	The boils, 9:8-11
vii.	The thunder and hail, 9:22-26

viii.   The locusts, 10:12-19
ix.   The darkness, 10:21-23
x.   The death of the firstborn, 12:29-30

The Terrors of the Trumpets (Rev. 8–11)

1. The coming of hail, fire and blood, through which one-third part of the trees and all the green grass are withered, 8:7
2. The flaming mountain cast into the sea, whereby one-third part of the sea become blood, 8:8
3. The fall of the star Wormwood into the waters, whereby the waters become bitter and poisonous, 8:10-11
4. The smiting of one-third part of the sun and the moon and the stars, whereby all is darkened, 8:12
5. The coming of the star who unlocks the pit of the abyss, from which there comes the smoke, out of which there come the demonic and terrible locusts, 9:1-12
6. The loosing of the four angels bound in the Euphrates, and the coming of the demonic cavalry from the east, 9:13-21
7. The announcement of the final victory of God, and of the rebellious anger of the nations, 11:15

The Terrors of the Bowls of Wrath (Rev. 16)

1. The coming of the ulcerous sores upon men, 16:2
2. The sea becomes like the blood of a dead man, 16:3
3. The rivers and fountains become blood, 16:4
4. The sun becomes scorchingly and burningly hot, 16:8
5. The darkness over the kingdom of the beast, and the agony of it, 16:10
6. The drying up of the Euphrates to open a way for the hordes of the kings of the east, 16:12
7. The pollution of the air and the accompanying terrors in nature, the thunder, the earthquake, the lightning and the hail, 16:17-19

1. The First Bowl of Wrath: Into the Earth, 16:1-2

16:1 Then I heard a loud voice from the temple, saying to the seven angels, "Go and pour out on the earth the seven bowls of the wrath of God." 2 So the first *angel* went and poured out his bowl on the earth; and it became a loathsome and malignant sore on the people who had the mark of the beast and who worshiped his image.

The first angel went to pour out his bowl on the land, and ugly and painful sores broke out on the people who had the mark of the beast and worshiped his image. There is a parallel here between the first trumpet and the first bowl of wrath. Also one notices the similarity between the first bowl of wrath and the sixth plague in Egypt. The consequences of evil are self-induced: ". . . if you do not obey the LORD your God, . . . the LORD will send upon you curses, confusion, and frustration" (Deut. 28:15, 20).

2. The Second Bowl of Wrath: Into the Sea, 16:3

16:3 The second *angel* poured out his bowl into the sea, and it became blood like *that* of a dead man; and every living thing in the sea died.

The parallel between this and the first plague in Egypt is obvious. But what does the sea represent? Is this to mean the a part of the whole creation, or does the sea represent the society of humans who are spiritually dead? A beast comes up out of the sea (13:1), which we have identified as society. In 8:8 the "sea" symbolizes the whole society of worldly mankind. The bowl of wrath portrays for us the utter filthiness of a dead society.

3. The Third Bowl of Wrath: Into the Rivers, 16:4-7

16:4 Then the third *angel* poured out his bowl into the rivers and the springs of waters; and they became blood. 5 And I heard the angel of the waters saying, "Righteous are You, who are and who were, O Holy

One, because You judged these things; 6 for they poured out the blood of saints and prophets, and You have given them blood to drink. They deserve it." 7 And I heard the altar saying, "Yes, O Lord God, the Almighty, true and righteous are Your judgments."

The third bowl corresponds even more closely with the first Egyptian plague. The angel of the waters denotes the angel whose special responsibility is to superintend the waters of the earth. Angels have special duties over different spheres of the earth. They control four winds (7:1), have power over fire (14:18), and, in this passage, have control over the rivers of the earth. Here is fresh water destruction even as we found in the third trumpet and again the figure of blood is used. The essence being the judgment once again is a complete judgment. There is no mercy with this judgment.

4. The Fourth Bowl of Wrath: Upon the Sun, 16:8-9

16:8 The fourth *angel* poured out his bowl upon the sun, and it was given to it to scorch men with fire. 9 Men were scorched with fierce heat; and they blasphemed the name of God who has the power over these plagues, and they did not repent so as to give Him glory.

Those who would not repent when the sun's light was darkened are now punished by having its heat intensified. There should have been repentance before now, but there is not. Since this is one of the last plagues, their impenitence is now incorrigible, and they show this by blaspheming the name of God and refusing to glorify Him. Their rebellion is bringing final judgment upon themselves.

5. The Fifth Bowl of Wrath:
Upon the Throne of the Beast, 16:10-11

16:10 Then the fifth *angel* poured out his bowl on the throne of the beast, and his kingdom became darkened; and they gnawed their tongues because of pain,

11 and they blasphemed the God of heaven because of their pains and their sores; and they did not repent of their deeds.

The beast is the Roman Empire and the throne of the beast is Rome, the capital of the empire. The darkness is reminiscent of the darkness which came upon Egypt (Exod. 10:21-23). In comparison with the partial darkness with the fourth trumpet blast, the darkness of this fifth plague is total. This indicates the total and complete judgment which entirely befits those who have allied themselves with the beast and Satan whose rule is a rule of darkness (cf. Eph. 6:12; Luke 22:53). It is in this darkness of ungodliness that Jesus came as the light (cf. John 1:5; 1 John 2:11). Christians are those who have been translated from the kingdom of darkness (Col. 1:13-14; cf. also 1 Pet. 2:9; Matt. 4:16; Acts 26:18; 2 Cor. 4:6; Eph. 5:8; 1 Thess. 5:4). Final judgment is this: "that the Light has come into the world, and men loved the darkness rather than the Light, for their deeds were evil" (John 3:19).

6. The Sixth Bowl of Wrath:
Upon the Great River, 16:12-16

16:12 The sixth *angel* poured out his bowl on the great river, the Euphrates; and its water was dried up, so that the way would be prepared for the kings from the east. 13 And I saw *coming* out of the mouth of the dragon and out of the mouth of the beast and out of the mouth of the false prophet, three unclean spirits like frogs; 14 for they are spirits of demons, performing signs, which go out to the kings of the whole world, to gather them together for the war of the great day of God, the Almighty. 15 ("Behold, I am coming like a thief. Blessed is the one who stays awake and keeps his clothes, so that he will not walk about naked and men will not see his shame.") 16 And they gathered them together to the place which in Hebrew is called Har-Magedon.

This sixth bowl of wrath is poured upon the River Euphrates. The Euphrates River always referred to the land of the enemy. It is from the area of the Euphrates that both the Assyrians and the Babylonians came. The significance of this being poured out upon the River Euphrates is a picture of it being poured out upon the enemies of God. God brings judgment upon those who are His enemies and they are gathered together for a battle against God.

There are a number of times in the Old Testament when the drying up of the waters is a sign and an action of the power of God. It was so at the Red Sea (Exod. 14:21). It was so at the River Jordan when the people under Joshua passed through the river (Josh. 3:17). In Isaiah the act of the power of God is that he will enable men to pass through the Egyptian sea dry shod (Isa. 11:16). The threat of God through Jeremiah is: "I will dry up her sea And make her fountain dry" (Jer. 51:36). Zechariah writes, "All the depths of the Nile will dry up" (Zech. 10:11).

Verses 13-16 present one of the most challenging sections in the chapter. There are several questions that concern us.

First, what does this phrase "three unclean spirits like frogs," which came out of the mouth of the dragon, the beast, and the false prophet, mean? There is a kind of play on words here in the Greek. The unclean spirit came out of the mouths of the three evil forces. The mouth is the organ of speech, and speech is one of the most powerfully influential forces in the world. The word for spirit is also the word for breath (*pneuma*). To say, therefore, that an evil spirit came out of a man's mouth is the same as saying that an evil breath came out of a man's mouth. As H. B. Swete puts it, the dragon, the beast, and the false prophet "breathed forth evil influences."

Second, why are these evil spirits like frogs? Frogs were considered unclean animals (Lev. 11:10). Frogs were connected with the plagues in Egypt (Exod. 8:5-11; cf. also Ps. 78:45; 105:30). The plague of frogs was something in Hebrew history which was not likely to be forgotten. To say that frogs came out of the mouth of these three evil forces is to say that their words were like plagues, that they were unclean, that they were empty futilities, that they were allies of the power of darkness.

Third, who is the false prophet? The dragon has been identified as Satan (12:3, 9). The beast is the Roman Empire with its Caesar worship (13:1). But this is the first time the false prophet has appeared. And he appears without any explanation. This indicates that while it may prove to be difficult for us, it was not likely so for John's original readers. The false prophet is mentioned again in 19:20 and 20:10. In 19:20 we learn that in the end the false prophet was taken, along with the beast, with those the beast deceived and who had received the mark of the beast and those that worshiped the image. In 13:13-14 we have a description of the second beast (land beast). He does great wonders and he deceives those that dwell on the earth by the means of those miracles which he had power to do in the sight of the false prophet. The land beast is identified with the provincial organizations and administration; i.e., the enforcer of emperor worship. The false prophet, then, stands for the whole organization which seeks to make men worship the emperor and to abandon the worship of the true God and of Jesus Christ.

Fourth, what is the battle of Armageddon? Verse 16 tells us where that battle is going to be fought and it is very significant for it is the battle called Har-Magedon, literally the mount of Megiddo. From a study of Old Testament history it is known especially to all Jews that the valley of Megiddo was the gathering place of invading forces where many battles had been fought (Judg. 5:19; 2 Kgs. 9:27; 2 Kgs. 23:28-29).

7. The Seventh Bowl of Wrath: Upon the Air, 16:17-21

16:17 Then the seventh *angel* poured out his bowl upon the air, and a loud voice came out of the temple from the throne, saying, "It is done." **18** And there were flashes of lightning and sounds and peals of thunder; and there was a great earthquake, such as there had not been since man came to be upon the earth, so great an earthquake *was it, and* so mighty. **19** The great city was split into three parts, and the cities of the nations fell. Babylon the great was remembered before God, to give her the cup of the wine of His fierce wrath. **20** And every island fled away, and the mountains were not found. **21** And huge hailstones, about one hundred pounds each, came down from heaven upon men; and men blasphemed God because of the plague of the hail, because its plague was extremely severe.

The seventh bowl of wrath presents the complete, everlasting, final, destruction of Rome, the intensity of which is found in verse 21. The language that is used here is language that is characteristic of the prophets (Micah 1; Nahum 1). The great city is Rome; there was not another city at this time that could fit this description. She is called Babylon in the picture because of her worldliness, but it is not literally Babylon because Babylon had long since been destroyed. When the destruction comes, the city is divided into three parts. The city falls under the seventh bowl. That fall will be described in chapter 18.

We already have seen the significance of the triumph of the righteousness of God. The triumph for the Christian comes when judgment is brought upon the wicked. In the first headline banner in chapter 14:6-7, we are told to fear God and give him glory for the hour of his judgment is come. Now it is come. With the pouring out of the seventh bowl of wrath, surely, "It is done!"

Revelation 17

X. THE JUDGMENT OF THE GREAT HARLOT, 17:1-21:8

In chapter 17, the second woman is introduced and she is just the opposite of the first woman. She is a harlot arrayed with all kinds of earthly splendor and glory. She has on her forehead a name that identifies her as the mother of the harlots of the earth and each woman will have an identity with a city. The woman of chapter 12 will be identified with the new Jerusalem, the heavenly city. The harlot carries an identity with Babylon. Chapter 17 is specifically going to tell us the judgment of the great harlot. This chapter will also show us what happens to Babylon, the sea beast and the great harlot that has already been introduced earlier.

A. The Vision of the Great Harlot, 17:1-5

¹Then one of the seven angels who had the seven bowls came and spoke with me, saying, "Come here, I will show you the judgment of the great harlot who

sits on many waters, [2]with whom the kings of the earth committed *acts of* immorality, and those who dwell on the earth were made drunk with the wine of her immorality."

[3]And he carried me away in the Spirit into a wilderness; and I saw a woman sitting on a scarlet beast, full of blasphemous names, having seven heads and ten horns. [4]The woman was clothed in purple and scarlet, and adorned with gold and precious stones and pearls, having in her hand a gold cup full of abominations and of the unclean things of her immorality, [5]and on her forehead a name *was* written, a mystery, "BABYLON THE GREAT, THE MOTHER OF HARLOTS AND OF THE ABOMINATIONS OF THE EARTH."

John is invited by the one of the angels with the seven bowls of wrath to view "the judgment of the great harlot." In the opening verses we are given material that assists in making clear the identification of the woman; and yet, this chapter is one of the most difficult in the book of Revelation. The various points of identification from the text help us draw the conclusion that the woman is the city of Rome, the center of the empire; and the beast is the Roman Empire itself. The woman who is judged does not have the appearance of one who faces judgment. She is decked with splendor and honor. Her dress is purple and scarlet and she is adorned with glittering gold and precious stones and pearls. She has in her hand a golden cup. The picture is one of a royal banquet feast, not a judgment. What are we to make of her? Who is she?

McGuiggan says the Harlot is Rome and gives the following reasons:[1]
1. She sits on seven hills: 17:9
2. She rules the earth in John's day: 17:18
3. She is a terrible persecutor of the saints: 17:6; 18:20, 24

4. She is the leading commercial power on earth: 18:3, 11ff, 15-19
5. She is supported by the military might of Rome: 17:3, 7
6. She is destroyed by her own military power, etc.: 17:16-17

In a word, she is Babylon (v. 5); that is to say, she is Rome. There are several points of identification which help us understand this picture:

First, she sits upon many waters. These waters are identified for us in verse 15 as, "peoples and multitudes and nations and tongues." It seems that the harlot is identified as one who covers the whole earth. That is to say, this is a reference to the worldwide dominion and influence of the woman.

Second, she is closely allied with the land beast of chapters 13. She sits "enthroned" (17:3) upon the beast and is "carried" by the beast (17:7).

Third, she is clothed in purple and scarlet and decked with all kinds of precious ornaments. This is a picture of the wealth and luxury of Rome. Rome is presented here as one who is decked out in all her fine dress in order to seduce men and to bring them into her immoral embraces.

Fourth, she is has a golden cup full of abominations. These words are used in the Old Testament to designate ceremonial or moral impurities, especially rites and ceremonies accompanying idolatrous worship. Jeremiah spoke of ancient Babylon when he wrote, "Babylon has been a golden cup in the hand of the LORD, Intoxicating all the earth. The nations have drunk of her wine; Therefore the nations are mad" (51:7).

Fifth, the woman has a name on her forehead" "BABYLON THE GREAT, THE MOTHER OF HARLOTS AND OF THE ABOMINATIONS OF THE EARTH." This is reference to a Roman custom where prostitutes in the public betrothals wore upon their foreheads a frontlet giving their names. These were the signs and trademarks of the Roman prostitutes. Seneca (*Rhet. Conro. x.2; Juvenal vs. 123*) mentions the custom of a prostitute wearing a headband on which was written her name or some descriptive phrase showing her occupation. This is another of the signs of a vivid picture of the corrupting influence of the Roman empire upon the nations of the earth. When he mentions the city of Babylon, John does not mean the earthly city (which still existed in John's day, but certainly did not rule the earth), but the "spiritual" Babylon of John's day, i.e., Rome. By the middle of the first century there are several places where the name "Babylon" is applied to the city of Rome (cf. 2 Baruch 11:1; Sibylline Oracles V, 143).

Sixth, the woman is said to be "drunk with the blood of the saints and the blood of the witnesses of Jesus." There is little doubt that this is a reference to the persecution of the Christians in the Roman Empire. She has reveled in her slaughter of Christians much like a drunken man revels in the wine he consumes.

Seventh, she has seduced the kings of the earth to commit fornication with her. Fornication is mentioned frequently in the Old Testament. When God's people make alliances with those who are following other gods, they are said to be guilty of fornication, or whoredom. Isaiah says that Tyre plays the harlot when she had no national relationship to God. Nahum (3:4) speaks of Nineveh as a "well-favored harlot" (ASV). The real crime of Israel was their following after other gods and failing to call upon Jehovah for their help. Israel is called an "adulteress" because God is her "husband" and she is playing the harlot. In what way? They made alliance with her and that is what made them rich (cf. 18:3, 11-14, 15, 17, 19).

Finally, she is said to have "seven mountains" and to be "the great city, which reigns over the kings of the earth" (v. 18): this could apply to no one other than Rome. The seven mountains of Rome were mentioned frequently by Latin writers (Vergil, *Aeneid* 11.784; Horace, *Carmen saeculare* 1.8; Ovid, *Tristia* 1.5.68-70; Martial, *Epigrams* LXIV.20).

B. The Beast Interpreted, 17:6-11

[6]And I saw the woman drunk with the blood of the saints, and with the blood of the witnesses of Jesus. When I saw her, I wondered greatly.
[7]And the angel said to me, "Why do you wonder? I will tell you the mystery of the woman and of the beast that carries her, which has the seven heads and the ten horns. [8]The beast that you saw was, and is not, and is about to come up out of the abyss and go to destruction. And those who dwell on the earth, whose name has not been written in the book of life from the foundation of the world, will wonder when they see the beast, that he was and is not and will come.
[9]"Here is the mind which has wisdom. The seven heads are seven mountains on which the woman sits, [10]and they are seven kings; five have fallen, one is, the other has not yet come; and when he comes, he must remain a little while. [11]The beast which was and is not, is himself also an eighth and is *one* of the seven, and he goes to destruction.

As John wonders about the woman and the beast, he is instructed by the angel that he will be given the answer. While the answer is given, it is not at all apparent just who (or what) is meant in this vision. The only clear part of the vision is that all of the meanings are closely connected Rome and with her empire.

The woman sits on the beast, and the beast is filled with blasphemous names which are insults to God (v. 3). If the woman is Rome, and she sits on the beast, then it seems the beast is the Roman Empire. The blasphemous names are a reference to the many gods of the empire. This beast is described as having seven heads and ten horns (v. 3). This is identical with the beast of 13:1, only the order is changed; i.e., "having ten horns and seven heads." The seven heads are said to be two things. (1) V. 9, the seven heads are seven hills. The identification of this with the city of Rome is usually acknowledged by everyone. Rome was a city built upon seven hills and is described this way numerous times in classical literature. The "seven-hilled" city was a common description given to Rome. This definitely identifies the beast with the imperial city and with the power of Rome. (2) Vv. 10-11, the seven heads are also seven kings: "five have fallen, one is, the other has not yet come; and when he comes, he must remain a little while." What are we to make of this?

"Five have fallen" — can only refer to five previous kings in Rome who no longer exist. The Roman Empire began with Augustus, then came Tiberius, Caligula, Claudius, and Nero. These are the five who have fallen. After the death of Nero there were two years of chaos in which Galba, Otho, and Vitellius followed in quick succession. These are not even considered by John (cf. our study on chapter 13).

"One is" — If our understanding is correct, this must be Vespasian. He is the first emperor to bring back stability to the empire.

"The other has not yet come, and when he comes, he must remain a little time" — Vespasian was succeeded by Titus. His reign lasted for only two years (79-81). After Titus came Domitian (81-96).

If "the one who is" has reference to Vespasian this implies that the book of Revelation was not written during Domitian's reign. While this seems to be a necessary conclusion, there is a solution to this problem. It is possible that John had been banished to the isle of Patmos during the reign of Vespasian and his banishment continued through the short reign of Titus into

Domitian's reign (thus giving rise to the tradition that John received his Revelation during the reign of Domitian). The writing would not have been available on the mainland until a later date. If tradition is correct about John being returned to Ephesus before his death, this would allow for his having received the Revelation while on Patmos, his writing it there to be copied when he came to the mainland, or having later written the visions he saw once he left the island.

C. The Horns and Woman Interpreted, 17:12-18

[12]"The ten horns which you saw are ten kings who have not yet received a kingdom, but they receive authority as kings with the beast for one hour. [13]These have one purpose, and they give their power and authority to the beast. [14]These will wage war against the Lamb, and the Lamb will overcome them, because He is Lord of lords and King of kings, and those who are with Him are the called and chosen and faithful."

[15]And he said to me, "The waters which you saw where the harlot sits, are peoples and multitudes and nations and tongues. [16]And the ten horns which you saw, and the beast, these will hate the harlot and will make her desolate and naked, and will eat her flesh and will burn her up with fire. [17]For God has put it in their hearts to execute His purpose by having a common purpose, and by giving their kingdom to the beast, until the words of God will be fulfilled. [18]The woman whom you saw is the great city, which reigns over the kings of the earth."

17:12 "The ten horns which you saw are ten kings who have not yet received a kingdom, but they receive authority as kings with the beast for one hour.

This is perhaps the most puzzling verse of the chapter. Who is this one who is "an eighth?" He is described

as one who (1) was and is not . . . (2) is one of the seven
. . . (3) and goes to destruction." If the one who is, is
Vespasian; and the one to rule for a short time is Titus,
then it follows that the eighth is Domitian. But this
one is described as "belonging to, or equivalent to" the
seven. This is generally understood to mean that the
emperor who followed Titus is identified with Nero
(*Nero redivivus*). He is evil, like Nero was evil. He is evil
incarnate; i.e., in him the evil of the Roman Empire is
consummated and epitomized. Who is the emperor
who followed Titus? That emperor is Domitian.

The biographer of Domitian is Suetonius, a Roman
historian. Suetonius paints a very grim picture of
Domitian. Early in his reign he would remain secluded
for hours, catching flies and stabbing them with a
sharpened stylus. He formed a homosexual attach-
ment with a famous actor called Paris. He executed
any historian who wrote anything he did not like.
Senators were slaughtered right and left. After a civil
war broke out in the provinces, Domitian became even
more cruel. Suetonius writes, "After his victory in the
civil war he became even more cruel, and to discover
any conspirators who were in hiding, tortured many
of the opposite party by a new form of inquisition,
inserting fire in their privates; and he cut off the
hands of some of them." He began his official edicts
with: "Our lord and god bids this to be done," and
soon this was the only way in which he might be
addressed. It was Domitian who first made Caesar
worship compulsory and who was responsible for
unloosing the flood-tides of persecution on the
Christian church. John saw in Domitian, the reincarna-
tion of Nero.

Since Nero the beast has not existed: he "was and is
not." But also Domitian, the eighth, belongs to the
seven; i.e., he partakes of the evil powers and influence
of the seven.

William Hendriksen says this represents the kingdoms that have ruled the world and that John has been taken back in history to understand all of the ungodly kingdoms that has ever been an affront to God's people. He begins describing the five that fell starting with Egypt, then Assyria, Babylon, Medo-Persia, and Greece. The one "who is" is Rome, and "the one to come" is any nation since Rome that functions in the same way that Rome did.[2] Others go back and try to get these to represent various kings. The trouble with that is, who do you begin counting as the first ruling king?

Homer Hailey's book on Revelation gives three different interpretations that have been handled by commentators on these verses. Hailey says the most popular view is that the angel had specific Roman emperors in mind, five of which were fallen, one was then on the throne and another was yet to come;[3] however there is no uniformity among those who hold this view as to where you begin numbering the emperors. Foy Wallace begins with Julius Caesar making Nero the sixth, omitting the subordinate mock rulers.[4] Where do you begin? This is the difficulty in trying to interpret this section of Scripture.

Hailey says the best solution to the problem is to remember the symbolic nature of the book. Repeatedly John has used seven as the symbol for completeness or perfection and ten for the fullness of power. The seven churches in chapter 1 were not the only congregations. They represented the church in its fullness. The same is said of the seven spirits, the seven lamps, etc. When the book was read to the churches, the members would have thought of Rome as they were told of the harlot, and of the empire when they heard of the beast on whom the harlot sat. The symbolism extends beyond this. The beast represented the total of forceful anti-Christian opposition and the harlot represented that which is lustful, enticing and seductive, all that appeals to the flesh. The seven kings therefore were a symbolic number representing all kings or all kingdoms, past, present, or future, that would oppose the kingdom of God. Each who would come would still be a part of the seven. Although kingdoms rise up out of the upheavals of the sea of society, their anti-God rulers originate in the abyss. Each continues for a little while, then goes down into perdition which is the end of all those who oppose God. By this, Hailey is suggesting that we do not necessarily have to take the seven kings to represent seven literal kings, but the emphasis is on the number seven and the significance of what it is to be a king rather than try to list out seven kings.[5] In verse 11 the beast that was, and is not, is himself also an eighth. Eighth what? Eighth kingdom. Verse 12 says they receive authority as kings with the beast for one hour. They are going to war with the Lamb, but the Lamb is going to overcome and win. The ten horns in verse 16 and the beast are going to hate the harlot. The pleasures of sin disappoint in the end. Jesus said, "Blessed are the meek for they shall inherit the earth; Blessed are those who do hunger and thirst after righteousness for they shall be filled." When Rome falls, those people who are a part of the empire, who have built their life around the empire, hate the woman. She fell and they are losing everything, and they hate her because they have lost it all. Those who are a part of the beast are a part of the empire. They will make her desolate and naked, and shall eat her flesh, and shall burn her utterly with fire.

NOTES

[1]Jim McGuiggan, *The Book of Revelation*, 239.

[2]William Hendricksen, *More Than Conquerors*, 200-204.

[3]Homer Hailey, *Revelation*, 353.

[4]Foy E. Wallace, *The Book of Revelation* (Nashville: Foy E. Wallace Jr. Publications, 1966), 371.

[5]Homer Hailey, *Revelation*, 353-357.

Revelation 18

D. Babylon's Fall Announced, 18:1-3

18:1 After these things I saw another angel coming down from heaven, having great authority, and the earth was illumined with his glory. 2 And he cried out with a mighty voice, saying, "Fallen, fallen is Babylon the great! She has become a dwelling place of demons and a prison of every unclean spirit, and a prison of every unclean and hateful bird. 3 "For all the nations have drunk of the wine of the passion of her immorality, and the kings of the earth have committed *acts of* immorality with her, and the merchants of the earth have become rich by the wealth of her sensuality."

As John begins chapter 18, he has a familiar phrase that we have seen many times which is "After these things I saw." It does not mean that a time limit has taken place in the midst of days or weeks or months, but simply that this vision came after the previous one. There is no time involved in it except in the sequence of events that John sees. Chapter 18 is going to describe the inevitable, complete, and irrevocable character of Babylon's fall. We have already been introduced to Babylon's fall earlier in chapter 14:8, and in chapter 16:19 when the seventh bowl of wrath was poured out. The great city was divided into three parts and the cities of the nations fell and Babylon the great was remembered in the sight of God to give unto her the cup of the wine of the fierceness of his wrath. In chapter 18 we will not only see the fall, but we will see the reason for the fall.

> The section consists of four subdivisions. First, there is a dirge or lament of an angel announcing that the city has fallen (18:1-8); next there is an accompanying dirge by the kings and merchants who mourn the loss of her trade (18:9-20); this is followed by an action parable in which an angel casts a great millstone into the sea, symbolizing the city's fall, which it then laments (18:21-24); and finally, voices from heaven and the elders praise the truth and justice of God's judgments upon the city (19:1-4).[1]

The fall of the harlot (ch. 17) is pictured here as the fall of the wicked city of Babylon. An angel descends to the earth lighted with the glory of God (cf. Ezek. 43:1-2). H.B. Swete says, "So recently has he come from the Presence that in passing he brings a broad belt of light across the dark earth." Those who come from the Presence of God bring with them the light of God.

The message of the angel is the fall of Babylon. So certain is fall that, even though it is yet to take place, it is spoken of as if it has already happened; a *fait accompli*. This is the third time that the fall of the city has been dealt with (cf. 6:12-17; 1:13; 16:18-19). We begin to wonder if the fall will ever take place.

Prophetic literature is used to present what is called "A Doom Song." It is the doom of the city of Rome pictured here as Babylon. There are Old Testament passages which are parallel. In Isaiah 34:11-15, we have the doom song of Edom:

But pelican and hedgehog shall possess it, And owl and raven will dwell in it; And He will stretch over it the line of desolation And the plumb line of emptiness. Its nobles — there is no one there *Whom* they may proclaim king — And all its princes shall be nothing. Thorns will come up in its fortified towers, Nettles and thistles in its fortified cities; It will also be a haunt of jackals *And* an abode of ostriches. The desert creatures shall meet with the wolves, The hairy goat also will cry to its kind; Yes, the night monster will settle there And shall find herself a resting place. The tree snake shall make its nest and lay *eggs* there, And it will hatch and gather *them* under its protection. Yes, the hawks shall be gathered there, Every one with its kind.

Jeremiah 50:39 and 51:37 are part of doom songs on Babylon, "Therefore the desert creatures will live *there* along with the jackals; The ostriches also will live in it, And it will never again be inhabited Or dwelt in from generation to generation. And Babylon will become a heap *of ruins*, a haunt of jackals, An object of horror and hissing, without inhabitants."

A doom song of Nineveh is found in Zephaniah 2:13-15:

And He will stretch out His hand against the north And destroy Assyria, And He will make Nineveh a desolation, Parched like the wilderness. Flocks will lie down in her midst, All beasts which range in herds; Both the pelican and the hedgehog Will lodge in the tops of her pillars; Birds will sing in the window, Desolation *will be* on the threshold; For He has laid bare the cedar work. This is the exultant city Which dwells securely, Who says in her heart, "I am, and there is no one besides me." How she has become a desolation, A resting place for beasts! Everyone who passes by her will hiss *And* wave his hand *in contempt*."

Resounding in the ears of the saints to which John writes are words that are familiar. When John reveals that an angel has pronounced the inevitable doom of

Babylon, the saints understand all too well what the end result would be.

The overthrow of the city would be like Sodom and Gomorrah; it would never be inhabited. Using Old Testament imagery, the city would be a dwelling place for wild beasts of the desert and all kinds of unseemly guests. Speaking of the Medes' overthrow of Babylon, God says through the prophet Isaiah,

> Behold, I am going to stir up the Medes against them, Who will not value silver or take pleasure in gold. And *their* bows will mow down the young men, They will not even have compassion on the fruit of the womb, Nor will their eye pity children. And Babylon, the beauty of kingdoms, the glory of the Chaldeans' pride, Will be as when God overthrew Sodom and Gomorrah. It will never be inhabited or lived in from generation to generation; Nor will the Arab pitch *his* tent there, Nor will shepherds make *their flocks* lie down there. But desert creatures will lie down there, And their houses will be full of owls; Ostriches also will live there, and shaggy goats will frolic there. Hyenas will howl in their fortified towers And jackals in their luxurious palaces. Her *fateful* time also will soon come And her days will not be prolonged" (Isa. 13:17-22; cf. Isa.14:3-23; Jer. 50:2).

Here is a glorious empire that once bragged about her beauty and glory. God says, "I will make you desolate; a barren place where no human would care to dwell. Your glory will be no more."

One of the reasons for Babylon's fall is that she had caused the kings of the earth to commit fornication with her. That is not to be taken as literal fornication, but it could be understood as adulterating themselves not only in the presence of their fellow men but also in the presence of God. Babylon (Rome) was responsible for other nations falling to pernicious and ungodly ways. She encouraged others in wickedness and because of this, God judges her and she will fall. God said the same thing of Nineveh, "[All] because of the many harlotries of the harlot, The charming one, the mistress of sorceries, Who sells nations by her harlotries And families by her sorceries" (Nahum 3:4).

Wantonness (*strenos*) usually means sensuality but often has a secondary sense of softness or luxury. The idea is that the idolatry and sensuality of the city demanded and consumed an abundance of products so that the merchants who supplied them grew wealthy in the trade (see list of articles in v. 12). Here is one of the keys to the hold that Rome had upon the world of her day. The *pax romana* ("Roman Peace"), brought about by the all-powerful military arm of the empire, held the world at bay. The vast travel and communication system of the empire provided the means of moving goods and building up of a world trade. The provinces which had long known war, revolution, piracy, and unrest grew rich under Rome's protection and trade. There is evidence of great gratitude to the emperor as the symbol of the government which made this safety and prosperity possible. All of this contributed to a feeling of self-sufficiency and luxury, plus a worship of wealth and lasciviousness, as well as of the state which made it possible.[2]

E. The Call to God's People Because of Approaching Punishment, 18:4-5

[4]I heard another voice from heaven, saying, "Come out of her, my people, so that you will not participate in her sins and receive of her plagues; [5]for her sins have piled up as high as heaven, and God has remembered her iniquities.

[6]"Pay her back even as she has paid, and give back to her double according to her deeds; in the cup which she has mixed, mix twice as much for her.

[7]"To the degree that she glorified herself and lived sensuously, to the same degree give her torment and

mourning; for she says in her heart, 'I SIT AS A QUEEN AND I AM NOT A WIDOW, and will never see mourning.'

[8]"For this reason in one day her plagues will come, pestilence and mourning and famine, and she will be burned up with fire; for the Lord God who judges her is strong."

18:4 I heard another voice from heaven, saying, "Come out of her, my people, so that you will not participate in her sins and receive of her plagues; 5 for her sins have piled up as high as heaven, and God has remembered her iniquities.

The call of withdrawal is appropriate. God is bringing judgment upon Rome and the righteous are to "come out" to avoid being part of the fall out. The call comes from God himself (cf. reference to "my people"). God has always issued a call for His people to remain aloof from the ways of the world or to leave the world behind (cf. Gen. 12:1; 19:12-14; Isa. 50:8; 51:6, 9, 45; 52:11). Christians are to be a separate people (cf. 2 Cor. 6:17) and "do not participate in the unfruitful deeds of darkness" (Eph. 5:11). If the Christian is to escape the impending destruction, there must be a separation from the ways of the world.

The amount of her sin has reached the point of saturation; judgment is inevitable. "For three transgressions, . . . and for four" (Amos 1,2) expresses the same idea (cf. also 2 Chron. 28:9; Jer. 51:9; Ezra 9:6 with Rev. 16:19). God is longsuffering, not willing that any should perish (2 Pet. 3:9); but God is also a God of justice; and justice demands that the fullness of iniquity be punished.

18:6 "Pay her back even as she has paid, and give back *to her* double according to her deeds; in the cup which she has mixed, mix twice as much for her. 7 "To the degree that she glorified herself and lived sensuously, to the same degree give her torment and mourning; for she says in her heart, 'I SIT AS A QUEEN AND I AM NOT A WIDOW, and will never see mourning.' 8 "For this reason in one day her plagues will come, pestilence and mourning and famine, and she will be burned up with fire; for the Lord God who judges her is strong.

These verses speak of punishment and vengeance. The vengeance is not from the people for they are forbidden such vengeance (cf. Rom. 12:7, 9) but the vengeance is from the Lord. There are two truths found in these verses: (1) A man will reap what he sows. In the Sermon on the Mount, Jesus said, "For in the way you judge, you will be judged; and by your standard of measure, it will be measured to you" (Matt. 7:2). The idea of double punishment and double reward is found in Exodus 22:4, 7, 9. The expression "the double" occurs several times in the writings of the prophets (Isa. 61:7; cf. Jer. 16:18; 17:18; Zech. 9:12). In Jeremiah 50:29 we read, "Summon many against Babylon, All those who bend the bow: Encamp against her on every side, Let there be no escape. Repay her according to her work; According to all that she has done, so do to her; For she has become arrogant against the LORD, Against the Holy One of Israel." (2) The second truth found in these verses is that all pride and arrogance will one day meet with humiliation. Rome has been filled with arrogance and pride ("I sit as a queen and I am not a widow, and will never see mourning," v. 7). To her self-glorification and wantonness is added arrogant boasting and pride. Three things are mentioned: (a) I sit a queen, (b) I am no widow, and (c) shall never see mourning. But she is wrong on all three accounts. While she may think she is a queen and no widow, the fact is that she is a harlot and has many illicit lovers. Solomon said, "When pride comes, then comes dishonor, But with the humble is wisdom" (Prov. 11:2), and also, "Pride goes

295

before destruction, And a haughty spirit before stumbling" (Prov. 16:18). This harlot's boasting is reminiscent of the boasting of old Babylon who said, "I will be a queen forever. . . I am, and there is no one besides me. I will not sit as a widow, nor know loss of children" (Isa. 47:7-8).

William Barclay observes,

> There is a sin which the Greek called *hubris*. *Hubris* is that arrogance, born of wealth and prosperity and success, which comes to feel that it has no need of God, and which eliminates God from life. The punishment for that sin is ultimate abasement and humiliation. Pride always goes before a fall.[3]

F. The Lament over the City, 18:9-24

[9]"And the kings of the earth, who committed *acts of* immorality and lived sensuously with her, will weep and lament over her when they see the smoke of her burning, [10]standing at a distance because of the fear of her torment, saying, 'Woe, woe, the great city, Babylon, the strong city! For in one hour your judgment has come.'

[11]"And the merchants of the earth weep and mourn over her, because no one buys their cargoes any more — [12]cargoes of gold and silver and precious stones and pearls and fine linen and purple and silk and scarlet, and every *kind of* citron wood and every article of ivory and every article *made* from very costly wood and bronze and iron and marble, [13]and cinnamon and spice and incense and perfume and frankincense and wine and olive oil and fine flour and wheat and cattle and sheep, and *cargoes* of horses and chariots and slaves and human lives.

[14]"The fruit you long for has gone from you, and all things that were luxurious and splendid have passed away from you and *men* will no longer find

them. [15]The merchants of these things, who became rich from her, will stand at a distance because of the fear of her torment, weeping and mourning, [16]saying, 'Woe, woe, the great city, she who was clothed in fine linen and purple and scarlet, and adorned with gold and precious stones and pearls; [17]for in one hour such great wealth has been laid waste!' And every shipmaster and every passenger and sailor, and as many as make their living by the sea, stood at a distance, [18]and were crying out as they saw the smoke of her burning, saying, 'What *city* is like the great city?'

[19]"And they threw dust on their heads and were crying out, weeping and mourning, saying, 'Woe, woe, the great city, in which all who had ships at sea became rich by her wealth, for in one hour she has been laid waste!' [20]Rejoice over her, O heaven, and you saints and apostles and prophets, because God has pronounced judgment for you against her."

Verses 9-20 is a threefold lamentation over Babylon's fall. Kings (v. 9), merchants (vv. 11-16) and shipmasters and sailors (vv. 17-19) all will wail and weep because Babylon falls. Again and again we hear of the greatness, the wealth and the wanton luxury of Rome. The picture painted is one that is impressive. Did Rome enjoy such luxury? Was she a city with this kind of wealth? Barclay[4] gives a good summary from the following books: *Roman Society from Nero to Marcus Aurelius* by Samuel Dill, *Roman Life and Manners* by Ludwig Friedlander, *Satires* of Juvenal, *Lives of the Caesars* by Suetonius and the works of Tacitus. From these he draws amazing facts about the wealth and wantonness of Rome, facts which enable us to see that John was not being a fanatic nor was he given to exaggeration. In the Talmud there is a saying that ten measures of wealth came down into the world, and that Rome received nine of them and all the rest only one. "If there is anything you cannot see at Rome, then it is a thing which does not exist and which never existed."

The "Woe, Woe," is an interjection of grief for "the great city, Babylon, the strong city." As the world counts greatness, none was greater than Rome. But she is no match for the Lord God in His judgment. Her fall shall be "in one hour" (cf. 17:12), which reminds us of the suddenness of Rome's fall.

The lament of the kings and the merchants should be read along with the lament over Tyre in Ezekiel 26-27 with which it shares many features in common. The merchants are purely selfish. The market from which they drew so much of their trade is gone. To see more of the luxury of Rome, look in detail at the items in the cargoes which came to Rome (vv. 11-16).

18:21 Then a strong angel took up a stone like a great millstone and threw it into the sea, saying, "So will Babylon, the great city, be thrown down with violence, and will not be found any longer. 22 "And the sound of harpists and musicians and flute-players and trumpeters will not be heard in you any longer; and no craftsman of any craft will be found in you any longer; and the sound of a mill will not be heard in you any longer; 23 and the light of a lamp will not shine in you any longer; and the voice of the bridegroom and bride will not be heard in you any longer; for your merchants were the great men of the earth, because all the nations were deceived by your sorcery. 24 "And in her was found the blood of prophets and of saints and of all who have been slain on the earth."

In these verses we have a picture of the final desolation and final obliteration of Rome. A strong angel takes a stone like a millstone and casts in into the sea. The sea consumes it as if it never existed. Such will be the fate of Rome. John takes his cue from the picture of ancient Babylon. Jeremiah writes, "And as soon as you finish reading this scroll, you will tie a stone to it and throw it into the middle of the Euphrates, and say, 'Just so shall Babylon sink down and not rise again because of the calamity that I am going to bring upon her; and they will become exhausted.' Thus far are the words of Jeremiah" (51:63-64). "In later days Strabo, the Greek geographer, was to say of the ancient Babylon that she was so completely obliterated that no one would ever have dared to say that the desert where she stood was once a great city. Rome is to be desolated, devastated, and obliterated."[5]

Never again will there be rejoicing (v. 22; cf. Ezek. 26:13). Never again will there be the sound of any craftsman plying his trade (v. 22). Never again will there be the sound of domestic activity be heard (v. 22). Never again will there be light on the streets or in the houses (v. 23). Never again will there be any sound of wedding rejoicing for even love will die (v. 23; cf. Jer. 23:20).

NOTES

[1]J.W. Roberts, *The Revelation to John*, The Living Word Commentary, vol. 19 (Austin, TX: Sweet Publishing Company, 1974), 145.

[2]Ibid., 148.

[3]William Barclay, *The Revelation of John, Vol. 2*, 200.

[4]Ibid., 201-208.

[5]Ibid., 215.

Revelation 19

G. The Hallelujah Chorus after the Fall of the Harlot, 19:1-10

[1]After these things I heard something like a loud voice of a great multitude in heaven, saying, "Hallelujah! Salvation and glory and power belong to our God; [2]BECAUSE HIS JUDGMENTS ARE TRUE AND RIGHTEOUS; for He has judged the great harlot who was corrupting the earth with her immorality, and HE HAS AVENGED THE BLOOD OF HIS BOND-SERVANTS ON HER."

[3]And a second time they said, "Hallelujah! HER SMOKE RISES UP FOREVER AND EVER."

[4]And the twenty-four elders and the four living creatures fell down and worshiped God who sits on the throne saying, "Amen. Hallelujah!"

[5]And a voice came from the throne, saying, "Give praise to our God, all you His bond-servants, you who fear Him, the small and the great."

[6]Then I heard something like the voice of a great multitude and like the sound of many waters and like the sound of mighty peals of thunder, saying,

"Hallelujah! For the Lord our God, the Almighty, reigns. ⁷Let us rejoice and be glad and give the glory to Him, for the marriage of the Lamb has come and His bride has made herself ready."

⁸It was given to her to clothe herself in fine linen, bright and clean; for the fine linen is the righteous acts of the saints.

⁹Then he said to me, "Write, 'Blessed are those who are invited to the marriage supper of the Lamb.' " And he said to me, "These are true words of God."

¹⁰Then I fell at his feet to worship him. But he said to me, "Do not do that; I am a fellow servant of yours and your brethren who hold the testimony of Jesus; worship God. For the testimony of Jesus is the spirit of prophecy."

When the fall of Babylon is complete, the rejoicing of the saints begins. "Rejoice over her, O heaven, and you saints and apostles and prophets, because God has pronounced judgment for you against her" (Rev. 18:20). At the beginning of chapter nineteen is the rejoicing which was called for.

19:1 After these things I heard something like a loud voice of a great multitude in heaven, saying, "Hallelujah! Salvation and glory and power belong to our God; 2 BECAUSE HIS JUDGMENTS ARE TRUE AND RIGHTEOUS; for He has judged the great harlot who was corrupting the earth with her immorality, and HE HAS AVENGED THE BLOOD OF HIS BOND-SERVANTS ON HER."

This rejoicing begins with the shout of a vast multitude in heaven. There is the great multitude of the martyrs (7:9) and the great multitude of the host of the angels (12:22). The great multitude here (19:1-2) is most likely the multitude of the angels for the praise of the saints is yet to come in verses 6-8. The chorus begins with hallelujah; a phrase which literally means

"Praise God." It comes from two Hebrew words, *halal* which means "to praise," and *Jah*, which is the name for God. Hallelujah occurs only in the New Testament in this scene (vv. 1,3,4,6). It occurs at the beginning and the end of numerous Psalms beginning with Psalm 104. One essential part of the education of every Jewish boy was the Hallel Psalms (113-118).

The praise to God is for his "salvation and glory and power." In the original there is a definite article before each noun giving to each a definitive emphasis. Salvation would refer to the salvation provided for the redeemed; glory ascribes honor and praise to Him for salvation; and power acknowledges the mighty strength and omnipotence by which He rules His universe.

The word translated "for" or "because" is a word in the original which introduces the cause or reason for the praise. The reason is "His judgments are true and righteous" (cf. 15:3; 16:7). But a second reason is offered: "He has judged the great harlot." Judgment is the inescapable consequence of sin. The worst of all sins is to teach others to sin, or to make it easier for others to sin. God's judgments on Rome is all the more inevitable and all the more stern, because Rome has seduced His people to forsake God and worship and follow after other gods.

19:3 And a second time they said, "Hallelujah! HER SMOKE RISES UP FOREVER AND EVER." 4 And the twenty-four elders and the four living creatures fell down and worshiped God who sits on the throne saying, "Amen. Hallelujah!"

There is a second Hallelujah in verse 3. Their praise is that the smoke of Babylon (Rome) rises for ever and ever. Her destruction is complete and final; she will never rise again to hurt or destroy.

The twenty-four elders then burst into praise. The last time we saw this group (14:3) they were before the throne. In fact, they have been prominent through the visions John received (4:4, 10; 5:6, 11, 14; 7:11; 11:16; 14:3). From the time the angels were given the seven bowls of wrath, no one was able to enter the sanctuary of God's presence until the seven plagues were completed (15:8). But now they have been finished (16:17) and again the throne and those before it come into view. They add their "Amen" and "Hallelujah" to what has been said.

19:5 And a voice came from the throne, saying, "Give praise to our God, all you His bond-servants, you who fear Him, the small and the great."

The voice from the throne is unidentified. Barclay says it is most likely the voice of one of the cherubim.[1] Hailey says it is neither God nor Christ, for the call is to give praise to "our God." "It is a universal summons to praise God for His mighty acts in history, and for his arm stretched out to save His people and His church. It is as if to say: 'Your time of triumph has come! You have suffered, but now you are vindicated! Praise God!'"[2]

Hailey writes,

The throne, from which the voice came, symbolized the majesty and power of Him who sat upon it. The address is to 'his servants,' His bondservants or slaves who had been purchased unto Him. Except for Moses (15:3), the Old Testament prophets (10:17; 11:18), and those who shall serve Him beyond the judgment (22:3), whenever God's servants are mentioned in this book, they are upon the earth. It was to them that John was to show the revelation of the things shortly to come to pass (1:1; 22:6); they were the ones threatened by the teaching of Jezebel in Thyatira (2:20), and the ones sealed upon the earth (7:3). From this it may be concluded that the exhortation of the voice is to the church on earth, all who fear His name, with no class or intellectual distinctions, 'the small and the great." If this is true then the three groups who shout the hallelujahs are (1) the redeemed in heaven, (2) the living creatures and elders, and (3) the saints on earth.[3]

19:6 Then I heard *something* like the voice of a great multitude and like the sound of many waters and like the sound of mighty peals of thunder, saying, "Hallelujah! For the Lord our God, the Almighty, reigns. 7 Let us rejoice and be glad and give the glory to Him, for the marriage of the Lamb has come and His bride has made herself ready." 8 It was given to her to clothe herself in fine linen, bright *and* clean; for the fine linen is the righteous acts of the saints.

The final shout of praise is the praise of the host of the redeemed. Their words are "Hallelujah, for the Lord our God, the Almighty, reigns!"

The reign of God is a recurring theme in the Apocalypse, and it is the equivalent to the universal acceptance or triumph of the gospel. John makes no distinction between the sovereignty of the Father and the Son. There are frequent references to the authority, the throne, and the right of both to rule (1:5; 4:11; 5:12f; 17:14; 19:16). Although the kingdom is treated as a reality (1:9), even to the affirmation that the saints participate in the reign of Christ (1:6; 5:10), the Apocalypse treats that reign as not actualized, in one sense, until the powers which prevented its earthly realization are defeated. Repeatedly the great persecution and martyrdom of the church are seen as the means of that realization (12:11; 17:14). Thus when the martyrdom is complete, God is declared the King of the ages and the universal acceptance of the gospel is proclaimed (15:3,4). And when Rome, the capital city which sits upon the beast is destroyed, the reign of God is declared to be a fact (cf. 11:17 and here, 19:6).[4]

The next picture is of the marriage of the Lamb and His Bride (church). Two women have been introduced: the radiant woman (ch. 12) and the harlot (ch. 17). Now there is a third, the bride. Her appearance is cause for rejoicing. With the removal of the harlot, the marriage feast of the Lamb has come; therefore let the saints "rejoice and be glad." The only other time these two verbs (rejoice and be glad) are found together in Scripture is when Jesus told His disciples of persecutions and false reproaches which would come upon them. He said, "Rejoice and be glad, for your reward in heaven is great; for in the same way they persecuted the prophets who were before you" (Matt. 5:12).

The relationship between God and His people as a marriage goes back to the Old Testament. The prophets often spoke of Israel as the chosen bride of God. "I will betroth you to Me forever; Yes, I will betroth you to Me in righteousness and in justice, In lovingkindness and in compassion, And I will betroth you to Me in faithfulness. Then you will know the LORD" (Hos. 2:19-20). "For your husband is your Maker, Whose name is the LORD of hosts; And your Redeemer is the Holy One of Israel, Who is called the God of all the earth" (Isa. 54:5). "'Return, O faithless sons,' declares the LORD; 'For I am a master to you, And I will take you one from a city and two from a family, And I will bring you to Zion'" (Jer. 3:14).

The figure of marriage also runs through the Gospels. We read of the marriage feast (Matt. 22:2); of the bridegroom and the wedding garment (Matt. 22:10-11); the sons of the bridegroom (Mark 2:19); of the bridegroom (Mark 2:19; Matt. 25:1); of the friends of the bridegroom (John 3:29).

Paul speaks of the church under the same figure or symbolism. He speaks of his betrothing the church as a pure virgin to Christ (2 Cor. 11:2), and of the relationship between a husband and wife being built upon the model of the Christ and the church (Eph. 5:21-33).

19:9 Then he said to me, "Write, 'Blessed are those who are invited to the marriage supper of the Lamb.'" And he said to me, "These are true words of

God." 10 Then I fell at his feet to worship him. But he said to me, "Do not do that; I am a fellow servant of yours and your brethren who hold the testimony of Jesus; worship God. For the testimony of Jesus is the spirit of prophecy."

Once again we have an anonymous speaker talking with John. He tells John to write a beatitude: "Write, 'Blessed are those who are invited to the marriage supper of the Lamb.'" This is the fourth of seven beatitudes found in the Apocalypse (cf. 1:3; 14:13; 16:15; 19:9; 20:6; 22:7, 14). And he said to me, "These are true words of God" (Rev. 19:9). Who gives this instruction? Is it the angel who invited John to come and see the judgment of the harlot (17:1); or the angel who had announced the fall of Babylon (18:1ff)? Perhaps it is the unidentified voice from heaven (18:4), or from the throne (19:5). Since a voice from heaven instructed John to write the beatitude concerning those who die in the Lord (14:13), is it possible that the present voice is the one from the throne? Perhaps it is the voice of verse 5. John's response of falling down to worship (v. 10) would seem to indicate the voice here is the voice of some angel. But the beatitude speaks of a blessing upon those who receive an invitation to the marriage supper of the Lamb. While the invitation is given, we never see the supper or the marriage scene.

John's response of falling down to worship makes some think that John at least thought the voice was from Christ himself. Either that, or John was so overwhelmed by the awesomeness of the whole scene that he impulsively fell at the speaker's feet as an act of homage. Surely John would not have willfully worshiped an angel; there must be some other explanation. But there is no definite answer to the question. The point of emphasis, however, is the response of the one in whose presence John is prostrate. "Do not do that," John is told. Worship belongs to God (cf. Matt. 4:10).

The speaker identifies himself as a "fellow-servant" with John and other Christians who hold the testimony of Jesus. This statement has caused some to think that the one who speaks to John is one of God's saints now on the throne with Jesus (cf. 3:21).

H. The Rider on the White Horse: The Conqueror, 19:11-21

[11]And I saw heaven opened, and behold, a white horse, and He who sat on it is called Faithful and True, and in righteousness He judges and wages war. [12]His eyes are a flame of fire, and on His head are many diadems; and He has a name written on Him which no one knows except Himself. [13]He is clothed with a robe dipped in blood, and His name is called The Word of God. [14]And the armies which are in heaven, clothed in fine linen, white and clean, were following Him on white horses. [15]From His mouth comes a sharp sword, so that with it He may strike down the nations, and He will rule them with a rod of iron; and He treads the wine press of the fierce wrath of God, the Almighty. [16]And on His robe and on His thigh He has a name written, "KING OF KINGS, AND LORD OF LORDS."
[17]Then I saw an angel standing in the sun, and he cried out with a loud voice, saying to all the birds which fly in midheaven, "Come, assemble for the great supper of God, [18]so that you may eat the flesh of kings and the flesh of commanders and the flesh of mighty men and the flesh of horses and of those who sit on them and the flesh of all men, both free men and slaves, and small and great."
[19]And I saw the beast and the kings of the earth and their armies assembled to make war against Him who sat on the horse and against His army. [20]And the beast was seized, and with him the false prophet who performed the signs in his presence, by which he

deceived those who had received the mark of the beast and those who worshiped his image; these two were thrown alive into the lake of fire which burns with brimstone. ²¹And the rest were killed with the sword which came from the mouth of Him who sat on the horse, and all the birds were filled with their flesh.

The harlot has been destroyed, but her two allies remain who are the enemies of God and His people; viz., the beast and false prophet, along with their leader, Satan. Their destruction is at hand.

Satan, the Sea Beast, the Earth Beast and the harlot are about to meet their defeat and destruction. They are presented in reverse order than which they were introduced in the book (chs. 12-17). Since they all stood together, they must fall together. In this vision a warrior-king conducts the war against His enemies. This is not the second or final coming of Christ, but the victorious war against the forces of the Roman Empire.

19:11 And I saw heaven opened, and behold, a white horse, and He who sat on it *is* called Faithful and True, and in righteousness He judges and wages war. 12 His eyes *are* a flame of fire, and on His head *are* many diadems; and He has a name written *on Him* which no one knows except Himself. 13 *He is* clothed with a robe dipped in blood, and His name is called The Word of God.

For the third time John writes, "And I saw heaven opened." The first reference is in 4:1 at the beginning of the vision in which the great scroll was disclosed. The second reference is in 11:19 when the vision of the scroll was completed.

Whether there is a similarity between the rider here and the one mentioned in chapter 6 is immaterial. The identification of this writer is complete with the title "Faithful and True" and "the Word of God" (v. 13).

This rider is the Christ. His eyes are a flame of fire (cf. 1:14; 2:18), indicating his penetration into the hearts of His enemies. On his head are many diadems, a crown worn by royalty. Satan even wore seven diadems and the sea-beast wore ten. Jesus, however, wears "many diadems," indicating the unlimited extent of His rule.

To identify the "name written on Him which no one knows" would be futile. And why should we try to "know," if we are told "no one knows"? Perhaps this is the writer's way of describing the ultimate mystery of his being and nature.

His garment is sprinkled with blood (older versions, "dipped in blood"). The blood here is not his own blood, or the blood of the Lamb that was slain (ch. 5), but rather the blood of His enemies. It is important to remember here that the heavenly leader in this vision is not the slain one, but the slayer. Hailey writes,

> Already a gory judgment has been described in which the winepress was trodden outside the city and blood covered the land (14:20). The scene depicted here of the blood-sprinkled garment is reminiscent of the one in which Jehovah was returning from Bozrah with His garments stained with blood. In response to the question posed, "Wherefore art thou red in thine apparel, and thy garments like him that treadeth in the winevat?" Jehovah replied, "I have trodden the winepress alone....I trod them in mine anger, and trampled them in my wrath; and their lifeblood is sprinkled upon my garments, and I have stained all my raiment" (Isa. 63:1-6; cf. also Joel 3:9-13). His garment was sprinkled with His enemies' blood when He tread the winepress. This parallel leads to the conclusion that the blood sprinkled upon the Rider's garment is that of His enemies and not His own or that of His own people who had died for His cause.[5]

19:14 And the armies which are in heaven, clothed in fine linen, white *and* clean, were following Him on white horses. 15 From His mouth comes a sharp

sword, so that with it He may strike down the nations, and He will rule them with a rod of iron; and He treads the wine press of the fierce wrath of God, the Almighty. 16 And on His robe and on His thigh He has a name written, "KING OF KINGS, AND LORD OF LORDS."

The armies of heaven which follow this rider on the white horse are the victorious saints whom the Lord leads in the defeat and overthrow of His enemies. It was said that those who overcame would be dressed in white garments (3:5); the martyrs underneath the altar each had a white robe (6:11); and those standing before the throne, who had come out of the great tribulation, were also arrayed in white robes (7:9, 14). And here they are; the army of heaven dressed in fine linen, white and pure.

The sword coming out of his mouth is not the gospel by which men are converted, but rather the sword of judgment. This sword was a characteristic of the description of the glorified Christ (1:16). With it He would make war against the unfaithful in the church (2:16), and in a far greater judgment he would smite the heathen nations.

19:17 Then I saw an angel standing in the sun, and he cried out with a loud voice, saying to all the birds which fly in midheaven, "Come, assemble for the great supper of God, 18 so that you may eat the flesh of kings and the flesh of commanders and the flesh of mighty men and the flesh of horses and of those who sit on them and the flesh of all men, both free men and slaves, and small and great." 19 And I saw the beast and the kings of the earth and their armies assembled to make war against Him who sat on the horse and against His army. 20 And the beast was seized, and with him the false prophet who performed the signs in his presence, by which he deceived those who had received the mark of the beast and those who worshiped his image; these two were thrown alive into the lake of fire which burns with brimstone. 21 And the rest were killed with the sword which came from the mouth of Him who sat on the horse, and all the birds were filled with their flesh.

These verses describe the doom of the enemies of Christ. A grim and terrible picture is painted. One is reminded of Matthew 24:28, "Wherever the corpse is, there the vultures will gather." These words of Jesus regarding the destruction of Jerusalem are similar for this picture. The picture of the birds of prey being invited to come from all over the sky and to feast on the corpses of the slain reminds us also of the slaughter and destruction of the forces of Gog and Magog of which Ezekiel wrote.

> As for you, son of man, thus says the Lord GOD, 'Speak to every kind of bird and to every beast of the field, . . . You will eat the flesh of mighty men and drink the blood of the princes of the earth, as *though they were* rams, lambs, goats, and bulls, . . . So you will eat fat until you are glutted, and drink blood until you are drunk, from My sacrifice which I have sacrificed for you. You will be glutted at My table with horses and charioteers, with mighty men and all the men of war," declares the Lord GOD (Ezek. 39:17-20).

This bloodthirsty picture is far more in line with the Old Testament apocalyptic expectations than with the gospel of Jesus Christ.

As this chapter comes to a close, we have seen the end of those with the mark of the beast in chapters 15 and 16; and the fall of Babylon in chapters 17 and 18; and Christ's victory over the beast and the false prophet here in chapter 19 — all of these who are allies of Satan have gone down in defeat. There is only one force that remains and that is Satan himself. That is what chapter 20 will show us.

NOTES

[1]William Barclay, *The Revelation of John, Vol. 2,* 220.

[2]Ibid., 221.

[3]Homer Hailey, *Revelation: An Introduction and Commentary,* 375-376.

[4]J.W. Roberts, *The Revelation to John,* The Living Word Commentary, vol. 19, 159.

[5]Homer Hailey, *Revelation: An Introduction and Commentary,* 383.

Revelation 20

I. The Thousand Year Reign, 20:1-6

¹Then I saw an angel coming down from heaven, holding the key of the abyss and a great chain in his hand. ²And he laid hold of the dragon, the serpent of old, who is the devil and Satan, and bound him for a thousand years; ³and he threw him into the abyss, and shut it and sealed it over him, so that he would not deceive the nations any longer, until the thousand years were completed; after these things he must be released for a short time.

⁴Then I saw thrones, and they sat on them, and judgment was given to them. And I saw the souls of those who had been beheaded because of their testimony of Jesus and because of the word of God, and those who had not worshiped the beast or his image, and had not received the mark on their forehead and on their hand; and they came to life and reigned with Christ for a thousand years. ⁵The rest of the dead did not come to life until the thousand years were completed. This is the first resurrection. ⁶Blessed and holy is the one who has a part in the first resurrection;

over these the second death has no power, but they will be priests of God and of Christ and will reign with Him for a thousand years.

This chapter occasioned much speculation through the centuries. It has served, and continues to serve, as the spawning ground for various millennial theories for a thousand year reign of Christ on earth. It is fundamental to the premillennial position. Alan Johnson begins his explanation of this text with these words, "The exegesis of this passages leads me to a premillennial interpretation."[1]

Homer Hailey gives a good summary of the general theory of millennialism in the following:

> Christ will come in the first phase of his return to earth (called "rapture"), and at this time the righteous dead will be raised, the living saints will be changed and both will be caught up in the air to meet the Lord. Then will come the marriage feast of the Lamb, during which there will be a great tribulation on earth. After the wedding, He and the bride, the church, will then complete the return to earth (called "the revelation"), where Christ will set up His kingdom, sit on David's throne and reign from Jerusalem for a literal thousand years — the millennium. According to some, the Jews will be converted and return to Palestine, Old Testament worship will be restored (with modifications) and there will be on earth an idealistic life which will continue for the definite period of one thousand years. At the end of the millennium Satan will be loosed for a short time and make a last furious effort to destroy the Lord's people and work. This will be followed by the resurrection of the wicked dead (for the righteous dead will have been raised at the beginning of the thousand years). The judgment will occur and the eternal destinies of heaven or hell will be meted.[2]

This section is composed of several parts each beginning with, "Then I saw" (or "And I saw," or "I saw") starting in chapter 19:11, 17, 19; 20:1, 4, 11, 12 and 21:1. This phrase appears to establish a sequence of visions which carries us from the rider on the white horse (19:11) to the establishment of the "new heaven and new earth" (21:1). The beast and the false prophet were cast in to the lake of fire that burned with brimstone, chapter 19:19-21. With the defeat of these two and the destruction of the harlot (chs. 17-18) Satan has lost his allies. Our present study (ch. 20) tell us what becomes of Satan — viz., he is defeated and the saints of God reign victorious. What becomes of him and the victory of the saints is the chief subject of chapter 20:1-10 rather than the 1000 years.

There are several things mentioned which are significant in the first ten verses of this chapter. How we understand these images (figures) will be important to our interpretation of this section of Scripture.

1. A thousand-year binding
2. A thousand-year reigning
3. A first resurrection
4. A thousand-year death
5. A little season of Satanic freedom
6. A Gog-Magog host
7. An invasion of a holy city
8. A (second) resurrection
9. A second death
10. A judgment scene
11. A lake of fire

20:1 Then I saw an angel coming down from heaven, holding the key of the abyss and a great chain in his hand. 2 And he laid hold of the dragon, the serpent of old, who is the devil and Satan, and bound him for a thousand years; 3 and he threw him into the abyss, and shut *it* and sealed *it* over him, so that he would not deceive the nations any longer, until the thousand years were completed; after these things he must be released for a short time.

The angel John sees coming down from heaven has "the key of the abyss and a great chain in his hand." The key represents power and the chain represents that by which Satan is bound. The "pit" (Gk, *abyssos*) is the spiritual underworld, the abode or stronghold of Satan (9:1; 11:7; 17:8). The Greeks saw the abyss as a vast subterranean cavern beneath the earth; sometimes the place where all the dead went. It was sometimes viewed as the place where special sinners were kept awaiting punishment. It was reached by a funnel or channel or chasm through the earth. It is the chasm which the angel locks in order to keep the Devil in the abyss.

The abyss is the place the devils fear the most. In the story of the Gerasene demoniac the request of the devils is that Jesus would not command them to depart from the man and return to the abyss (which seems to imply it was their proper place of habitation), Luke 8:26-31.

All four names by which the great deceiver of the whole world[3] was called in 12:9 are repeated here. Each of these names has a significance. As a dragon,[4] strong and ferocious, he was defeated in heavenly combat by Michael and his angels (12:8). As the old serpent,[5] he is the cunning deceiver, who from Eden has beguiled with his craftiness (2 Cor. 11:3). But, he unsuccessfully tries to sweep away the people of God by a river from his mouth (12:15). As the devil,[6] he has been the accuser and slanderer, the malignant enemy of God and man; and as Satan,[7] he is the adversary, opponent and antagonist of all that is good. He knows that his time is short (12:12).

The sealing of this abyss is reminiscent of the tomb of Jesus which was sealed so no one could tamper with it and or steal the body (Matt. 27:66; cf. also Dan. 6:17). The purpose of the sealing is confinement not punishment. That is found later (v. 10). It is to prevent him from the deceiving the nations.

The great chain signifies a manacle or handcuff such as was used to chain the demoniac (Mark 5:4) or was ordinarily used to retrain Roman prisoners (Acts 12:7; 28:20). The chaining of the devil did not render him powerless but only limited his power and what he was able to accomplish. As Satan himself had for eighteen years bound a woman with sickness whom Jesus had healed (Luke 13:16; Matt. 12:9), so now he will be chained (bound).

The binding of Satan was to be for a thousand years. The number 1000 is a complete number which stands for an undetermined but full period of time (cf. Job 9:3; 33:23; Ps. 50:10; 90:4; Eccl. 6:6; 7:28; 2 Pet. 3:8).

This time period relates to events we have already seen in the book of Revelation: (1) the holy city was to be trodden under foot forty-two months, 11:2; (2) the witnesses were to prophesy under persecution twelve hundred sixty days, 11:3; (3) the radiant woman was to be in the wilderness, protected from Satan and cared for by God and the Lamb, twelve hundred sixty days, 12:6; or "time, times and a half a time," three and a half years, 12:1; (4) the beast with authority to persecute and blaspheme would continue his unholy work forty-two months, 13:5 (cf. Dan. 7:25). Hailey says, "This period was the same for each and was interpreted to be the period of the Roman persecution . . . the thousand years symbolizes that period of victory beginning with Constantine, when Roman persecution ended, and continuing until some time before the Lord's return when Satan will be loosed from his present restraint."[8] But does this refer to a "period of time" or to "a state of affairs"? The later seems more likely; i.e., it refers to the ways things are since the death of Jesus.

The casting down of the dragon to the abyss coincides with his being cast out of heaven (12:7-9). When Jesus sent the seventy out on the limited commission, they returned with joy saying, "Lord, even the demons

are subject to us in Your name" (Luke 10:17). Upon saying this, Jesus responded by saying to them, "I was
watching Satan fall from heaven like lightning" (Luke
10:18). This relates to Jesus' assertion to entering the
strong man's house and plundering his good by first
binding the strong man (cf. Matt. 12:24-30; Mark 3:22-
27). With His eye on the victory of the cross, Jesus said,
"Now judgment is upon this world; now the ruler of
this world will be cast out. And I, if I am lifted up from
the earth, will draw all men to Myself" (John 12:31-32).
As Jesus instructs His disciples to take the gospel to all
the nations (Matt. 28:18-20; Mark 16:15-16), we understand that throught to mean that "the great dragon
was thrown down, the serpent of old who is called the
devil and Satan, who deceives the whole world; he was
thrown down to the earth, and his angels were thrown
down with him" (Rev. 12:9). Jesus is the one who is
stronger than Satan. In His incarnation He ". . . par-
took of the same, that through death He might render
powerless him who had the power of death, that is, the
devil, and might free those who through fear of death
were subject to slavery all their lives" (Heb. 2:14-15).

The "thousand years" then refers to a "state of affairs"
which began with the Incarnation, was achieved in the
crucifixion, and assured in His resurrection from the
dead and continues to be expressed in His ascension
and enthronement at the right hand of God (cf. Heb.
1:3; 12:12).

20:4 Then I saw thrones, and they sat on them, and
judgment was given to them. And I *saw* the souls of
those who had been beheaded because of their testimony of Jesus and because of the word of God, and
those who had not worshiped the beast or his image,
and had not received the mark on their forehead and
on their hand; and they came to life and reigned with
Christ for a thousand years. 5 The rest of the dead did
not come to life until the thousand years were com-

pleted. This is the first resurrection. 6 Blessed and holy is the one who has a part in the first resurrection; over these the second death has no power, but they will be priests of God and of Christ and will reign with Him for a thousand years.

In the next vision John sees thrones and someone ("they") sat on them. Judgment is given to those on the throne, which is related to two specific groups. First, there are "those who had been beheaded because of their testimony of Jesus and because of the word of God." Second, there are those who "had not worshiped the beast or its image and had not received its mark on their forehead or on their hand."

The saints mentioned in these verses have been faithful to Christ and have been given the kingdom. This is what Jesus promised to the ones who overcome (2:26-27; 3:21). Daniel had prophesied concerning this many years before (cf. Dan. 7). Beginning with verse seventeen, Daniel is told of four kingdoms which would rise up but "the saints of the Highest One will receive the kingdom and possess the kingdom forever, for all ages to come" (7:18). In Daniel 7:21-22, we read of the little horn making war with them and prevailing "until the Ancient of Days came and judgment was passed in favor of the saints of the Highest One, and the time arrived when the saints took possession of the kingdom" (Dan. 7:22). That is the background for the vision found here. The ones sitting on thrones have received a kingdom (that is why they are on thrones) and judgment was given to them (cf. 18:20). In Revelation 2:26-27, Jesus promises those who overcome a share in the kingdom. In Revelation 11:15, the kingdom of the world becomes the kingdom of our God and of His Christ. Then, the saints get their reward with Jesus and share in His kingdom. The same thing is going on in Daniel 7. In verse 21-22 the saints get the kingdom at the destruction of the beast. Then we read, "'But the court will sit *for judgment,* and his dominion will be taken away, annihilated and destroyed forever. 'Then the sovereignty, the dominion and the greatness of *all* the kingdoms under the whole heaven will be given to the people of the saints of the Highest One; His kingdom *will be* an everlasting kingdom, and all the dominions will serve and obey Him'" (Dan. 7:26-27).

20:4 Then I saw thrones, and they sat on them, and judgment was given to them. And I *saw* the souls of those who had been beheaded because of their testimony of Jesus and because of the word of God, and those who had not worshiped the beast or his image, and had not received the mark on their forehead and on their hand; and they came to life and reigned with Christ for a thousand years.

Several questions confront us in this verse. (1) What are these thrones? (2) Who is on them? (3) What is the judgment given to them?

The word "throne" is used to refer to: (1) God's throne, Acts 7:39; Rev. 4:2; (2) Christ's throne, Heb. 1:8f; Rev. 3:21; (3) the throne of David on which Christ now sits, Luke 1:32; Acts 2:30; (4) thrones of judgment occupied by the apostles in the present dispensation, Matt. 18:28; Luke 22:30; (5) the elders' thrones, 4:4; 11:16; (6) the throne of judgment, 20:11; (7) the throne of grace, Heb. 4:16; (8) Satan's throne, the seat of paganism, 2:13; (9) the throne of the dragon, 13:2; (10) the throne which Satan gave to the beast, 13:2; (11) the throne of princes or rulers, Luke 1:52; and (12) the thrones of the souls beheaded for the testimony of Jesus, 20:4.

The second question is answered in this verse. The ones on the thrones are "the souls of those who had been beheaded for the testimony of Jesus, and because of the word of God, and those who had not worshiped the beast or his image, and had not received the mark on their forehead and on their hand." Two classes are mentioned here. First, those who have actually been martyred for their loyalty to Christ. The word used here for "beheaded" is a very strong word, occurring only here in the New Testament. It means "to cut with an axe." Second, those who have not worshiped the beast and have not received his mark on their hand or on their forehand. H. B. Swete identifies these, as those who, although they were not actually martyred, willingly bore suffering, reproach, boycotting, imprisonment, loss of their goods, the disruption of their homes and their personal relationships for the sake of Jesus Christ. These are those who were purchased with His blood and who "reign upon the earth" (Rev. 5:9-10).

Third, what is the judgment given to them? The judgment is that rendered against Satan on behalf of the saints. It is a judgment on their behalf that had been executed against the harlot as she was burned with fire (18:20). Now judgment is executed against the beast and the false prophet as they are cast into the lake of fire and brimstone (v. 10).

20:5 The rest of the dead did not come to life until the thousand years were completed. This is the first resurrection. 6 Blessed and holy is the one who has a part in the first resurrection; over these the second death has no power, but they will be priests of God and of Christ and will reign with Him for a thousand years.

Who are the "rest of the dead?" They are the dead who died in service of the beast. They neither live nor reign with anyone. They remain dead for the 1,000 years. John calls this "the first resurrection." Those who view this as the future bodily resurrection miss the point. A pronouncement of "blessedness" is declared upon those who participate in the "first resurrection," for they escape the "second death" (v. 6). John goes on to say that they "will reign with Him [Christ] for a thousand years." Those who experience the "first resurrection" will not experience the "second death" (2:11; 20:14; 21:8). The "second death" is identified later as "the lake that burns with fire and brimstone" (21:8).

Let us take a moment and reflect on what we have seen. John mentions a "first resurrection" and implies "a second resurrection." He mentions a "second death" and implies a "first death." To what do each of these refer?

The first resurrection is a resurrection to life; it is living and reigning with Christ. Some say it is the resurrection to life experienced by a person in obedience to the gospel of Christ (cf. Rom. 6:1-17). The Christian has no fear of the second death; i.e., eternal destruction, for as one who has experienced the first resurrection, the second death has no power.

Those who participate in the first resurrection are "priests of God and of Christ and will reign with Him for a thousand years." John has already stated that Christians have been made a kingdom of priests (1:6). Peter writes that Christians are a "holy nation" (1 Pet. 1:5) and a "royal priesthood" (1 Pet. 2:9).

J. Satan is Loosed for a Little Season, 20:7-10

[7]When the thousand years are completed, Satan will be released from his prison, [8]and will come out to deceive the nations which are in the four corners of the earth, Gog and Magog, to gather them together for the war; the number of them is like the sand of the seashore. [9]And they came up on the broad plain of the earth and surrounded the camp of the saints and the beloved city, and fire came down from heaven and devoured them. [10]And the devil who deceived them was thrown into the lake of fire and brimstone, where the beast and the false prophet are also; and they will be tormented day and night forever and ever.

When the thousand years are completed, Satan is released out of his prison to continue in his deceiving of the nations. This loosing is first introduced in verse 3 and called "a little season" or "a short time." Whatever is bound in verse 3, is released in verse 7. Gog and Magog are familiar symbols of invading nations attacking Israel. The background for this vision is Ezekiel 38-39. Ezekiel is not clear at what point in the messianic age this attack is expected. In apocalyptic literature these two mythlike symbols come to stand for forces which fight against the Messiah (Sibylline Oracles 3:512; 2 Esdras 13:34; Enoch 56:5-8; 90:13-15; Test. Jos. 19:8). John may not have intended the sequence to be chronological. He simply means that once the thousand years of the martyrs' reign have begun (that is, when the victory is complete), though Satan has lost his power at large (in Rome's defeat), he will continue the battle as local conditions and situations permit. The lesson is that even in times of the church's greatest triumph, saints are in danger of Satan's deception. Only in keeping God at the center of their lives are Christians safe.

K. End of Conflict: Final Judgment, 20:11-15

[11]Then I saw a great white throne and Him who sat upon it, from whose presence earth and heaven fled away, and no place was found for them. [12]And I saw the dead, the great and the small, standing before the throne, and books were opened; and another book was opened, which is *the book* of life; and the dead were judged from the things which were written in the books, according to their deeds. [13]And the sea gave up the dead which were in it, and death and Hades gave up the dead which were in them; and they were judged, every one *of them* according to their deeds. [14]Then death and Hades were thrown into the lake of fire. This is the second death, the lake of fire. [15]And if

anyone's name was not found written in the book of
life, he was thrown into the lake of fire.

We have already seen several judgment scenes in
the Apocalypse: the judgment of the nations on behalf
of the saints (11:18); a judgment on those who poured
out the blood of the saints (16:5); a judgment on the
harlot (11:18); and one on the beast and the false
prophet (19:11-21).

John sees a great white throne and "Him who sat
upon it." Throughout the book of Revelation the One
sitting upon the throne is the Father (4:2, 9; 5:1, 7, 13;
6:16; 7:10, 15; 19:4; 21:5). Furthermore, all judgments
of the book have been ascribed to God the Almighty
(16:5, 7; 18:8, 20; 19:2). But, it was the Word of God, the
King of Kings who came forth to judge and make war
(19:11). Jesus had said that the Father had given all
judgment unto the Son (John 5:22-27; cf. Matt. 25:31-48;
Acts 17:31; 2 Tim. 4:1; 2 Cor. 5:1:10). The idea that the
Father and the Son both judge should not pose any
problem. Jesus taught that both He and the Father are
one (John 10:30), and that to see Him is to see the
Father (John 14:10). Barclay says the reason why the
Father is viewed as the one judging is because the fla-
vor of the book is Jewish.

The judgment begins with the passing away of this
present world. Earth and heaven fled away from the
presence of the One seated on the throne. The nature
of this disappearance is like that where the islands and
mountains fled away (16:20). It has been abundantly
foretold that the heaven and earth would pass away.
Psalm 102:25-27 reads, "Of old You founded the earth,
And the heavens are the work of Your hands. "Even
they will perish, but You endure; And all of them will
wear out like a garment; Like clothing You will change
them and they will be changed. "But You are the same,
And Your years will not come to an end.

Isaiah 51:6 says, "Lift up your eyes to the sky, Then

look to the earth beneath; For the sky will vanish like smoke, And the earth will wear out like a garment And its inhabitants will die in like manner; But My salvation will be forever, And My righteousness will not wane." It is symbolic of the events which are to happen at the end of time. Peter wrote, "But the day of the Lord will come like a thief, in which the heavens will pass away with a roar and the elements will be destroyed with intense heat, and the earth and its works will be burned up" (2 Pet. 3:10).

Judgment involves the great and the small. There is none so great as to escape the judgment of God, and there is none so unimportant as to fail to receive the vindication of God. The scene presupposes the resurrection of all who have lived and died from Adam until the end of time. Jesus said, "Do not marvel at this; for an hour is coming, in which all who are in the tombs will hear His voice, and will come forth; those who did the good *deeds* to a resurrection of life, those who committed the evil *deeds* to a resurrection of judgment" (John 5:28-29). The tombs from which these shall come forth are not limited to the rock-hewn sepulchers, but includes whatever graves hold the dust of the dead. Regardless of the destruction of the body in death, and no matter what the condition of the body caused by death, all will be raised and stand before Him in the great day of judgment.

"The books were opened" is reminiscent of Daniel 7:10, where the books were opened in the judgment of the fourth great beast who was judged, slain, and burned. Two kinds of books are mentioned, the first of which is the book which contains the records of the deeds of men. The idea here is simple symbolism which declares that all through life we are writing our own destiny; we are compiling a story of success or failure in God's sight. We are acquiring a record which will bring us either honor or shame in the presence of God. Every man is the author of his own story; it is not so much God who judges us as it is that we write our own judgment. This is not a judgment of the wicked only, "For we must all appear before the judgment seat of Christ, so that each one may be recompensed for his deeds in the body, according to what he has done, whether good or bad" (2 Cor. 5:10).

The second book is the Book of Life. This phrase, the "book of life," occurs often in Scripture. In order to save the people of Israel, Moses was willing for his name to be blotted out of the Book of Life (Exod. 32:32). Psalm 69:28 says, "May they be blotted out of the book of life And may they not be recorded with the righteous." Isaiah speaks of those who are written among the living (Isa. 4:3) and Paul speaks of his fellow-laborers whose names are in the Book of Life (Phil. 4:3; cf. Mal. 3:16; Luke 10:20; Rev. 3:5; 13:8; 17:8; 21:27).

John adds, "and the dead were judged from the things which were written in the books, according to their deeds." Ecclesiastes 12:14 says, "For God will bring every act to judgment, everything which is hidden, whether it is good or evil." Hebrews 4:13 says, "And there is no creature hidden from His sight, but all things are open and laid bare to the eyes of Him with whom we have to do."

20:14 Then death and Hades were thrown into the lake of fire. This is the second death, the lake of fire. 15 And if anyone's name was not found written in the book of life, he was thrown into the lake of fire.

When the word *Hades* occurs in the book it is associated with death (cf. 6:8) and now they end together. Death, our final enemy (1 Cor. 15:26) is cast into the lake of fire. This is the second death (cf. 2:11; 20:6). Up to this point the harlot, the beast, the false prophet, Satan and now death and Hades, have been brought to their end in the lake of fire.

There remains only one group to be dealt with: those "not found written in the book of life." "These would be 'the rest' who had fought with the beast and false prophet against the Lord, and those who had been slain with the sword out of His mouth (19:21), those who had rallied about Satan in his last effort to destroy the camp of the saints (20:9), and all others who, in their indifference to the Lord, had to taken a stand for Him, or had turned away from Him (Heb. 10:26, 31). The defeat of Satan and his forces against God and truth is total — complete and final."[9]

NOTES

[1]Alan Johnson, *Book of Revelation*, The Expositor's Bible Commentary, vol. 12, 578.

[2]Homer Hailey, *Revelation: An Introduction and Commentary*, 389-390.

[3]Rev. 12:9; 13:14; 18:23; 19:20.

[4]Rev. 12:3-4,7,9,13,16-17; 13:2,4,11; 16:13.

[5]Rev. 12:9,14-15.

[6]Rev. 2:10; 12:9,12.

[7]Rev. 2:9,13,24; 3:9; 12:9.

[8]Homer Hailey, *Revelation: An Introduction and Commentary*, 392.

[9]Ibid., 403.

Revelation 21

L. The New Heaven and New Earth, 21:1-8

[1]Then I saw a new heaven and a new earth; for the first heaven and the first earth passed away, and there is no longer any sea. [2]And I saw the holy city, new Jerusalem, coming down out of heaven from God, made ready as a bride adorned for her husband. [3]And I heard a loud voice from the throne, saying, "Behold, the tabernacle of God is among men, and He will dwell among them, and they shall be His people, and God Himself will be among them, [4]and He will wipe away every tear from their eyes; and there will no longer be any death; there will no longer be any mourning, or crying, or pain; the first things have passed away."

[5]And He who sits on the throne said, "Behold, I am making all things new." And He said, "Write, for these words are faithful and true."

[6]Then He said to me, "It is done. I am the Alpha and the Omega, the beginning and the end. I will give to the one who thirsts from the spring of the water of life without cost. [7]He who overcomes will inherit

these things, and I will be his God and he will be My son. ⁸But for the cowardly and unbelieving and abominable and murderers and immoral persons and sorcerers and idolaters and all liars, their part will be in the lake that burns with fire and brimstone, which is the second death."

The war is over, the smoke is cleared, and the people of God are the only ones left standing. The victory belongs to the people. All this time Rome had declared that Caesar was god, the most powerful, and that those who followed after him were the real "saints." Now, after Rome has taken her fall and the people of God are all standing with their leader, the Lamb, guess who looks like they won. Right! The saints won! Now the Christian can live in a "new atmosphere." The pressure is off, the persecution is over, the people of God are vindicated. The persecution suffered from the tyranny of a Domitian now fades into insignificance as we realize as Christians what we have and enjoy, as we see the world in its proper perspective. We live in a new universe when we understand the victory to be ours, and know that God is in control and not Rome. The old universe of fear and uncertainty is gone (cf. 2 Pet. 3:13; also Isa. 65-66).

21:1 Then I saw a new heaven and a new earth; for the first heaven and the first earth passed away, and there is no longer *any* sea.

The "new heaven and new earth" indicates a new order of things (Isa. 34:3-4; 51:4-6; 65:16-25; 66:22-24). The Greek word for "new" is *kainos* and it emphasizes newness in quality rather than in point of time. They may be living in the old heavens and the old earth, but they have a new aspect, a new character; it is an environment adapted to a new end. It is a universe in victory. This new heaven and new earth replaces the old heaven and the old earth that "fled away" (20:11). It speaks of the works of evil fleeing from the presence of God. When all of the evil was destroyed and righteousness reigns.

> We cannot be sure how he [i.e., John] viewed the new heaven and new earth, but the context of this statement suggests that his real concern is not with physical geography, but to describe a context of life for God's people which accords with the great and glorious purpose God has in mind for them.[1]

"There is no longer any sea" can be understood in two ways. First, there is the idea of separation. If this is meant, John is saying there is no more separation, either from God or from one another. What separates in 4:6 is done away with in 21:1. Second, in the book of Revelation the beast comes up out of the sea (13:1), and the great harlot sits upon many waters (17:1). To take away the sea means there will be no more worry about the beast nor the harlot in the new heaven and new earth; they are gone.

21:2 And I saw the holy city, new Jerusalem, coming down out of heaven from God, made ready as a bride adorned for her husband.

The holy city, new Jerusalem, is seen as coming down out of heaven. This suggests origin rather than distinctions. The new Jerusalem is from God and pictured as a bride ready for her husband. The details of her adornment are given in verses 11-21. In 19:7 the people of God were presented as a bride; here the same figure is used of the place of their abode, the New Jerusalem. The contrast between the earthly city with the harlot and the heavenly city with the bride is obvious. The holy city is not an actual city but a symbol of the church in its glorified and eternal state. This is familiar language used for the church (cf. Eph. 5:21-32; et. al.) There is nothing discussed in this text that is not already a possession of the church, or a description of the church in other passages. Uninspired Jewish apocalyptic literature speaks of the glorified Jerusalem in similar terminology (Sib. Or. 5:420ff; Tobit 13:16ff; 4 Ezra 7:26; 10:44ff; 2 Baruch 4:2ff).

21:3 And I heard a loud voice from the throne, saying, "Behold, the tabernacle of God is among men, and He will dwell among them, and they shall be His people, and God Himself will be among them,

In verse 3 the voice from the throne is once again not identified, though it may be the speaker of 16:17 or 19:5. Or, it may be either God (the Father) or Christ (the Lamb).

The Holiness Code of Leviticus 26 is apparent, "'I will also walk among you and be your God, and you shall be My people" (Lev. 26:12).

Twice the tabernacle in heaven has been in view (13:6; 15:5). The word "tabernacle" means a tent or booth, a lodging or dwelling place. The word *skēnē* is the word used here and was originally used for the dwelling place of God in the wilderness. It is also closely related to the Hebrew *shekinah*. The same word is used of Jesus in John 1:14.

21:4 and He will wipe away every tear from their eyes; and there will no longer be *any* death; there will no longer be *any* mourning, or crying, or pain; the first things have passed away."

The compassionate and loving character of God is seen in that he will "wipe away every tear from their eyes. . ." Whatever causes the heart to ache and break will be taken away. The bliss of being in the presence of God is described with five negatives: no tears, no death, no mourning, no crying, and no pain. The reason for this is because sin which caused them is no more; sin and death are swallowed up in victory.

Death, mourning, crying and pain are all a part of the "first things" which now are gone. They belong to the previous order of things. They are now history (cf. Isa. 35:10; 65:19; also Rev. 7:16-17).

Death entered the world through sin (Gen. 3; Rom. 5:12). Man fears death and is subject to it (Heb. 2:15; 9:27). But as God said through Isaiah, "He will swallow up death for all time" (25:8). Or as Paul pronounced, "DEATH IS SWALLOWED UP in victory" (1 Cor. 15:54). Now the final declaration of the victory over death finds its fulfillment. With death, mourning, crying and pain also disappear.

21:5 And He who sits on the throne said, "Behold, I am making all things new." And He said, "Write, for these words are faithful and true." 6 Then He said to me, "It is done. I am the Alpha and the Omega, the beginning and the end. I will give to the one who thirsts from the spring of the water of life without cost.

The throne upon which God sits represents his sovereignty and majesty (Rev. 4:2, 9; 5:1, 7; 6:16; 7:10, 15; 19:14). As He speaks, He speaks words of promise and comfort. He says, "Behold, I am making all things new." This makes one think of 2 Corinthians 5:17; when one becomes a new creature in Christ, "the old things passed away; behold, new things have come." The grandeur of "all things made new" indicates that everything will surely surpass and exceed anything that our imagination can conceive.

The one who instructs John to write is either an angel, God, or Christ. If it is not an angel, it could be either God or Christ since both sit on the throne (3:21). Yet it is Christ who acts in behalf of His Father in carrying out His purpose (5:7). It really makes no difference; the fact is, someone with authority (i.e., sitting on a throne) instructs John once again to write.

The words heard by the apostle are "faithful and true" because it is impossible for God who spoke them to lie (Heb. 6:18; 2 Tim. 2:13). They are faithful and true because of the integrity and trustworthiness of the speaker. He is in sovereign control. He claims to be the "Alpha and Omega, the beginning and the end." The claim of 1:18 is repeated here and again in 22:13, where a phrase is added "the first and the last." The meaning here is that God is our everything. Using the first and last letters of the Greek alphabet the implication is that God is first, last, and all the letters in between. God's claim to be the only deity is also found in other passages (Isa. 41:4; 43:10; 44:6; 48:12).

The Scripture often uses the figure of thirst to indicate the desire of the soul for God. The Psalmist wrote, "As the deer pants for the water brooks, So my soul pants for You, O God" (42:1; cf. Ps. 36:9; 63:1; Isa. 55:1). Jesus himself claims to give the water of life to those who are thirsty (cf. John 4). And, in the final end, God will provide from His throne and the throne of the Lamb, "a spring of the water of life" (Rev. 22:1).

21:7 "He who overcomes will inherit these things, and I will be his God and he will be My son.

We are familiar with the overcomer in this book. Throughout the letters to the seven churches there are several promises made to those who overcome. We learn there that the overcomer will eat of the tree of life (2:7); not be hurt by the second death (2:11); be given hidden manna and a white stone (2:17); receive power over the nations (2:26); not have his name blotted from the book of life (3:5); be a pillar in the temple of God (3:12); and sit with Christ on his throne (3:21). But here, John gives the greatest promise of all, "I will be his God and he will be my son" (cf. Gen. 17:7; 2 Sam. 7:14; Gal. 3:27-28; 1 John 3:1-4).

21:8 "But for the cowardly and unbelieving and abominable and murderers and immoral persons and sorcerers and idolaters and all liars, their part *will be* in the lake that burns with fire and brimstone, which is the second death."

The list of those who find their part in the lake of fire and brimstone sounds like a list of the "who's who of hell." The "cowardly" are those who fear and serve men rather than God. They are those who retreat because they fear for their own safety rather than strive to be faithful to Christ. These are the ones in which God has no pleasure (Heb. 10:38f). The "unbelieving" are those have betrayed the trust committed to them (Luke 12:46). They are not the unbelievers of the secular pagan world, but believers who denied their faith in a time of trial. The "abominable" are those who joined in the unholy ritual of emperor worship. They have given themselves over to the practice of unnatural vices. They are the morally and spiritually foul, who are abhorred by God. They have taken of the harlot's cup of abominations, "even the unclean things of her immorality" (17:4). The "murderers" are those who count human life cheap and whose hands are stained with innocent blood. They are those who have no respect for the sanctity of human life. The lack of respect for the sanctity of human life has been punishable by death from the days of Noah (Gen. 9:6), under the law (Exod. 21:12), and under the present dispensation (Rom. 13:4). This may also refer to those who committed acts of homicide under the tyranny of the beast. The "immoral persons" are the sexually immoral. Those who indulge their lust in promiscuity without respect for the sanctity of the marriage bond. The "sorcerer" is one who allows his life to be governed by potions and the stars. He practices demonic magic instead of living by the wisdom of God and His word. The idolater is the one who worships the creature rather than the Creator (cf. Rom. 1:25), a worshiper of a false god, whether a visible image or an invisible mental image. And "all liars" have committed themselves to falsehood instead of truth (cf. Acts 5, the first problem in the local church was lying). Liars is appropriate in John's list in view of his emphasis on truth (cf. 1 John 2:21-22; 3:19; 4:6). Throughout the book of Revelation, deviation from truth has been seen as wrong (2:2; 3:19; 14:5; 21:27; 22:15).

XI. THE VISION OF THE NEW JERUSALEM, 21:9-22:5

A. John is Invited to View the Holy City, 21:9-11a

The Lamb's bride and the marriage supper (19:7f) is now shown in greater detail. The angel seen here may be the same angel who spoke in 17:1 and showed him the judgment of the great harlot. Now John is shown another woman, the bride, who is the wife of the Lamb.

⁹Then one of the seven angels who had the seven bowls full of the seven last plagues came and spoke with me, saying, "Come here, I will show you the bride, the wife of the Lamb." ¹⁰And he carried me away in the Spirit to a great and high mountain, and showed me the holy city, Jerusalem, coming down out of heaven from God, ¹¹having the glory of God.

The angel of 17:1 who had invited John to witness the judgment of the great harlot now commands him to come and see the bride, the wife of the Lamb. Attention is drawn to the contrast between the great harlot (the wicked city, Babylon) and the bride of the Lamb (the holy city, Jerusalem). One is of the earth, the other descends from heaven. The contrast seems both obvious and intentional. The angel wants John (and us) to notice the striking difference between these two women. One is ungodly, sinful and disgusting; the other is pure, lovely and holy.

The phrase "in the Spirit" (cf 1:10; 4:2; 17:3) is reminiscent of the language of Ezekiel 40:2, where the prophet Ezekiel begins his description of the restored city of Jerusalem and its temple.

John is carried away to a "great and high mountain" and shown the holy city, the new Jerusalem. John had already been taken away into a wilderness and had seen the wicked Babylon (17:3), but now he is taken to a high mountain and sees the holy city. In the visionary experience the mountain really existed. Mountains have always played an important part in God's dealing with man. Moses' received the Ten Commandments from God on Mt. Sinai (Exod. 19-20); Elijah challenged and defeated the prophets of Baal with the power of God on Mt. Carmel (1 Kgs. 18). Ezekiel's vision of the restored temple was given on "a very high mountain" (Ezek. 40:2). Jesus was transfigured on a mountain (Matt. 17).

John now sees the holy city, Jerusalem, coming down out of heaven in the splendor and radiance of the glory of God. As the glory of God was reflected in the face of Moses at Mt. Sinai (Exod. 19-20; 2 Cor. 3:7-15) and in Jesus' face at the Mount of Transfiguration (Matt. 17), so also the holy city radiates with the glory of almighty God. In Ezekiel 45:5, the word "glory" designates God's presence.

The phrase "New Jerusalem" occurs only twice in Scripture (Rev. 3:12; 21:1). "The Holy City" occurs three times (Rev. 11:2; 21:1; 22:19); and "the beloved city" once (20:9). It is now called "the holy city, Jerusalem." The holy city signifies the favor of God. "The Great City" (see comments on 11:8) is the harlot city of Babylon. "The Holy City" is the New Jerusalem, coming down out of heaven from God.

The descending from heaven should only be seen as a "real event" within the vision. The "descent" metaphor is simply a way of expressing God's entrance into our earthly existence. The city comes down from heaven indicating that the final state of man is a gift from God.

B. The City's Outward Appearance, 21:11b-23

Her brilliance was like a very costly stone, as a stone of crystal-clear jasper. [12]It had a great and high wall, with twelve gates, and at the gates twelve angels; and names were written on them, which are the names of the twelve tribes of the sons of Israel. [13]There were three gates on the east and three gates on the north and three gates on the south and three gates on the west. [14]And the wall of the city had twelve foundation stones, and on them were the twelve names of the twelve apostles of the Lamb.

[15]The one who spoke with me had a gold measuring rod to measure the city, and its gates and its wall. [16]The city is laid out as a square, and its length is as great as the width; and he measured the city with the rod, fifteen hundred miles; its length and width and height are equal. [17]And he measured its wall, seventy-two yards, according to human measurements, which are also angelic measurements. [18]The material of the wall was jasper; and the city was pure gold, like clear glass. [19]The foundation stones of the city wall were adorned with every kind of precious stone. The first foundation stone was jasper; the second, sapphire; the third, chalcedony; the fourth, emerald; [20]the fifth, sardonyx; the sixth, sardius; the seventh, chrysolite; the eighth, beryl; the ninth, topaz; the tenth, chrysoprase; the eleventh, jacinth; the twelfth, amethyst. [21]And the twelve gates were twelve pearls; each one of the gates was a single pearl. And the street of the city was pure gold, like transparent glass.

[22]I saw no temple in it, for the Lord God the Almighty and the Lamb are its temple. [23]And the city has no need of the sun or of the moon to shine on it, for the glory of God has illumined it, and its lamp is the Lamb.

The holy city is the most beautiful and perfect institution upon the earth in spite of her faults or weaknesses. Her light was like a precious stone, clear, radiant, and beautiful (Matt. 5:14; Phil. 2:14ff). She has a great and high wall (Ps. 31:2-3; Isa. 26:1; 60:18; Zech. 2:5). She has twelve gates, twelve angels, twelve names of the twelve tribes of Israel. The gates were distributed equally on the four sides of the city.

John is not satisfied with a general picture of the greatness of the New Jerusalem. As Ezekiel measured the city, so John must measure the city. It is a perfect cube, 12,000 furlongs (1500 miles). So a Jerusalem of 1500 miles is to be built in every direction, in the land of Canaan, and with a wall of only 266 feet. The literalist obviously runs into a problem here. Barclay says the city would have a total area of 2,250,000 miles. This is a symbolism showing that there is ample room for everyone.

21:11b Her brilliance was like a very costly stone, as a stone of crystal-clear jasper.

"Her brilliance" (*phōstēr*, "luminary, a light-giving body") occurs only here and in Philippians 2:15. This brilliance certainly reflects the glory of God. Her brilliance is describe as "like a crystal-clear jasper." In ancient times the word "jasper" was used for any opaque precious stone. John had already seen this stone shining from the throne of God (4:3).

21:12 It had a great and high wall, with twelve gates, and at the gates twelve angels; and names *were* written on them, which are *the names* of the twelve tribes of the sons of Israel. 13 *There were* three gates on the east and three gates on the north and three gates on the south and three gates on the west.

What was introduced in verse two now continues. Here is a city surrounded by a great and high wall. It has twelve gates with twelve angels guarding the gates. On the gates are written the names of the twelve tribes of Israel. In John's day, no city could endure without a strong wall for protection. But what protection is needed here? The enemy of God's people has been destroyed. Walls separate the clean from the unclean. But what separation is needed here? There is no one left from whom to separate. What, then, does this mean? The wall should be understood as a part of an ideal city as conceived by ancient people. The fact that there is no need for separation or for protection is beside the point. God's people are given a picture in the vision of the most ideal city in which to dwell. One which is so great that there need be no fear, but provides them with a sense of great security.

The twelve gates are evenly distributed on each side. In Ezekiel 48:30-34, the twelve gates are named after the twelve tribes of Israel. John's order of the twelve gates is the same order given to Ezekiel in measuring the temple (Ezek. 42:15ff); i.e., east, north, south, and west; rather than north, south, east, and west. Many believe both Ezekiel and John avoided arranging the gates in the same order observed by the astrologers of his day.

The twelve angels as gatekeepers may reflect Isaiah's picture of watchmen upon the wall (Isa. 62:6). An ideal city would have watchmen on the wall for security purposes.

21:14 And the wall of the city had twelve foundation stones, and on them *were* the twelve names of the twelve apostles of the Lamb.

The wall of the city had twelve foundation stones with the names of the twelve apostles on them. It is futile to try to put literal names on either the twelve gates or the foundation stones. In the twelve tribes of Israel, Levi is assigned a gate, and Ephraim and Manasseh are combined in Joseph. With the twelve apostles who would be omitted — Matthias or Paul? Both were genuine apostles but that would make the number thirteen, not twelve.

The fact is, the number twelve is not to be taken literally, but figuratively to represent the full or complete number of the tribes of Israel and the twelve apostles. The number twelve is a corporate use; i.e., the number twelve is sometimes used to refer to the select group of the apostles when all twelve are not in view — John 20:24 has ten; 1 Corinthians 15:5 has eleven.

The apostles laid the foundation for the church (Eph. 2:20; 1 Cor. 3:10), carried out the great commission by preaching the gospel (Mark 16:15-16; Col. 1:23), and sat upon twelve thrones judging the twelve tribes of Israel by the word (Matt. 19:18).

21:15 The one who spoke with me had a gold measuring rod to measure the city, and its gates and its wall. 16 The city is laid out as a square, and its length is as great as the width; and he measured the city with the rod, fifteen hundred miles; its length and width and height are equal. 17 And he measured its wall, seventy-two yards, *according to* human measurements, which are *also* angelic *measurements.*

In chapter 11:1, John is told to measure the temple of God, the altar, and those who worship there. Here, the holy city is measured by an angel (cf. 21:9), who uses a reed or staff approximately ten feet long. The measuring of chapter 11 was for separation and protection. The meaning here, however, is to portray the immensity of the size of the holy city; the eternal dwelling place of the faithful.

John writes, "the city is laid out as a square." Its length, width, and height are "all equal" (v. 16). The measurement is fifteen hundred miles. It is said to be "according to human measurements, which are also angelic measurements." The NIV says it was "by man's measurement, which the angel was using" (21:17).

The shape would remind the reader within the Jewish community of the inner sanctuary of the temple (1 Kgs 6:20), the place of the presence of God. The fact that the city is foursquare means that God has taken up residence with His people.

21:18 The material of the wall was jasper, and the city was pure gold, like clear glass.

The wall (lit., "the material of the wall") is described in words appropriate for "the holy city, Jerusalem." Jasper is a most precious stone and symbolizes the radiance of God (4:3; cf. Isa. 54:11-12; Zech. 2:5). The city itself is built upon transparent glass (21:21).

21:19 The foundation stones of the city walls were adorned with every kind of precious stone. The first foundation stone was jasper; the second, sapphire; the third, chalcedony; the fourth, emerald; 20 the fifth, sardonyx; the sixth, sardius; the seventh, chrysolite; the eighth, beryl; the ninth, topaz; the tenth, chrysoprase; the eleventh, jacinth; and the twelfth, amethyst.

The materials of the city contain beautiful gems and stones. It has a wall of "jasper." This was a translucent rock crystal, green in color. A city of gold. The foundations of the wall were adorned with all manner of precious stones. Jasper was thought to be the diamond, a most precious stone even today. "Sapphire" is sky blue or of various shades of blue, flecked with gold. "Chalcedony" is a green silicate of copper found in the copper mines in Calcedon in Asia Minor. "Emerald" is the greenest of all stones. "Sardonyx" is an onyx in which the white was broken by layers of red and brown. "Sardius" is a blood red stone, often used for carving or cameos. "Chrysolite," whose identity is uncertain, was probably a yellow beryl or gold-colored jasper. "Beryl" is a sea blue or green. "Topaz" is a transparent greenish gold stone. "Chrysoprase" is a green quartz. "Jacinth" is a violet, bluish purple stone, like a sapphire. "Amethyst" is a purple quartz and similar to jacinth but more brilliant.

21:21 And the twelve gates were twelve pearls; each one of the gates was a single pearl. And the street of the city was pure gold, like transparent glass.

There are two descriptions which remain: (1) the gates are of pearl, and (2) the streets are of pure gold. Along with gold and expensive clothing, pearl was a mark of affluence (1 Tim. 2:9). They are considered of great value (cf. Matt. 7:6; 13:45-46). The gold is unlike any known to us for it is described as "transparent glass."

> The gold, like that of verse 18, is unlike any known to us; for it is as transparent glass, transcending the beauty of any metal known on earth. The beholders of the great harlot city cried as they beheld her burning, "What city is like the great city?" (18:18). In her class there was none like her. And so shall the beholder of this city say, To what shall we compare such a city? It is as incomparable as the God from whom it comes. Isaiah issued the following challenge to the people of his day, "To whom then will ye liken God? or what likeness will ye compare unto him?" (Isa. 40:18). There was no one or likeness to which to make a comparison. And so might John challenge the whole creation, "To what will ye liken this city? or to what will you compare it?" The answer is that there is nothing in the universe with which it can be compared.[2]

21:22 I saw no temple in it, for the Lord God the Almighty and the Lamb are its temple. 23 And the city has no need of the sun or of the moon to shine on it, for the glory of God has illumined it, and its lamp *is* the Lamb.

There is no "temple" here. The need for sun or moon is obsolete. The holy city is illumined by the glory of God (*shekinah*). Isaiah used the same term to picture the restoration of Jerusalem. He wrote, "The sun will no more be your light by day, nor will the brightness of the moon shine on you, for the LORD will be your everlasting light, and your God will be your glory. Your sun will never set again, and your moon will wane no more; the LORD will be your everlasting light, and your days of sorrow will end" (Isa. 60:19-20, NIV).

It was just as Jesus said it would. It receives all the "light" it needs from the Lamb, and the glory of God. We see the nations walking by the light of the church. Without the church, they walk in darkness. What an ugly and dark world it would be. Kings bring their glory into it. Important people will come and be a part of it. And when we have a "nation of kings" what a glorious people that would be. And that is exactly what we are. Kings pay homage to us (Isa. 2:2-4; 49:6; Jer. 3:17; 16:19ff; Zech. 8:20ff). The gates of this great city are never shut. Anyone who has washed his robe in the blood of the Lamb has the right to enter the city, regardless of race, color, or ethnic group. . . There is no reason to shut the gates, for there is no night there. We live in a world of light; a light from the glorious gospel of Christ (Col. 1:10ff). All of the shadows have vanished. Jesus referred to himself as the "light of the world" (8:12; cf. 3:18; 12:35). Now, as the light, he continues to illuminate even heaven itself.

C. The Inhabitants of the City, 21:24-27

[24]The nations will walk by its light, and the kings of the earth will bring their glory into it. [25]In the daytime (for there will be no night there) its gates will never be closed; [26]and they will bring the glory and the honor of the nations into it; [27]and nothing unclean, and no one who practices abomination and lying, shall ever come into it, but only those whose names are written in the Lamb's book of life.

21:24 The nations will walk by its light, and the kings of the earth will bring their glory into it.

In earlier visions "the nations" refer to those that dwell on the earth (13:14) and are deceived by the devil (17:2). But all the enemies of Christ have been destroyed (chs. 17-18, 20), therefore this reference to the nations cannot refer to the wicked but must be the fulfillment of the song of the redeemed, ""Who will not fear, O Lord, and glorify Your name? For You alone are holy; For ALL THE NATIONS WILL COME AND WORSHIP BEFORE YOU, FOR YOUR RIGHTEOUS ACTS HAVE BEEN REVEALED" (Rev. 15:4).

The model for this is Isaiah 60. The glory of the Lord is seen Jerusalem, and the nations and kings are attracted to it (60:1-3). The wealth of the nations comes back to Zion as her sons and daughters return from afar (60:4-5; also vv. 6, 9, 11, 13, 17).

21:25 In the daytime (for there will be no night there) its gates will never be closed;

The gates of the city are open because there is no need for them to be shut. No one is excluded from entering. Security measures are no longer necessary since evil has been destroyed. Day extends indefinitely because darkness never comes. Zechariah 14:7 serves as a background for this part of the vision.

21:26 and they will bring the glory and the honor of the nations into it;

And they (i.e., the nations and kings) will bring their glory and honor into the city. The nations will walk in the city and the kings of the earth will bring their glory and honor within it; but the city is not defiled. These have been brought into the city by the redemptive work of the Lamb.

21:27 and nothing unclean, and no one who practices abomination and lying, shall ever come into it, but only those whose names are written in the Lamb's book of life.

The defiant shall not enter the city. Nothing unclean shall enter therein. Only those whose names are written in the Lamb's Book of Life. Nothing which is contrary to the holiness of God will find its way into the city.

There is an obvious similarity between Genesis 1 and Revelation 21. In Genesis 1 God created the heavens and earth; in Revelation 21 God creates a new heaven and a new earth. In Genesis 1 God created the sun, moon and stars; in Revelation 21 the city has no need for sun nor moon to shine on it for the glory of God lights it and the Lamb is the lamp. In Genesis there was paradise lost; in Revelation there is paradise regained. Genesis tells us the story of the cunning power of the devil; Revelation tells us he is bound and cast into a lake of fire. Genesis pictures man fleeing from God and hiding from the presence of Jehovah; Revelation pictures for us a beautiful relationship and redeemed man. Genesis shows us an angel that keeps man out of the tree of life; Revelation shows us that man has access once again to that tree of life.

NOTES

[1]G.R. Beasley-Murray, *The Book of Revelation*, 308.
[2]Homer Hailey, *Revelation: An Introduction and Commentary*, 417.

Revelation 22

D. The Provision of the City, 22:1-5

[1]Then he showed me a river of the water of life, clear as crystal, coming from the throne of God and of the Lamb, [2]in the middle of its street. On either side of the river was the tree of life, bearing twelve kinds of fruit, yielding its fruit every month; and the leaves of the tree were for the healing of the nations. [3]There will no longer be any curse; and the throne of God and of the Lamb will be in it, and His bond-servants will serve Him; [4]they will see His face, and His name will be on their foreheads. [5]And there will no longer be any night; and they will not have need of the light of a lamp nor the light of the sun, because the Lord God will illumine them; and they will reign forever and ever.

Here is a paradise garden with a "river of life." We partake of this river as the people of God (cf. Ezek. 47:1ff; Ps. 46:4; Joel 3:18; Zech. 14:8). The tree of life (Gen. 3:22) is the source of life and the leaves are for the healing of the nations (i.e., all people).

22:1 Then he showed me a river of the water of life, clear as crystal, coming from the throne of God and of the Lamb, 2 in the middle of its street. On either side of the river was the tree of life, bearing twelve *kinds of* fruit, yielding its fruit every month; and the leaves of the tree were for the healing of the nations.

The opening verses of chapter 22 are a continuation of the previous chapter, even though the phrase "then he showed me" indicates a break. The vision of the Lamb's bride, was introduced in 21:9. The expression "water of life" is peculiar to John's writings (cf. 7:17; 21:6; 22:1, 17) and is similar to the phrase "living water" found in the Gospel of John (4:10-11; 7:38). Does the phrase "water of life" signify water possessing life-giving powers? Or, is it water which restores and supports life? Or, is it water which "is" life?

The water which is mentioned here is described as water "clear as crystal," a phrase found only here and in 4:6. This indicates both the purity and beauty of the stream, that it is unpolluted or uncorrupted.

Connecting the river of the water of life with the tree of life (v. 2) indicates that John has in mind the original scene from the garden of Eden (Gen. 2:9-10). This picture is also similar to Ezekiel's vision (Ezek. 47:1-12). Ezekiel does not speak of "living water" but does say, "It will come about that every living creature which swarms in every place where the river goes, **will live**. And there will be very many fish, for these waters go there and *the others* become fresh; so everything **will live** where the river goes" (v. 9, bold added for emphasis). Notice the words "will live" in Ezekiel's prophecy. In Ezekiel's visions the river flowed eastward from the threshold of the temple toward the Dead Sea. Its waters were for the healing of the salt waters providing abundance of fish (cf. "very many fish," v. 9; "very many," v. 10) and on either side of the river grows all kinds of trees for food.

In John's vision the river flows from the "throne of

God and of the Lamb," and continues through "the middle of its street" and has no termination. It sustains (or is) life.

The source of this river is "coming from the throne of God and of the Lamb." This is the first time the phrase "throne of God and of the Lamb" occurs. Prior to this it has been "Him who sits on the throne" (5:13; 6:16; 7:10); or the Lamb whom John sees either "between the throne" (5:6) or "in the center of the throne" (7:17). Now the Lamb is seen sitting on the throne in heaven with the Father.

The phrase "tree of life" occurs twice in Genesis (2:9; 3:22). This tree, placed in the Garden of Eden, provided man with the potentiality of eternal life; i.e., eating of this tree would have allowed man to live forever. But man sinned causing his removal from the garden and no longer had access to the tree of life. Now, he must find life in a different tree, the one on which the Savior was hanged (Acts 5:30; 10:39; Gal. 3:13; 1 Pet. 2:24).

The tree provides fruit to be eaten and leaves for the healing of the nations. In other words, the nations, once marred by sin and separated from God in their rebellious state, may now upon their repentance and obedience, stand in the presence of God in the New Jerusalem.

22:3 There will no longer be any curse; and the throne of God and of the Lamb will be in it, and His bond-servants will serve Him; 4 they will see His face, and His name *will be* on their foreheads.

"There will no longer be any curse" reminds us once again of Eden. The curse was upon the serpent (Gen. 3:14), the ground (v. 17) and upon Adam and Eve (vv. 16-19). Curses continue through out the Old Testament upon those who are disobedient: Cain, because of murder (Gen. 4:11); those who curse Abraham or his descendants (Gen. 12:3; 27:29); and those who violate God's law (Deut. 27:15-26; 28:15-68).

But the greatest blessing of all eternity is reflected in "they will see His face, and His name will be on their foreheads." To see the face of God is something man has never been able to do. Moses was not allowed to see the face of God because God declared, "You cannot see My face, for no man can see Me and live!" (Exod. 33:20). However, Moses was allowed to see the backside of God (Exod. 33:23). Philip declared a universal desire of the human soul when he asked the Lord, "Show us the Father" (John 14:8). That desire is inherent within the human soul. Christians live with the promise that his name will be written on us (3:12) and as servants of God we are sealed on our foreheads (7:3). Those standing on Mt. Zion have the name of the Lamb and of His Father written on their foreheads (14:1).

22:5 And there will no longer be *any* night; and they will not have need of the light of a lamp nor the light of the sun, because the Lord God will illumine them; and they will reign forever and ever.

What was said earlier is repeated here, there is no need for light of lamp or the light of the sun (cf. 21:23, 25). In the book of Revelation the thought has developed from walking in the light (21:24), to serving in the light (22:3), and now to reigning in the light (22:5). This will consist together with a reign which will be "forever and ever" as opposed to the one thousand year reign mentioned in Revelation 20:1-8.

XII. THE EPILOGUE: CLOSING WORDS, 22:6-21

[6]And he said to me, "These words are faithful and true"; and the Lord, the God of the spirits of the prophets, sent His angel to show to His bond-servants the things which must soon take place.

[7]"And behold, I am coming quickly. Blessed is he

who heeds the words of the prophecy of this book." [8]I, John, am the one who heard and saw these things. And when I heard and saw, I fell down to worship at the feet of the angel who showed me these things. [9]But he said to me, "Do not do that. I am a fellow servant of yours and of your brethren the prophets and of those who heed the words of this book. Worship God." [10]And he said to me, "Do not seal up the words of the prophecy of this book, for the time is near. [11]Let the one who does wrong, still do wrong; and the one who is filthy, still be filthy; and let the one who is righteous, still practice righteousness; and the one who is holy, still keep himself holy."

[12]"Behold, I am coming quickly, and My reward is with Me, to render to every man according to what he has done. [13]I am the Alpha and the Omega, the first and the last, the beginning and the end."

[14]Blessed are those who wash their robes, so that they may have the right to the tree of life, and may enter by the gates into the city. [15]Outside are the dogs and the sorcerers and the immoral persons and the murderers and the idolaters, and everyone who loves and practices lying.

[16]"I, Jesus, have sent My angel to testify to you these things for the churches. I am the root and the descendant of David, the bright morning star."

[17]The Spirit and the bride say, "Come." And let the one who hears say, "Come." And let the one who is thirsty come; let the one who wishes take the water of life without cost.

[18]I testify to everyone who hears the words of the prophecy of this book: if anyone adds to them, God will add to him the plagues which are written in this book; [19]and if anyone takes away from the words of the book of this prophecy, God will take away his part from the tree of life and from the holy city, which are written in this book.

[20]He who testifies to these things says, "Yes, I am

coming quickly." Amen. Come, Lord Jesus.
²¹The grace of the Lord Jesus be with all. Amen.

The final division of the book is an urgent appeal to
be faithful. Two subjects are stressed: (1) The exhortation to faithfully keep and preserve "the words of the
prophecy of this book, vv. 7,9,18-19; and (2) Jesus'
pledge to "come quickly" and accomplish his words in
the book for his saints, vv. 7,10,12,20.

The importance of the book is stressed in the following: (1) A twofold exhortation to keep the words of the
book (vv. 6-9). John assures us that the words of the
book are genuinely from God and he will soon perform his words (vv. 6-7). Hence, "Blessed is he who
heeds the words of the prophecy of this book." John's
assurance of the genuineness of the book and the
angels' promise to serve "those who heed the words of
this book" (vv. 8-9). (2) The immediate needs of the
righteous are the words of the book (vv. 10-15).
Daniel's prophecy pertained to the future needs of the
saints and was to be sealed or shut up "until the end of
the time" (Dan. 12:4). But in great contrast the book of
Revelation pertains to the immediate needs of the
saints in all generations. Thus the commandment to
John was, "Do not seal up the words of the prophecy of
this book; for the time is near," for Christ to come and
fulfill the promises of the book to His church.

Those who "have the right to the tree of life, and
may enter by the gates into the city" (21:1-22:5) must
have the words of this book.

John closes with a great invitation (v. 17) and a
strong word of warning to preserve the words of this
book (vv. 18-19). His final promise is: "He who testifies
to these things says, 'Yes, I am coming quickly.' Amen.
Come, Lord Jesus. The grace of the Lord Jesus be with
all. Amen" (vv. 20-21)

Verses 6-21 form the Epilogue of the Book of
Revelation. It is difficult, at times, to discern who is

doing the speaking. But that does not take away from the wonderful words of exhortation with which John closes this book. As we come to the end there remains three things for John to leave his readers: (1) the witness of God and His Son to the vision, (2) some final exhortations to the original readers, and (3) an exhortation for the Lord's return.

The similarities between the Prologue and the Epilogue are often pointed out. First, this book is a genuine book of prophecy (cf. 1:3 with 22:6, 9-10, 18-19); second, the writing is by one who is a genuine prophet (cf. 1:1, 9-10 with 22:8-10); third, the book is to be read to the churches (1:3, 11 with 22:18); and fourth, it is to encourage the faithful (1:3 with 22:7, 12, 14).

22:6 And he said to me, "These words are faithful and true"; and the Lord, the God of the spirits of the prophets, sent His angel to show to His bond-servants the things which must soon take place.

The identity of the speaker in this verse is uncertain. Is it the angel of 21:9, 15? Or, is it the angel who had given the Revelation (1:1; 22:16)? Or is it Jesus himself? While we cannot be certain, it seems that the context would indicate that it is the angel of the preceding paragraph who showed John the eternal city, the New Jerusalem.

As in the opening verses (1:1), the book closes with the words that what has been seen and written by John. These are "the things which must soon take place" (22:6). The sources of these visions is said to be "the God of the spirits of the prophets" (22:6). The word "spirits" is plural and does not refer to the Holy Spirit but rather the prophets as a group (both Old and New Testament prophets).

22:7 "And behold, I am coming quickly. Blessed is he who heeds the words of the prophecy of this book."

The word "Behold" is an imperative and asks the

reader to pay special and close attention. "I am coming quickly" signifies an action that is swift (cf. Matt. 5:25; 28:7-8; John 11:29). Robert Mounce writes concerning this verse,

> It is best to take the utterance at face value and accept the difficulty of a foreshortened perspective on the time of the end rather than to reinterpret it in the sense that Jesus 'comes' in the crises of life and especially at the death of every man. Revelation has enough riddles without our adding more. Matthew 24:42-44 counsels every generation to be on the alert for the return of the Son of man. An infallible timetable would do away with that attitude of urgent expectation which has been the hallmark of the church through the centuries.[1]

The sixth beatitude pronounces a blessing on the one who "heeds the words of the prophecy of this book" (v. 7). This repeats the principle of the first beatitude, "Blessed is he who reads and those who hear the words of the prophecy, and heed the things which are written in it; for the time is near" (1:3). To heed means "to observe, fulfill, or pay attention to." The words written herein are important and ought to be given serious consideration (cf. 22:18-29).

22:8 I, John, am the one who heard and saw these things. And when I heard and saw, I fell down to worship at the feet of the angel who showed me these things. 9 But he said to me, "Do not do that. I am a fellow servant of yours and of your brethren the prophets and of those who heed the words of this book. Worship God."

John now attests to what he saw and heard; i.e., the things which are written in this book. The impulse of John to worship the angel is curious in light of the fact that a similar impulse was recently rejected (19:10). Some offer conjectures as to why John does this, but the fact is that we really do not know why. Some think

John may be simply making a second reference to the previous incident because it seems unlikely that he would once again make such a gesture. Others think this may be a reference to the fact that it is likely that people in Asia Minor had been practicing the worship of angels (cf. Col. 2:18), but that does not seem likely either. Nonetheless, John is corrected (not rebuked, for his heart is right) and told to "worship God" (v. 9b; cf. Matt. 4:10). In giving this instruction, the angel identifies himself as one who is a "fellow-servant" to John, the prophets, and other Christians.

22:10 And he said to me, "Do not seal up the words of the prophecy of this book, for the time is near.

"Do not seal up . . . the time is near." The prophet Daniel is told "seal up the book until the end of time" (12:4). The things about which Daniel writes pertain to the end of Hebrew history and are not for the immediate future (Dan. 8:26; 10:14; 12:4, 9). John was told to "seal up the things which the seven peals of thunder have spoken" (10:4), so we cannot know what they were. But here, John is told that his prophecy is not to be sealed for the time is near. This indicates an immediate fulfillment of the things recorded in this book.

The raises a question for some regarding the problem of a postponed consummation. Nearly two millennia have passed since this was announced and some have concluded John was simply wrong in his eschatological expectations. But this is not a necessary conclusion. This book has a twofold perspective: it is concerned with the struggle between Christ and Satan (chs. 12-22) which climaxes at the end of the ages. But this struggle was manifesting itself between the church and the evil influences within the Roman government. It surfaces anytime a government makes similar demands. Therefore, while the book itself has a primary fulfillment in the immediate future for the church and the Roman government, the principle remains the same for every generation until the end of time and the message will continue to serve as a blessing for those who read and heed its words.

22:11 "Let the one who does wrong, still do wrong; and the one who is filthy, still be filthy; and let the one who is righteous, still practice righteousness; and the one who is holy, still keep himself holy."

The end is close and John is told that things will remain as they are. The one who does wrong, will continue to do wrong; the one who is filthy, will continue in his filth. On the other hand, the one who is righteous will practice righteousness and the one who is holy, will keep himself holy. This seems reminiscent of Jesus' words, "He who believes in Him is not judged; he who does not believe has been judged already, because he has not believed in the name of the only begotten Son of God. This is the judgment, that the Light has come into the world, and men loved the darkness rather than the Light, for their deeds were evil. For everyone who does evil hates the Light, and does not come to the Light for fear that his deeds will be exposed" (John 3:18-20).

22:12 "Behold, I am coming quickly, and My reward *is* with Me, to render to every man according to what he has done.

"I am coming quickly" is another emphasis given to the immediacy and swiftness of the Lord's coming. Several phrases in this section indicate that: "the things which must soon take place" (v. 6); "behold, I am coming quickly" (v. 7); "for the time is near" (v. 10); and "I am coming quickly" (vv. 12, 20). Remember, the book is not sealed, the time is near, and the Lord is coming quickly. These cannot refer to the Lord's second or final coming. This coming must be related to God's judgment (in time) on the Roman Empire.

The word for "reward" (*misthos*) means pay or

wages, and is used twice in the book of Revelation, here and in 11:18 where the prophets and servants are mentioned. The distribution of reward on the basis of works is taught throughout Scripture (cf. Jer. 17:10; Rom. 2:6; 1 Pet. 1:17). The reward will be a spiritual blessedness for those who are righteous but judgment against those who are evil (cf. Gal. 6:7-8).

22:13 "I am the Alpha and the Omega, the first and the last, the beginning and the end."

In 1:8 and 21:6 God was identified as the Alpha and Omega, now it is Christ. The phrase "alpha and omega," "first and last," and "beginning and end," are all parallel to each other and have the same significance attached to them.

22:14 Blessed are those who wash their robes, so that they may have the right to the tree of life, and may enter by the gates into the city.

"Blessed are those who wash their robes" refers to the ones who have not defiled themselves by complying with the demands of the beast. Our ability to overcome is based on the blood of Christ. "And they overcame him because of the blood of the Lamb and because of the word of their testimony, and they did not love their life even when faced with death" (Rev. 12:11). The blood of Christ has released us from our sins (1:5), purchased us unto God (5:9), and our robes have been made white "in the blood of the Lamb" (7:14). Thus, the Christian has a right to the tree of life and to enter into the holy city by way of the open gates (chs. 21-22).

22:15 Outside are the dogs and the sorcerers and the immoral persons and the murderers and the idolaters, and everyone who loves and practices lying.

Here is a description of those who have no right to the tree of life and who may not enter the holy city.

Five of the six designations mentioned here are listed in 21:8. Their end is the lake of fire and brimstone. The new term here is the word "dog." In the Bible the word "dog" is used to refer to various kinds of impure and evil persons. For example, the immoral or the prostitutes (Deut. 23:17-18); the vicious (Ps. 22:16; Phil. 3:2); and the moral scavengers (Ps. 59:6-7; 2 Pet. 2:7-8). Dog describes the abominable and filthy.

22:16 "I, Jesus, have sent My angel to testify to you these things for the churches. I am the root and the descendant of David, the bright morning star."

The testimony of the angel is now authenticated by Jesus himself. He describes himself as "the root and descendant of David," i.e., the fulfillment of Messianic prophecy (Isa. 11:1, 10). In Revelation 5 he was "the Lion that is from the tribe of Judah, the Root of David" (v. 5). He is also the "bright and morning star" (cf. 2:28) and as the morning star, he announces the beginning of a new day, an eternal day, a never ending day of wonderful and glorious blessings to those who answer his invitation.

22:17 The Spirit and the bride say, "Come." And let the one who hears say, "Come." And let the one who is thirsty come; let the one who wishes take the water of life without cost.

There are four invitations in this verse. The Spirit (Holy Spirit), the bride (the church), and "the one who hears" (individual Christians) all say, "Come." Throughout the letters to the seven churches we were told "'He who has an ear, let him hear what the Spirit says to the churches" (cf comments on 2:7 and other related passages). The invitation given by the Spirit, joined by the church (collectively and individually) is an open invitation. John adds, "let the one who is thirsty come . . . and take of the water of life without cost." Isaiah wrote, "Every one who thirsts, come to the waters; And you who have no money come, buy and eat. Come, buy wine and milk Without money and without cost" (55:1). Jesus said, "I am the bread of life; he who comes to Me will not hunger, and he who believes in Me will never thirst" (John 6:35). Such sentiments, then, are not new but seem to offer those in need the sustenance available for life everlasting.

22:18 I testify to everyone who hears the words of the prophecy of this book: if anyone adds to them, God will add to him the plagues which are written in this book; 19 and if anyone takes away from the words of the book of this prophecy, God will take away his part from the tree of life and from the holy city, which are written in this book.

A severe warning is now issued to anyone who tampers with this prophetic message. Do not add to, nor take away from, this prophecy. These words are not spoken to future scribes who might hand copy the words of Scripture. These words are for those listeners in the seven churches of Asia to whom this book would be read.

Often someone will say, "Is not this talking only about the book of Revelation?" And the answer is, "yes." But one should not infer that this means he can add to or take away from any other book of Scripture and it be acceptable to God. The principle "of adding to or taking away from" is found several times in Scripture.

God has always warned against tampering with His word. "You shall not add to the word which I am commanding you, nor take away from it, that you may keep the commandments of the LORD your God which I command you" (Deut. 4:2). "Whatever I command you, you shall be careful to do; you shall not add to nor take away from it" (Deut. 12:32). "Every word of God is tested; He is a shield to those who take refuge in Him. Do not add to His words Or He will reprove you, and you will be proved a liar" (Prov. 30:5-6). "I am amazed that you are so quickly deserting Him who called you by the grace of Christ, for a different gospel; which is *really* not another; only there are some who are disturbing you and want to distort the gospel of Christ" (Gal. 1:6-7).

22:20 He who testifies to these things says, "Yes, I am coming quickly." Amen. Come, Lord Jesus.

The testimony of Christ is, "Yes, I am coming quickly" and John add, "Amen. Come, Lord Jesus." This is the Greek equivalent to the Aramaic in 1 Corinthians 16:22, *"maranatha."*

22:21 The grace of the Lord Jesus be with all. Amen.

The word "grace" is found only twice in the book, at the beginning in 1:4-5 and here in 22:21. Therefore, John closes his book with a formal benediction similar to what Paul used (Rom. 16:20; 1 Cor. 16:23; Gal. 6:18; Phil. 4:23). There can be no higher desire for others than that the grace of the Lord be with them, and with these words John closes his book.

NOTES

[1]Robert H. Mounce, *The Book of Revelation*, 391.

Selected Bibliography

Aune, David E. *Prophecy in Early Christian and the Ancient Mediterranean World*. Grand Rapids: Eerdmans, 1983.

Barclay, William. *The Revelation of John, 2 Vols.* Philadelphia: Westminster, 1960.

Beasley-Murray, G.R. *The Book of Revelation.* New Century Bible Commentary. Grand Rapids: Eerdmans, 1978.

Boring, M. Eugene. *Revelation.* Interpretation. Louisville: John Knox Press, 1989.

Bullinger, E.W. *The Apocalypse.* Old Tappan, NJ: Revell, 1972 Reprint.

Caird, G.B. "On Deciphering the Book of Revelation." *Expository Times* (1962-63).

_____ *A Commentary on the Revelation of St. John the Divine.* New York and Evanston: Harper & Row, 1966.

Charles, R.H. *A Critical and Exegetical Commentary on the Revelation of St. John, 2 Vols.* The International Critical Commentary. New York: Scribner's, 1920.

Chilton, David. *The Days of Vengeance: An Exposition of the Book of Revelation*. Ft. Worth: Dominion Press, 1987.

Collins, Adela Yarbro. *Crisis and Catharsis: The Power of the Apocalypse*. Philadelphia: Westminster, 1984.

Corsini, Eugenio. *The Apocalypse: The Perennial Revelation of Jesus Christ*. Wilmington, DE: Michael Glazier, Inc., 1983.

Court, John M. *Revelation*. New Testament Guides (JSOT Press). Sheffield, England: Sheffield Academic Press Ltd, 1994.

Danner, Dan. "A History of Interpretation of Revelation 20:1-10 in the Restoration Movement." *Restoration Quarterly* 7 (1963): 27-35.

Ford, J. Massyngberde. *Revelation: Introduction, Translation and Commentary*. The Anchor Bible. Garden City, NY: Doubleday, 1975.

Hailey, Homer. *Revelation: An Introduction and Commentary*. Grand Rapids: Baker, 1979.

Harrington, Wilfrid J. *Revelation*. Sacra Pagina Series, vol. 16. Collegeville, MN: The Liturgical Press, 1993.

Hemer, Colin J. *The Letters to the Seven Churches of Asia in Their Local Setting*. Journal for the Study of the New Testament, vol. Supplement Series 11. Sheffield: The University of Sheffield, 1986.

Hendriksen, William. *More Than Conquerors*. Grand Rapids: Baker, 1939.

Hughes, Philip Edgcumbe. *The Book of Revelation: A Commentary*. Grand Rapids: Eerdmans, 1990.

Isbell, Allen. "The Dating of Revelation." *Restoration Quarterly* 9 (1966): 107-17.

Jenkins, Ferrell. *The Old Testament in the Book of Revelation*. Marion, IN: Cogdill Foundations Publications, 1972.

Johnson, Alan. *Book of Revelation*. The Expositor's Bible Commentary, vol. 12. Grand Rapids: Zondervan, 1981.

Jones, Joe D. *Victory in Jesus*. Searcy, AR: Joe D. Jones, 1990.

Ladd, George Eldon. *Commentary on the Revelation of John*. Grand Rapids: Eerdmans, 1972.

Mauro, Philip. *Of Things Which Soon Must Come To Pass*. Swengel, PA: Reiner Publications, 1971.

McGuiggan, Jim. *The Book of Revelation*. Let The Bible Speak. West Monroe, LA: William C. Johnson, Inc., 1976.

Michaels, J. Ramsey. *Interpreting the Book of Revelation*. Guides to New Testament Exegesis. Grand Rapids: Baker, 1992.

Mounce, Robert H. *The Book of Revelation*. Grand Rapids: Eerdmans, 1977.

Ogden, Arthur M. *The Avenging of the Apostles and Prophets*. Louisville: Ogden Publications, 1985.

Pack, Frank. *The Message of the New Testament: The Revelation, 2 Vols*. The Way of Life Series, vol. 176. Abilene, TX: Biblical Research Press, 1984.

Pieters, Albertus. *The Lamb, The Woman and The Dragon*. 2d ed. Grand Rapids: The Church Press, 1946.

Ramsay, Sir William M. *The Letters to the Seven Churches of Asia*. London: Hodder & Stroughton, 1904.

Richardson, Donald W. *The Revelation of Jesus Christ*. New York: Pillar Books, 1977.

Roberts, J.W. "The Interpretation of the Apocalypse: The State of the Question." *Restoration Quarterly* 8 (1965): 154-62.

_____. "The Meaning of the Eschatology in the Book of Revelation." *Restoration Quarterly* 15 (1972): 95-110.

_____. *The Revelation to John*. The Living Word Commentary, vol. 19. Austin, TX: Sweet, 1974.

Strauss, James D. *The Seer, The Savior, and The Saved*. Joplin, MO: College Press, 1963.

Summers, Ray. *Worthy is the Lamb*. Nashville: Broadman Press, 1951.

Swete, Henry Barclay. *Commentary on Revelation*. Grand Rapids: Kregel, 1977 Reprint.

Thomas, Robert L. *Revelation 1-7, an Exegetical Commentary*. Chicago: Moody, 1992.

Thompson, Leonard L. *The Book of Revelation: Apocalypse and Empire*. New York / Oxford: Oxford University Press, 1990.

Trench, Richard C. *Synonyms of the New Testament*. Grand Rapids: Eerdmans, 1958 reprint of 1880.